1968

may be kept

D1496357

Caxton's Mirrour of the World

EARLY ENGLISH TEXT SOCIETY

Extra Series, No. 110

1913 (for 1912) ; reprinted 1966

PRICE 42s.

Caxton's
Mirrour of the World

EDITED BY

OLIVER H. PRIOR

Published for
THE EARLY ENGLISH TEXT SOCIETY
by the
OXFORD UNIVERSITY PRESS
LONDON NEW YORK TORONTO

FIRST PUBLISHED 1913
REPRINTED 1966

𝕰xtra 𝕾eries, No. 110

ORIGINALLY PRINTED BY
RICHARD CLAY & SONS LTD., LONDON AND BUNGAY
AND NOW REPRINTED LITHOGRAPHICALLY IN GREAT BRITAIN
AT THE UNIVERSITY PRESS, OXFORD
BY VIVIAN RIDLER, PRINTER TO THE UNIVERSITY

INTRODUCTION.

CAXTON'S *Mirrour* has a double claim to the notice of all book-lovers and students of mediæval literature: it is the first work printed in England with illustrations, and one of the earliest encyclopædias in the English language.

As Caxton himself tells us in his introduction, the *Mirrour* was translated in 1480 from the French, at the request of his friend Hugh Bryce,[1] a fellow member of the Mercers' Company, who wished to present it to Lord Hastings. The translation was made from a MS. at Bruges which, as we show later, is now in the British Museum. The book was printed at Westminster.[2] Definite dates mark the various stages of the work, all the facts connected with it being accurately stated. Thus we know that it took nearly ten weeks to translate the whole of the *Mirrour* (Jan. 2 to March 8, 1480).[3] This gives us a fair idea of the rate of work in the Middle Ages, and is a testimony to the great printer's industry.

Caxton's choice was in every way a happy one. He could have selected any one of many Latin works of great value, which contained the sum of the knowledge of the times. But these were too learned or too cumbersome for the use of ordinary readers and laymen. There were many didactic works treating of one or two scientific subjects only, which were drawn out to an inordinate length, with long moral disquisitions.

---

[1] Hugh Bryce, like Caxton, was a Kentish man. He was knighted about 1472. In 1473 he was sent on a trade embassy to Bruges "de difficultatibus super intercursu Burgundiæ removendis." He held the offices of Keeper of the King's Exchange, London, Governor of the King's Mint in the Tower, under Lord Hastings, and was Mayor of London in 1494. He died in 1496. (Cf. Blade's *Caxton*.)

[2] Cf. p. 7.   [3] Cf. p. 185.

The French *Image du Monde* alone fulfilled the
necessary conditions of a popular encyclopædia. For
two centuries this work had been read and appreciated,
as the vast number of manuscripts which we still
possess testifies.

The English version met with equal success. Caxton
himself produced two editions of the *Mirrour*. Later,
about 1527, Lawrence Andrewe thought it worth while
to reprint the book with some alterations and additions.[1]

We do not know for certain when Caxton's *Mirrour*
was printed; the date 1480, already mentioned, refers
only to the translation. The first edition, of which
at least 33 copies are known to exist,[2] was probably
produced in the course of the same year, or in 1481,
the type used, (2*), being the same as that of the
Kendale *Letters of Indulgence*, first issue, dated 1480.[3]
The second edition, of which we know 19 copies, must
have been printed about 1490.[4] The type used, (6), is
definitely dated 1489 in the *Fayttes of armes and
chyualrye*.

The differences between the first and second edition
are very slight. One of the original figures [5] (God
with an orb and cross, Fig. 3, p. 11) has been replaced

[1] The British Museum copy of Lawrence Andrewe's edition is
catalogued " c. 11. b. 13." 89 leaves, without pagination ; sig. b i–
y ii. Imperfect : wanting the leaves between the title-page and b i ;
containing preliminary matter. The title-page is mutilated.

[2] The copy reproduced in our text is catalogued in the British
Museum IB 55041 = c. 10. b. 5.—The first edition and the copies
of it known are described in Seymour de Ricci's *Census of Caxtons*,
pp. 93–96.—Folio, 100 ff., the first a blank : a–m⁸, n⁴, 29 lines.
—The copy in the Göttingen University Library was bought by
the Government at the sale of F. W. von Duve's collection, and
then given to the library. By a slight mistake Seymour de Ricci
states that von Duve *bequeathed* it to Göttingen University
(p. 94).—In April 1909 Mr. E. Stanley paid £2600 at Sotheby's
for a volume containing five productions of Caxton's press. These
were *The Mirrour, 1481 ; Dictes or Sayings ;* Tully, *on Old Age ;*
Cicero, *de Amicitia ;* and *Cordyale.* This tome is mentioned as
being the property of a gentleman living in the North. It does not
seem to appear in S. de Ricci's list.

[3] British Museum copy, catalogued IB. 55024.

[4] Second edition : folio ; 88 ff. ; a–l⁸, 31 lines. (Cf. Seymour
de Ricci *o.c.*, pp. 96–98.)

[5] The figures and diagrams, which form such a striking feature
of the *Mirrour*, have all the explanations inserted in ink. Oldys
suggests that the writing is that of Caxton himself ; but of this, of
ourse, there is no proof.

by a woodcut, which is here quite out of place, representing the Transfiguration. A few mistakes have been corrected,[1] and thus we get definite evidence as to the proper sequence of the two editions. On the whole it seems as if Caxton had taken greater pains over the first issue than over the second, in which misprints are numerous and abbreviations far more frequently used.

The English printer was undoubtedly a good French scholar. Obscure passages are sometimes rendered rather freely; but in the whole work we only find ten mistakes in translation.[2] With his usual modesty he apologises beforehand for his shortcomings, and warns the reader not to blame him for strange statements which are entirely due to the French author. And indeed Caxton seldom departs from his original. When he does, his motives are evident: he is thoroughly patriotic. To the mention of Paris as a seat of learning he invariably adds Oxford and Cambridge; the King of France becomes King of France and England; Bath is mentioned among the great health-giving resorts of Europe; the disparaging story about men with tails in England is omitted. Otherwise he keeps strictly to his text, though occasionally expressing surprise at some geographical eccentricity of the French work, or doubt about some mediæval legend, such as that of St. Patrick's Purgatory.

According to Caxton himself the French MS. on which his translation is based was written at Bruges in 1464.[3] This MS. is now beyond a doubt in the British Museum: the MS. Roy. 19A IX. In it we find the date and place, *Bruges 1464*, duly given[4]; a long prologue, which appears in no other MS., has been translated, word for word;

[1] In the first edition Saxony is called "Sapronye" (p. 92), which is also the spelling of the Old French text. In the second edition Caxton solves the riddle and spells correctly "Saxonye."
[2] For these mistakes, see pp. 79, 81, 84, 91, 95, 99, 100, 145, 147, 170.
[3] Cf. p. 7.
[4] Cf. fo. 4 vo. in MS. Roy. 19A IX.: "Ci fu grossé et de tous poins ordonné, comme dist est, en la ville de Bruges l'an de l'incarnation nostre seigneur Jhesu Crist mil quatre cens soixante et quatre."

and all the mistakes and omissions peculiar to Roy.
19A IX reappear in the *Mirrour.*

A further coincidence enables us to say what MS. the
Bruges scribe used for his copy. In his preface he
states that the *Image du Monde* was translated from
Latin into French in the year 1245, by order of the
noble Duke John of Berry and Auvergne. This son of
Jean le Bon, king of France, lived 1340–1416, and is
well known in English history. He was present at the
battle of Poitiers, and went to England as hostage for
his father after the peace of Bretigny. Some time
later he returned home, Edward III having granted
him permission to remain a year in France; *but,* as
Froissart says, *he acted so prudently and made so many
different excuses that he never went back.*[1]

Obviously the *Image du Monde* could not have been
written in 1245 by order of Jean de Berry, who lived in
the fourteenth century.

We find the explanation of this strange error in a MS.
of the Bibliothèque Nationale in Paris (Fonds fr. 574).[2]
On the first page, and again at the end of the volume,
we read : " Ce livre est au Duc de Berry . Jehan B."

The scribe of Roy. 19A IX, evidently deceived by these
inscriptions, ascribed to Jean de Berry, the owner of the
MS., the suggestion of a work written more than a
century earlier—an historical mistake which Caxton does
not correct, and which, worse still, Blades perpetuates.

This alone would not be a sufficient proof of the close
relationship between the two MSS., but our opinion is
further strengthened by other points which they have
in common. The most striking mistakes which we
find in the Paris MS. have been faithfully rendered
in Royal 19A IX, and consequently in Caxton's
Mirrour ; the omissions also are the same in all three
texts of the same work.[3]

[1] Cf. Froissart, *Chronicles*, ch. 249 (ed. Johnes. London, 1839.
Vol. I. p. 397).
[2] We shall in future refer to this particular MS. as "MS. A."
[3] For further details on this point, and generally on the Old
French work, cf. *L'Image du Monde de Maître Gossouin* (Lausanne,
1913).

The French MSS. we have mentioned so far belong to the prose version of the *Image du Monde.*

In its original form, this encyclopædia was a rhymed poem of 6594 octosyllabic verses, divided, like the prose version, into three parts. Twice in the course of his work the author states that the poem was completed in January 1245 (O.S.). There is no reason for doubting the accuracy of this date which is confirmed by the measure of the verses and by mathematical calculations, based on the date 1245 (O.S), in the Astronomical part of the *Image.*

In 1247 (O.S.) a second rhymed version appeared, in which the poem, increased by some 4000 verses, was divided into two parts only, and the order of the chapters altered.

We possess further two Hebrew translations; also a shameless plagiary by a man called Buffereau, who published the poem under his own name at Geneva in 1517; and two very scarce and valuable French editions of the prose version, printed in Paris in 1501 by Michel le Noir, and in 1520 by Alain Lotrian respectively.

As usual, much has been written and much argument expended on the subject of the place of origin and authorship of the *Image du Monde.*[1]

There is little doubt that it was written at Metz in Lorraine; the frequent mention of that town in the course of the work, the intimate knowledge of the neighbourhood, the mention of local monasteries, and especially the use of the Lorraine dialect in the poem, are sufficient proofs.

Paul Meyer[2] gives the author's name as Gauthier de Metz. Ch. V. Langlois[3] disputes this opinion. He points out that *Gauthier* occurs only in one MS. of the *second* rhymed version,[4] which in many respects is a new

[1] The arguments for and against are given in full in the French edition.

[2] Paul Meyer in *Notices et extraits des Manuscrits,* XXXIV. 1, p. 174.

[3] Ch. V. Langlois. *La Connaissance de la Nature et du Monde au Moyen Age* (Paris: Hachette et Cie. 1911), p. 64 *seq.*

[4] MS. Phillipps, No. 3,655 in the library of Sir Thomas Phillipps, Cheltenham.

and a different work, while the name *Gossouin* is found
under different forms in one verse MS., now lost, of
the first original edition and in three prose MSS.   The
balance of arguments seems to be rather in favour of
Gossouin.[1]

The prose version follows very closely the poem composed in 1245 (O.S.), and seems to have been written
at about the same period.   It may be the work of
Gossouin himself, whose name, as we have just said, is
given in three of the MSS.   There is, moreover, some
internal evidence in the prose version itself which
strengthens this presumption.[2]

The *Image du Monde* is the work of a well-read man.
Many classical authors are quoted fairly accurately, and
the sources are numerous and varied.   It is not likely
that Gossouin had any direct knowledge of Greek, but
an acquaintance with Hellenic literature was far more
widespread in the XIIIth century than is generally
supposed.   Latin translations of several of Aristotle's
works and of Plato's *Timaeus* were certainly available.
Such men as Neckam and Albertus Magnus are known
to have lectured on Greek philosophy and expounded
texts in Paris and at other Universities.[3]

Our encyclopædia is not a translation from any one
Latin writer, but a compilation in which we find
passages taken word for word from various sources.
Jacobus de Vitriaco, Honorius Augustodunensis,
Neckam have been used freely.   We shall have occasion
to mention many others.   By a curious mistake, in Duff
and Seymour de Ricci's works the *Mirrour* is found
under the name "Vincentius."   The few passages which
can be traced back to that prolific writer appear likewise in the works of Adelard of Bath and other writers.
The translations from the latter sources are sufficiently

---

[1] In the rolls of the town of Metz for the thirteenth century we
find both the names *Gauthier* and *Gossouin* frequently mentioned.
But these references give us no further clue to the identity of our
author.   Cf. Dr. K. Wichmann, *Die Metzer Bannrollen des XIII[ten]
Jahrhunderts* (Metz, 1912)

[2] Cf. *L'Image du Monde*, p. 7 s.

[3] Cf. Sandys, *A History of Classical Scholarship* (Cambridge,
1906-8, 8°), vol. I.

literal not to require the assumption of a lost work of Vincentius, an unknown *Speculum vel Imago Mundi*, which might be the original used by Gossouin.

The study of sources is an interesting and fruitful one. We discover thereby the origin of many a myth. Even a most serious and scientifically valuable work may produce the strangest result at the hands of a scribe or translator. Solinus may talk of a nation living on fish as "ex mari viventis"; a scribe or Jacques de Vitry himself renders this by "ex mari bibentis." We understand then Gossouin's account of a nation which drinks nothing but sea-water.

But not once do we find in the *Image* statements merely due to gross mistakes of the kind on the author's part. However extraordinary the facts mentioned by Gossouin, they are due, not to his carelessness or ignorance when translating, but to his sources.

Caxton is not so blameless ; for instance, he describes the slingers of the Balearic Islands as people skilful "in the maner of meltyng of metals," mistaking O.F. *la fonde*, the sling, for *la fonte*, melting. This is one of the mistakes we alluded to before.

In the following pages we give a summary of the first book by chapters, and some remarks about the next two books. Especially in the first part, Gossouin is apt to expatiate at length upon subjects of great moral and theological interest at the time ; but to us all this may seem drawn out and tedious. Moreover the logical sequence of ideas is ·not always obvious, and this alone would render a help both justifiable and necessary.

PART I

In the first chapter, Gossouin describes the power of ch. 1 God :—

" All things come from Him and return to Him.

"There can be no evil in Him; if there were He would be mortal like ourselves.

" Everything that is good rises up to Him ; the bad goes down like dregs in wine.

"He is both immoveable and motionless : yet all motion has its origin in Him.[1]

"Time does not exist for Him nor for the elect. Even before the world was created God knew all that was to happen in it.

ch. 2.   "God created the world out of kindness, so that others might share in His bliss, which we must therefore strive to deserve.

"He has given us all the power to do so.[2]

ch. 3.   "God created man in His own image, and made him master of all creation. He gave him intelligence, to remember His blessings and share in His bliss.

"The man who does good is superior even to angels.

ch. 4.   "God gave man the power to do good or evil. There would be no merit attached to a man who could not sin, for then his virtue would not be due to himself.

"Angels, who cannot sin, are not rewarded as we are.

"By God's will, it was to be within our power to attain to the bliss which is His ; for this purpose He endowed us with reason and common-sense.

"A man must be mad who imagines that he is helping God by abstaining from evil ; for even if the world did not exist, God would be none the worse.

ch. 5.   "In former days men strove to discover the reason of things, the secrets of the firmament. They did not merely think of their food, as people do nowadays. They endeavoured to acquire the sciences which would give them the knowledge of God. They studied His work, for the workman is known by his works.

"They suffered persecution for love of truth, just as the Saints suffered martyrdom for the love of Jesus.

"By means of their science, certain philosophers, and among them Virgil, were able to foretell the coming of Christ."

---

[1] Gossouin adopts the new Aristotelian ideas which were beginning to spread in the first half of the thirteenth century. Plato's Deity merely creates, and then rests, leaving to nature the care of reproduction and increase.

[2] This chapter and the two next are based apparently on St. Augustine. We give the parallel passages in the notes to the text.

In the third part, a whole chapter is devoted to Virgil the magician who here appears as a prophet. We need only briefly refer to this well-known legend of the Middle Ages, about which so much has been written.

Virgil's 4th *Eclogue*, which contains the Sibylline oracles about the golden age, gave rise to his supposed prophecy. Even St. Augustine (*Patrol.*, t. 33, col. 1073) quotes verses 13 and 14, and adds : " Quod ex Cumæo, id est, ex Sibyllino carmine se fassus est transtulisse Virgilius, quoniam fortassi etiam illa vates aliquid de unico Salvatore in spiritu audierat, quod necesse habuit confiteri."

Gossouin tells us that on reading Virgil's verses St. Paul exclaimed : " If only you had lived until my time, I would have made of you a child of God !" These very words formed part of a hymn sung as late as the fifteenth century during the mass of St. Paul at Mantua.[1] Chapter 5 continues with a scornful reference to those wealthy people who buy many books in order to be thought learned ; the author applies to them the fable of the Cock and the Pearl.

Next he gives us the list of the seven liberal arts which formed the subjects of teaching in the School of Alexandria : the trivium (grammar, logic, rhetoric), the quadrivium (arithmetic, geometry, music and astronomy).

Philosophers at Athens divided men into three classes : ch. 6. labourers, who must provide for the needs of others ; knights, who must defend others ; clerks, who must teach them.

Since the time of the Emperor Charles the Great, the kings of France have always upheld the liberal arts, which are cultivated with most care by the " fratres

---

[1] " Quem te, inquit, reddidissem,
  Si te vivum invenissem,
  Poetarum maxime ! "

Cf. Comparetti, *Virgilio nel medio evo* (Livorno, 1872), p. 72 *s.*; also Bettinelli, *Delle lettere e delle arti Mantovane* (Mantua, 1775). We often find quoted also the old Christmas song of the Church, beginning : " Maro, Maro, vates gentilium, da Christo testimonium."

minores " (minorites or Franciscans), and the " Jacobins " (Black friars or Dominicans).[1]

ch. 7 to 13.   Chs. 7–13 contain a detailed account of the seven liberal arts. Medicine is not one of them, because it is concerned with the body alone ; and only sciences which affect the soul deserve the name of " liberal."

ch. 14.   In this chapter Gossouin further develops his ideas about God and nature.

" First God created nature, which causes the stars to move ; it gives them light, and brings things to life at will. Without nature nothing can exist.

" Nature in the hand of God is like the carpenter's axe : the axe cuts, but the hand which holds it guides it wherever it wishes.[2]

" According to Gossouin, Plato describes nature as a power which makes like bring forth like. Aristotle calls it a principle which gives to things the power of movement.

ch. 15.   " The world is in the shape of a ball.

" The heaven surrounds both the world and ether, a pure air from which the angels assume their shape. This ether is of such startling brilliance that no sinner can gaze at it with impunity : this is why men fall down in a faint when angels appear before them.

ch. 16.   " Ether surrounds the four elements placed in the following order : earth, water, air, fire. Gossouin compares this to the different parts of an egg : the shell, the white, the yolk, the drop of grease.

ch. 17.   " In the middle of the world lies the heaviest of all elements, the earth.

[1] In France the Black Friars were named " Jacobins," when, in 1218, they settled in a house of the " rue St. Jacques " in Paris. This fact alone, without any other data, would enable us to say that the *Image du Monde* could not have been written before 1218.

[2] A similar comparison occurs in the works of St. Thomas Aquinas, who wrote some twenty years later than Gossouin, and whose *Summa Theologica* is an echo of contemporary thought. We quote from Migne's *Patrologia*, series secunda, t. I. col. 1313. " Deus movet non solum res ad operandum, quasi applicando formas et virtutes rerum ad operationem (sicut etiam artifex applicat securim ad scindendum, qui tamen interdum formam securi non tribuit)."

No further proof is needed that Gossouin's theories had nothing subversive, and were in accordance with the ideas held by theologians of his time.

" A man could walk round it, just as a fly can go round an apple. Two men going away from each other, one due east the other west, would meet again at the antipodes.

" By means of a series of examples with explanatory figures, Gossouin proves that stones thrown to the centre of the earth could go no further, since they would then be at an equal distance all round from the firmament.

" If these stones were of different weights, the heaviest would reach the centre first.

" If we could rise up to a sufficient height, mountains and valleys would vanish and the round shape of the earth would become evident. Large rivers would look no bigger than a hair on a man's finger. ch. 18.

" No shape is more favourable to motion than the round. As everything in this world is in a state of motion God made the earth round. ch. 19.

" The sky is so far away from us that a stone would fall for 100 years before reaching us. ch. 20.

" Seen from the sky, the earth would be in size like the smallest of the stars.

" The sky turns from east to west, the sun and the other planets from west to east. This motion can be compared to that of a fly moving one way on a wheel while the wheel revolves in the opposite direction."

PART II

Gossouin's geography is in some respects the most interesting part of his work.

We read there descriptions of all the strange countries, nations and animals which are so frequently mentioned in mediæval literature.

In most maps and works of the Middle Ages, we find Jerusalem situated in the middle of the world; but Gossouin assigns this position to a mysterious city, round in shape, called " Aaron."—According to the Arab legend this place lies on the extreme limits of the inhabitable world; it is the refuge of demons and the seat of Iblys, their prince and master. " Aaron," or ". Arym," is occasionally mentioned in works of the fo. 34, vo.

thirteenth century[1]; but it is difficult to say how this Eastern legend found its way into Gossouin's work; it certainly appears in none of his usual sources.

In the chapter on "Africa," Caxton, though conscientiously translating all the information given, cannot help protesting mildly against the inclusion of Greece, Tuscany, Lombardy, Gascony, Spain and other countries in that continent. This same fact has puzzled all modern critics of the *Image du Monde,* who see in it a mere mistake of the original transcriber perpetuated by careless scribes.

Yet this apparent mistake is found in every MS. of all three versions of the French encyclopædia. The explanation is simple enough. Many writers looked upon Africa as merely a province of Europe. Passages to that effect can be quoted from many authors belonging to widely different periods; in the note [2] we mention a few names which by no means exhaust the list.

Gossouin himself tells us (p. 93) that the southern limit of Europe is Mount Jus (Mons Jovis, *i. e.* the Great St. Bernard). He thus settles in an arbitrary fashion the somewhat vague boundary between the two continents, ascribing to Africa the whole of Southern Europe and the shores of the Mediterranean generally. Thus Thessaly, Epirus, "part of Constantinople," are in Europe, but Italy, Greece, Spain, Palestine belong to Africa.

"Maron" provides us with one of those riddles which

---

[1] Cf. Miller. *Mappœmundi,* iii. 127 (Stuttgart, 1895).

[2] Varro (*De ling. lat.,* 4): "Ut omnis natura in cœlum et terram divisa est, sic cœlum in regiones, terra in Asiam et Europam."

Sallust (*Jugurt.,* ch. 17): "In divisione orbis terræ plerique partem tertiam Africam posuere: pauci tantummodo Asiam et Europam esse, sed Africam in Europa."

Orosius (*Histor.,* I. 2): ". . . quamvis aliqui duas (partes), hoc est Asiam, ac deinde Africam in Europam accipiendam putarint" [*Patrol.,* t. 31, col. 673].

Gervase of Tilbury (*Otia Imp.,* II. 11): ". . . sed potius in Europa deputantes Africam, hoc est secundæ partis portionem appellare maluerunt" [ed. Hanover, 1707].

Ranulph Higden (*Polychron.,* I. 7): "Idcirco qui res humanas evidentius agnoverunt duas tantum orbis partes accipiendas censuerunt, scilicet Asiam solummodo et Europam; Africam vero censuerunt Europæ finibus deputandam . . ."—[ed. Babington, London, 1865-86].

are common owing to the carelessness of scribes. The name of that island appears in the MSS. in the most varied forms: Naaron, Varon, Anon. One MS. only spells it correctly "Naxos." The letter *x* has always proved a stumbling-block to scribes, and is the most frequent source of error. We have another instance of this in "Sapronye" (p. 92) for Saxony.

Gossouin tells us that Naxos was the birthplace of St. Denis the martyr who was beheaded in France.

As early as the ninth century this first Bishop of Paris was identified with Dionysius the Areopagite converted by St. Paul.[1] One of the gravest accusations against Abailard was his refusal to acknowledge this identity on the authority of a passage in Bæda. Hilduin's *Areopagitica* gave rise to this error.

According to Suidas, the Areopagite was an Athenian by birth. Gossouin is apparently the first author who connects St. Denis with Naxos. His mistake is due to a strange confusion between names. As Isidore tells us,[2] Naxos, on account of its wealth in vineyards, was surnamed "Dionysias," the island of Dionysus or Bacchus. The connection of the god of wine with the Saint and Martyr is even more remote than that of the Areopagite.

The queen of Samos who prophesied the coming of Christ was one of the most famous of the sibyls whose oracles were held in reverence, even by the Church, during the first three centuries of the Christian era. The Nuremberg *Chronicle* gives us a list of the ten great sibyls, of which Samos is the sixth.[3]

fo. 50.

Caxton is very sceptical about the well-known legend of St. Patrick's Purgatory.[4] He admits that such

[1] Cf. de Launoy, *Duo Dionysii* (Paris, 1660).

[2] Isidore (*Etym.*, XIV. 6): "Naxos insula a Dionysio dicta, quasi Dionaxos, quod fertilitate vitium vincat ceteras."

[3] Bæda wrote *Sibyllinorum verborum interpretatio*, in which he says of one of the sibyls: "Tiburtina Græce, Albunea Latine vocatur, ex cujus carminibus multa de Deo et Christo scripta continentur."

[4] See: T. Wright, *St. Patrick's Purgatory* (London, 1844); S. Baring-Gould, *Curious Myths of the Middle Ages* (London, 1884). H. L. D. Ward, *Catalogue of Romances*, II. (London, 1893), pp. 435–492; G. P. Krapp, *The Legend of St. Patrick's Purgatory* (Baltimore, 1900).

strange events may have happened in ancient times "as the storye of Tundale and other witnesse." But since then things have changed, and he calls to witness "a certain high canon of Waterford," and a knight of Bruges, Sir John de Banste,[1] who, being strong-minded men, went into the cave in Lough Derg which led to the Purgatory, slept there, and came out, without having experienced anything at all thrilling.

That this spirit of scepticism was gaining ground is proved by the fact that the Purgatory was closed by orders of the Pope, Alexander VI, on St. Patrick's Day, 1497. Except the canon of Waterford, whose anonymity was perhaps wisely preserved (pilgrims still flocked to the shrine when Caxton wrote the *Mirrour*), the other names mentioned are well known.

An account of Tundale is found in *Helinand*,[2] and the "Vision of Tundale" has given rise to a small literature of its own in modern times.[3]

Sir John de Banste, if not quite a historical character, was certainly more than a mere local celebrity. Jean de Bænst, to call him by his correct name, belonged to a distinguished family of Bruges. He was three times burgomaster, "chef-homme" in 1461, and died in 1485.[4]

fo. 52, 1o.   For centuries the English were nicknamed by the French "coués," *i. e.* tailed men.

The passage of the *Image du Monde*[5] which refers to this legend has been omitted by Caxton, obviously for patriotic reasons. It is a curious instance of a tradition, at first purely local, gradually gaining ground and being made to apply at last to a whole nation.

---

[1] Cf. p. 99.

[2] Cf. *Helinandi frigidi montis monachi chronicon.* (Patrol., t. 212, col. 1038 *seq.*)

[3] Cf. A. Wagner. *Das mittelenglische Gedicht über die Vision des Tundalus* (Halle a/S, 1893); Ward, *o.c.*, pp. 416–435, and an article "Vision de Tindal, etc.," in *Bibliothèque Méridionale*, Série I. t. 8, 1903.

[4] For further details about Jean de Bænst, see J. Gailliard, *Bruges*, I. (Bruges, 1857).

[5] *Image du Monde*, fo. 72B: "En Bretaingne ot une maniere de genz qui avoient keues par darrieres." As Jacobus de Vitriaco, from whom this passage is translated, says definitely, "in *Majori Brittania*," there can be no doubt that the story applies to England.

S. Baring-Gould,[1] who has a chapter on the subject, does not quote any very early authorities ; we mention here what is apparently the first form in which the legend appeared. The inhabitants of the country round Dorchester, having mockingly tied fish-tails on St. Augustine of Canterbury's garments, or thrown them at him, were cursed as well as their descendants by the apostle, and had tails ever after.

According to Baring-Gould the same accusation was levelled against men of Kent and even Cornwall. Caxton's evident sensitiveness on the subject may be an argument in favour of the Kentish origin of this myth.

By some unaccountable oversight a whole chapter has been omitted, both in MS. Roy. and in Caxton's translation, between those numbered 30 and 31 in the *Mirrour.* fo. 65, vo.

In the old French Text this chapter is entitled "Du dragon qui samble cheoir, et que ce est." [2]

Gossouin describes meteors, in which people in the Middle Ages saw the shape of a dragon, as a dry vapour which catches fire, falls to the earth and disappears. This is based on Neckam's *De Laudibus* (I. 319), in which we read :

> " Impetus in longum nubem producit et illam
> Serpentis formam visus habere putant."

PART III

Several passages of the *Image* have been borrowed from the *Almagest* of Ptolemy. fo. 79.

Claudius Ptolemy, who taught at the renowned school of Alexandria in the second century after Christ, was born at Ptolemais, and has of course no connection with King Ptolemy of the Legidæ Dynasty. His work was translated into Latin from the Arabic by order of Frederic II in 1230. It is not surprising, therefore, that Gossouin should use what is evidently

---

[1] S. Baring-Gould, *o.c.*, pp. 146, 147.
[2] *i. e.* "About the dragon which seems to fall, and what it is."

an Arabic title, for a work originally written in Greek.

A homily, somewhat lengthy but by no means without merit, fills the greater part of the chapter. In it the author speaks to us about the proper use of time, punctuality, and the punishment of those who strive after wealth and forget the service of God.

fo. 82.   Both the historian Josephus [1] and Gervase of Tilbury [2] mention the following legend : The Philosophers, knowing that the world must perish twice, once through fire, a second time through water, erected two columns on which they inscribed the seven arts. One was of stone to resist water, the other of bricks to resist fire. According to the Hebrew historian these two columns still existed in his time in Syria, but had been erected

fo. 83.   by Seth. To the latter, Josephus also ascribes the discovery of astronomy after the Deluge. Gossouin confuses names, and mentions Abraham and Sem, son of Noah, instead of Seth.

It is impossible to say on what authority our author states that Aristotle believed in the Holy Trinity. Certainly no passage in the known works of the philosopher can have given rise to this statement, which, besides, is nowhere to be found in the writings of the Fathers of the Church. As for Plato the case is different : his belief in the Trinity is frequently referred to in theological writings of the Middle Ages. Clement of Alexandria, [3] the first to write on Plato and the Trinity, quotes Timæus, and discusses at length the passage on which his opinion is based.

fo. 84.   We come now to the chapter on Virgil and his miracles. We read of him before as a prophet. He earned his reputation as a magician through the eighth *Eclogue* and a passage in the *Æneid* (vi. 263 *seq.*)

Except one, [4] all the prodigies mentioned in the *Image*

---

[1] Josephus, *Antiq. Jud.*, I. 2.
[2] Gervase of Tilbury, *o.c.*, I. 20.
[3] Cf. Clement of Alexandria, *Stromata V.*, ch. 14. (*Patrol.* Series Græca., t. 8, col. 155, 158).
[4] The miracle of the two candles and the lamp which burn buried in the ground.

du Monde as having been performed by the Latin poet
are found in numerous authors in the Middle Ages.
The most widely known is the miracle of the brazen fly
near which no fly could live.

This legend appears to have existed also in the East.
In the travels of Evliya Efendi (published by the
Oriental Translation Committee), p. 17, the author,
speaking of some ancient columns at Constantinople,
says : On one of them, erected by the Hakím Fílikús
(Philip), lord of the castle of Kaváláh, was the figure of
a black fly, made of brass, which by its incessant
humming, drove all flies away from Istámból.

We found this note in a copy of the *Image du Monde*,
MS. Add. 10015, made by Thomas Wright himself.[1]
In his *Popular Treatises* [2] the learned author mentions
his intention of editing the Old French encyclopædia,
with copious notes. His inability to carry out his plan
is a grievous misfortune and a loss to literature.

So far, no critic has been able to trace the origin of
the miracle of the lamp and candles such as Gossouin
relates it. It seems as if the story were, in part at
least, original, and the result of a process of association
very similar to that by which our author connects
St. Denis with Naxos.

The legend of the *lamp* was well known in the Middle
Ages, even before the *Image* was written. Thus we read
in William of Malmesbury's *Gesta Regum Anglorum* [3] :
" Epitaphium hujusmodi repertum :

      ' Filius Evandri Pallas, quem lancea Turni
      Militis occidit more suo, jacet hic.'

Quod non tunc crediderim factum, licet Carmentis,
mater Evandri, Latinas litteras dicatur invenisse ; sed
ab Ennio, vel alio aliquo antiquo poeta compositum.
Ardens lucerna ad caput inventa arte mechanica, ut

---

[1] This copy is now in the library of the Halle University
Romanisches Seminar, where we had access to it.

[2] T. Wright. *Popular Treatises on Science written during the
Middle Ages in Anglo-Saxon, Anglo-Norman, and English* (London,
1841), p. 8.

[3] ed. W. Stubbs. London, 1887. I. pp. 258, 259 Account
of the discovery of the body of Pallas at Rome.

nullius flatus violentia, nullius liquoris aspergine valeret exstingui."

The same account is found in the *Roman de Troie* of Benoît de Sainte-More.

The train of thought which led Gossouin to attribute to the Latin poet the miracle of the lamp seems now to be fairly obvious: Virgil the Magician, author of the *Æneid*, easily becomes, in the writer's mind, the inventor of the lamp in the tomb of Pallas.

As for the candles, Gossouin probably added this detail himself.

We end our introduction to Caxton's translation with some remarks about the mathematical calculations in the *Image du Monde;* in these we shall endeavour to justify our corrections of the numbers as found in the *Mirrour.*

Caxton gives the distance from the earth to the moon as equal to *15* times the circumference of the earth.[1] This number ought to read *12*, as stated in some of the MSS. The distance from the earth to the moon, according to the Old French text $= 34\frac{11}{12}$ times the earth's diameter (6500 miles) $= 226,958\frac{1}{3}$ miles; $= 12$ times (to a fraction) the circumference of the earth.

fo. 91.

The earth is **39** times (and a little more) larger than the moon. **29**, as given by Caxton, is a mistake, as both the MSS. and Ptolemy give **39**.

The figure $34\frac{11}{12}$ mentioned above is altogether wrong in the *Mirrour* [2]. We read there $24\frac{1}{2}$. $34\frac{11}{12}$ is confirmed not only by the calculation which we have just given, but also by the measure of the line in the rhymed version of the *Image*, which is too short by one syllable if we read xx (vingt) instead of xxx (trente).

fo. 92.

When reckoning the time taken by Adam to walk from the earth to heaven, starting at the Creation, the Prose MSS. of the *Image du Monde* base their calculations on an average of 20 miles a day, which produces an absurd result. Caxton corrects the figure to *25*, which is in accordance with the Verse MSS. According to these calculations Adam would still have to walk

[1] Cf. p. 124.   [2] Cf. p. 170.

for 713 years after the date when the *Image* was finished, *i. e.* in 1245 (not 1246 as Caxton says).

If we work out this sum we find that the Creation must have taken place in the year 5199½ before Christ. This is the date given by Orosius. The figure *25* is thereby proved to be correct.

We reproduce here the interesting passage which fixes this last date [1]:

" Sunt autem ab Adam, primo homine, usque ad Ninum magnum (ut dicunt) regem, quando natus est Abraham, anni tria millia centum octoginta et quatuor. . . . A Nino autem vel Abraham usque ad Cæsarem Augustum, id est, usque at Nativitatem Christi . . . anni duo millia quindecim."

All these numbers must have been well known and acknowledged as correct in the Middle Ages, since Gossouin uses them as a basis for his calculations without even mentioning them.

In the following pages we give Caxton's full text without any corrections or emendations, as copied by us, only the stops being inserted as a help towards the correct reading. The extension of abbreviations is given in italics. Capitals are used in all cases for the initial letters of proper names.

Otherwise the present edition can in no sense be called critical : it is a reprint. All mistakes, as far as lay in the editor's power, have been mentioned and corrected in the notes. A careful comparison with the Old French Version, and with a perfect copy of the second edition, belonging to the Cambridge University Library, have also been the means of explaining some obscure passages of which a paraphrase is given in the foot-notes.

Here and there the text, often incorrect, of the old French MS. Royal 19A IX., seems to have baffled Caxton. In such cases he either gives us a free translation or an approximate meaning of the original, or else he translates word for word and sacrifices clearness to accuracy.

[1] Orosius, *Hist.*, I. 1 (*Patrol.*, t. 31).

Differences in spelling between the two English editions will form part of a separate work, undertaken at the suggestion of the late Dr. Furnivall, dealing with the influence, often most striking, of Old French idioms and syntax on Caxton's translation. This subject, so interesting in itself, is proving more extensive than was at first supposed, and could not have found room in the present volume. A separate vocabulary was deemed unnecessary. The few exceptional words, not to be found in Mayhew and Skeat's *Middle English Dictionary*, are either translated in the notes, or Caxton himself explains them by means of pairs of words which answer the purpose of a glossary.[1]

Before closing this Introduction, we must add that any point which may seem to have been passed over rather lightly and without sufficient references to authorities, will be found fully dealt with in the French edition of the *Image du Monde*. The reader will also find there a complete bibliography of the subject.

The editor has to thank many scholars for kindly help and advice: Professor H. Suchier, of Halle University, who first suggested the editing of the Old French text ; Dr. Pietschmann, Director of the Göttingen University Library ; Mr. A. de Poorter, town-librarian at Bruges ; Mr. J. A. Herbert, of the British Museum, who, in addition to revising some of the proofs, has been a source of invaluable assistance and never-failing information ; Mr. John Munro, thanks to whose efforts a work begun some years ago is at last seen in print.

A student in search of material for his work is not received everywhere with the kindness and courtesy shown by the Cambridge University Librarians.

The inception of this edition was due to Dr. Furnivall. It is through him that the Early English Text Society undertook its publication.

[1] Cf. p. 10. deffete or vnmake.
14. ewrous and happy.
17. enhaunsed and lyft up.
26. ouche or gemme.
50. araye and atourement.
68. conduyted and brought.
78. aryse ne releue, etc.

We append a list of works to which we frequently refer as sources. For the sake of brevity, the author's name alone, printed in italics, is given in the notes to the text.

Adelard of Bath, *Quaestiones Naturales* (Louvain, 1480).

Gervase of Tilbury, *Otia Imperialia* (ed. Leibnitz, 2 vol., Hanover, 1707).

Giraldus Cambrensis, *Topographia Hibernica* (Opera, ed. Brewer and Dimock, 8 vol., London, 1861–1891, vol. 5).

Honorius Augustodunensis, *Imago Mundi* (Migne, *Patrologia*, t. 172).

Isidore of Seville, *Etymologiae* (Migne, *Patrologia*, t. 81–84).

Jacobus de Vitriaco, *Historia Hierosolomitana* (Douai, 1597).

Neckam, *De Naturis Rerum* and *De Laudibus Divinae Sapientiae* (ed. T. Wright, London, 1863).

Orosius, *Historiarium libri septem* (Migne, *Patrologia*, t. 31).

Philosophia Mundi (Migne, *Patrologia*, t. 172).

Ptolemy, *Almagest* (ed. Halma, Paris, 1813).

Solinus, *Polyhistor* (Biponti, 1794).

Besides the above, other authors are occasionally mentioned as sources. In such cases we give in full, in the notes, the title and edition of the work quoted.

The Mirrour of the World

---

[1] The numbering of the chapters in Caxton differs very much
from that of the O.F. text. This can be accounted for by the
fact that chapters in Royal 19A, IX., the O.F. MS. used by Caxton
for his translation, are not numbered, the references in the table
being not to chapters, but to pages in the text.

[2] Chapters vii to xiii, Part 1, form one chapter only in the O.F.
original, which has therefore only fourteen chapters.

2

Contents.

[1] The second part in the O.F. original contains only nineteen
chapters. The chapters correspond as follows:—

O.F.	Caxton.
i	= i and ii.
ii	= ii–x.
iii, iv, v	= xi, xii, xiii.
vi	= xiiii–xvi.
vii, viii, ix, x	= xvii, xviii, xix, xx.
xi, xii, xiii, xiv	= xxi, xxii, xxiii, xxiv.
xv	= xxv, xxvi, xxvii, xxviii.
xvi	= xxix.
xvii	= xxx.
xviii	= xxxi, xxxii.
xix	= xxxiii.

Contents.

Here endeth the second partie of the table of the
  Rubrices of this present booek.

[1] This chapter is wrongly numbered xxxii. It ought to be
xxxiii. The correct number is given p. 128.

Contents.

---

[1] The O.F. version has only twenty-two chapters in the third part.
 O.F. ch. i corresponds to Caxton's ch. i, ii, iii.

After this foloweth the Recapitulacion of the thinges   [fo. 4]
    aforsaid .   .   .   .   .   capitulo xxiiii.
Hier endeth the table of the Rubrices of this
    present book.

Prologue declaryng to whom this book apperteyneth.[1]

FIG. 1.

Consideryng that wordes ben perisshyng, vayne &
forgeteful, and writynges duelle & abide permanent, as I rede *Vox audita perit, littera scripta
manet*, thise thinges haue caused that the faites and
dedes of Anncyent menn ben sette by declaracion in
fair and Aourned volumes, to thende that science and
Artes lerned and founden of thinges passed myght be
had in perpetuel memorye and remembraunce ; ffor the
hertes of nobles in eschewyng of ydlenes at suche tyme
as they haue none other vertuouse ocupacion[2] on hande
ought texcersise them in redyng, studyng & visytyng
the noble faytes and dedes of the sage and wysemen

---

[1] In the wood-cut reproduced here, a scroll, issuing from the magi-
ster's mouth, with the words "*audita pereunt,*·*scripta manent,*" has
been inserted in ink.   [2] Caxton: *ocupacōn*; 2nd ed. *occupaciō*.

somtyme travaillyng in prouffytable vertues; of whom
it happeth ofte that sommen ben enclyned to visyte the
bookes treatyng of sciences particuler, and other to
rede & visyte bookes spekyng of faytes of armes, of
loue, or of other mervail*-lous histories. And emonge
alle other this present booke, whiche is called the ymage
or myrrour of the world, ought to be visyted, redde &
knowen, by cause it treateth of the world and of the
wondreful dyuision therof. In whiche book a man
resonable may see and vndrrstande more clerer, by the
visytyng and seeyng of it and the figures therin, the
situacion [1] and moeuyng of the firmament, and how the
vnyuersal erthe hangeth in the myddle of the same, as
þe chapitres here folowyng shal more clerly shewe and
declare to yon. Whiche said book waz [2] translated out
of latyn in to ffrensshe [3] by the ordynaunce of the
noble duc Johan of Berry and Auuergne, the yere of Our
Lord .M.CC.xlv. [4], and now at this tyme rudely translated out of ffrensshe [5] in to Englissh by me symple
persone William Caxton, [6] at the request, desire, coste
and dispense of the honourable & worshipful man
Hugh Bryce, Alderman and Cytezeyn of London, [7]
entendyng to present the same vnto the vertuous, noble
and puissaunt lord, Wylliam [8] lord Hastynges, lord
Chamberlayn vnto the most Crysten kynge, kynge
Edward the fourthe, kynge of England and of Ffraunce,
etc., and lietenaunt [9] for the same of the toun of Calais [10]
and marches there, whom he humbly bescheth to resseyue in gree and thanke. [11] Whiche booke conteyneth
in alle lxxvii chapitres and xxvii figures, [12] without
whiche it may not lightly be vnderstande.

[1] Caxton: *situacōn ;* 2nd ed. *sytuacion.* Cf. also "recommendacion," p. 77; signefycacions," p. 143, etc.
[2] 2nd ed. was.   [3] 2nd ed. frensshe.
[4] We find in the first part of this Prologue the strongest
evidence in favour of Caxton's use of the British Museum MS.
Royal 19A. IX, for his translation. The striking information which
this Prologue contains is not found in any of the other O.F. MSS.
[5] 2nd ed. frensshe.   [6] 2nd ed. Wyllm Caxton.
[7] 2nd ed. Londen.   [8] 2nd ed. Wyllm.
[9] Caxton: lietenaunt ; 2nd ed. lieutenaunt.   [10] 2nd ed. Caleys.
[11] The passage from "And now at this tyme . . ." to ". . . and
thanke." is not in the O.F. text.
[12] O.F. text contains 55 chapters and 28 designs, including two
designs not in the text. (2nd ed. says ".xxvii. chapitres.")

And for to declare more openly, it is ordeyned in thre parties, of whiche the firste conteyneth xx chapitres and viii figures, the seconde partie xxxiii chapitres and ix figures, and the therde conteyneth xxiiii chapitres and * [* fo. 5] x figures[1]; whiche was engrossed and in alle poyntes ordeyned by chapitres and figures in ffrenshe in the toun of Bruggis the yere of thyncarnacion of Our Lord .M.CCCC.lxiiii. in the moneth of Juyn, and emprised by me ryght vnable and of lytil connyng to translate and brynge it in to our maternal tongue þe second day of the moneth of Janyuer the yer of our said Lord .M.CCCC.lxxx. in thabbay of Westmestre by London,[2] humbly requyryng alle them that shal fynde faulte, to correcte and amende where as they shal ony fynde, and of suche so founden that they repute not the blame on me, but on my copie whiche i am charged to folowe as nyghe as God wil gyue me grace; whom i most humbly beseche to gyue me scyence, connyng and lyf taccomplysshe and wel to fynysshe it, etc.[3]

Thenne who so wylle comprise and vnderstande the substaunce of this present volume, for to lerne and knowe specially the creacion of this world, the gretnes of the firmament and lytilnes of therthe in regard of heuen, how the vii sciences were ffounden and what they bee, by whiche he may the better auaylle in knowleche alle the dayes of his lyf, thenne late hym rede this said volume treatably, auisedly and ordynatly, that, in suche thing as he shal rede, he suffre nothyng to passe but that he vnderstonde it right well; and so may he knowe and vnderstonde veritably the declaracion of this said volume. And he thenne that so wille obeye this commandement may, by the contente of the same, lerne grete partie of the fourme and condicion of this worlde, and how, by þe wyll of Our Lord *, it was by Hym [* fo. 5, vo.] created, made and accomplisshed, and the cause

[1] O.F. text: 1st part 14 ch., 8 designs
　　　　2nd ,, 19 ch., 9 ,,
　　　　3rd ,, 22 ch., 9 ,,
[2] 2nd ed. Londen.
[3] The passage from "and emprised by me ..." to "... fynysshe it, etc." is not in the O.F. text.

C

wherfor it was establisshid; wherof the debonayr Lord
hath don to vs so grete grace that we euer ben bounden
to gyue hym lawde and worshyp, or ellys we had
not ben of ony valew ne worth ony thyng, no more
than vnresonable beestis.

Thenne late vs praye the maker and creatour of alle
cratures, God all myghty, that at the begynnyg of this
book it liste hym of his most bounteuous grace to
departe with vs of the same, that we may lerne, and
that lerned to reteyne, and that reteyned so teche that
we may haue so parfyght scyence and knowleche of
God, that we may gete therby the helthe of our sowles,
and to be partyners of his glorye permanent and without
ende in heuen.   Amen.

[* fo. 6]   * Hier begynneth the book callid the myrrour of the
worlde,

And treateth first of the power and puissaunce of God.
capitulo primo.[1]

FIG. 2.

Ye ought to knowe that whan Our Lord God made the
world and that he had made alle thinges of nought,

[1] O.F. text Ch. I[1].

he had no nede of it ; ffor as moche had he bifore as he
had afterward.   Certainly God was to fore, and shal be
incessantly after, without ende and withoute begynnyng.
Thenne he shal nothyng amende ne be better, ffor hym
faylled neuer ony thynge.   He seeth all, hereth all,
knoweth alle, and holdeth alle thynge in his honde ; he
had neuer hunger, ne thurste, ne tyme, ne daye, ne hour,
but abydeth contynuelly in alle good : ffor to hym ne
apperteyneth soone ne late ; and of alle them that euer
were, that ben and shal be, haue alway ben and shal be
to fore his eyen as wel the ferre as the nyghe, and the
euyll as the good.[1] He sawe as wel the world er it was
made and fourmed as he doth now at this daye.

And yf he had neuer made the worlde, as moche had
he ben thenne worth, and of as grete valewe, as he euer
myght haue be ; ffor other wise he myght not be God yf
he knewe not, sawe and herde alle that myght be ; and
yf he were not soo, he shold be lackyng * and not myghty   [* fo. 6, vo.]
of euery thynge ; and of so moche he was and shold be
a mortal man.

Bus[2] his nature was not suche, ffor he is God entierly
and hool without begynnyng and without ende. Nothyng
is to hym newe ne olde.   Alle weel and good thingis
ben his by right, and by nature go on and retourne
agayn to hym ; ffor fro hym alle thynge procede and
meue, and retornyng to hym in holdyng the right
waye.[3]

He retcheth neuer of ony harme, ffor hys bounte
is alle pure, clene, hool and clere without ony espece
of euyll. Certes alle euyllis ben to hym contraryes.
And therfor it is pure necessite that they wythdrawe
them vnder hym and fro alle his goodnes ; ffor it is
nothyng but donge and ordure whiche muste nedes
descende in to the deppest. And the good thingis
must nedes goo vpward tofore the souerayn creatour

---

[1] "and of alle . . . good": All those that ever were, or are,
or will be, whether far or near, whether good or bad, have always
been before His eyes, and always will be.
[2] "bus" stands of course for "but"; 2nd ed. "but."
[3] "ffor fro hym . . . waye": (O.F. text, p. 60) for all good
things come from Him and move through Him, and return to
Him by keeping on the right way.

whiche is clere, net and pure. And the synnes, whiche
ben obscure, horrible and derke aboue alle other thyng,
leuen the good whiche is aboute God and auale and goo
doun ; ffor so behoueth it to be by rayson and nature,
alle in lyke wyse as we see the ordure of the wyn that
is put in the vessel, and the foule departeth fro the clere,
in suche wyse as the good and clere abydeth aboue. And
the lye,[1] whiche is thordure, abideth byneth in the bottom
as infecte and not good. And the good wyn that is
aboue abideth alway clere and fyn. And that whiche is
not good, that is byneth in the bottom, abideth alway
obscure, fowle and black. And so moche the more as the
wyn is good and more clere, so moche more reteyneth
the lye more of filthe and obscure.

Thus is it of the good and euyll ; ffor the euyll
[* fo. 7] muste descende in to *places derke and horrible and
ful of all sorow and bitternesse. And so moche more as
the good shyneth to fore God and the more it ioyeth,
so moche the more sorowe and derknesse is in helle,
where it is contynuell and shal be as longe as God shal
be in heuen, where as God hath alle goodnesse to fore
hym and alle way shall haue without payne, wythout
trauayl, and without grief or Annoye ; he hath alle, and
alle he enlumyneth without ony defaulte and withoute
ony terme.

God may make alle thyng, and alle deffete or vnmake
without changyng hym self in ony thing that may be ;
ffor he may alle and conceyueth alle. Ther is nothyng
that may hurte hym. He is establed without ony
meuyng, and alle meuynges meue of hym.

An hondred thousand yere mounte not to hym so
moche as the thousand parte of one only houre of this
world, ne to alle them that be in heuen ; of whiche the
leste that abideth there hath more Joye in an hour
only, and of deduyte, soulace, gladnes and of honour of
whiche he shal neuer be wery ne full, than ony man
may thynke ne knowe ne esteme in this world in an
hondred thousand yere, yf he myght so longe lyue and
endure, thaugh he were the most subtyl of alle the men

---

[1] lye : dregs of wine.

that euer were born or euer shal be, thaugh he thought
the beste he myghte.

Of this so grete and inestimable glorye is God the
veray and souerayn lord without ony other, as God that
alle knoweth and alle seeth, alle that euer that hath
ben, alle that is, and alle that euer shal be, and all that
belongeth to hym. Hym faylled neuer ony thynge
that is good; he hath hem alleway to fore hym; ner
ther was neuer ony good * thynge, ne neuer shal be, but   [* fo. 7, vo.]
that it was pourtrayed to fore hym byfore the creacion
of the world.

Now ye shal here why and wherfore God created and
made the world.

Wherfor God made and created the world.
capitulo ii°.[1]

FIG. 3.

[1] O. F. text, Ch. II [1].

G od made and created all the world of his only wylle
by cause that he myght haue somme thynge that
myght be suche as myght deserue of his weel and goodnes, yf it were not in his defaulte. And therfore he
establisshid this worlde, nothynge for that he shold be
the better, ne that he had ony nede. But he dyde it for
charyte and by his grete debonairte; ffor, as right
charitable, he wolde that other shold parte with hym of his
weel and goodnes, and that alle other creatures, euerich
after his nature, sholde fele of his puissance after that it
myght apperteyne to hym.[1]

Thus wold God establisshe this world, that suche
thinge shold yssue that myght vnderstande and knowe
the noblesse of his power and of his sapyence, and also
of the good that he made for the man erthely, that he
myght serue hym in suche maner, that by hym he
myght deserue the grete weel and good that he had
made for hym.

[* fo. 8]   Thenne ought we aboue alle other thynge to loue hym
and thanke * hym that made and fourmed vs, whan we
haue suche power and suche auctorite by hym that, yf
we wil loue hym, we shal be lordes of alle goodes. Now
loue we hym thenne with alle our myght, and thenne
shal we doo as wise men. And yf we do not, we shal
haue grete harme and dammage; ffor yf we by our
cause lose suche goodes as Our Lord hath made for vs,
yet for alle that God shal lese nothing. Certaynly he
made them to thende that we shold haue them, syth
that by our good dedes we myght conne deserue them
and that he of his grace hath gyuen to vs the wytte,
thentendement and the power.

Wherfor God fourmed man like vnto his ymage and
to his semblaunce. capitulo iii°.[2]

[1] "God made . . . apperteyne to hym": St. Augustin, *Liber
de diligendo Deo,* c. II (Migne's *Patrologia,* t. 40): "Sciendum est
ergo rerum creatarum, coelestium et terrestrium, visibilium et
invisibilium, causam non esse nisi bonitatem Creatoris, qui est
Deus unus et verus; cujus tanta est bonitas, quod alios suae
beatitudinis qua aeternaliter beatus est, velit esse participes."
[2] O.F. text, Ch. III [1].

FIG. 4.

Whan God fourmed man, he wolde make and create hym like vnto his ymage and semblaunce, to thende that he shold haue remembraunce of the goodes that he had lente hym, and that he myght deserue them alle by right and raison; ffor he shewde to hym so grete loue, that aboue alle other creatures he fourmed hym to his figure and semblaunce, and gaf to hym naturelly right parſyght vnderstondyng for to loue and knowe hym more than ony * other thyng, to thende that he myght [* fo. 8, vo.] parte¹ more largely of his goodes than ony other creature.²

Ne God dyde neuer ne made for other creature so many good thynges as he hath made for man. But who is he that wyll deserue them? And yf he doo not, it is Reson that he sorowe; ffor he doth to God no bounte, that doth wel for to haue hys grace and his loue; ffor he doth it

---

¹ parte : share in.
² "Whan God . . . creature": St. Augustin, *De Trinitate*, xiv. 12 (Migne's *Patrologia*, t. 42, col. 1048): "Non propterea est Dei imago in mente, quia sui meminit et diligit se, sed quia potest etiam meminisse, intelligere et amare Deum, a quo facta est."

more for his owen prouffyt than he doth it for other. And ther for he doth well that loueth and seruyth hym; ffor moche may he calle hym self Caytyf and meschaunt that by his folye leseth so hye, so noble and so excellente glorye ffor his synne that prouffyteth hym nought. And hath not in thende but shame and blame, and draweth hym in to suche a place where is no thinge but payne, yre, sorowe and heuynesse, of whiche he shal neuer see hym delyuerd as longe as he lyueth.

Thus hath he loste the grete joye that was gyuen to hym, whiche is taken away by his synne. And myght haue ben a lord yf he had wolde, yf he had mayntened hym self in doyng alway good werkes, and wold haue absteyned and kepte hym fro doyng euyll; ffor who that doth wel in this world, he hath so moche good and honour that thangels of heuen make hym their lord and maistre by fore God kynge of alle kynges. Thenne he may wel holde hym for ewrous [1] and happy that doth so moche good in erthe duryng his lyf, that may conquere and haue this honour. And that may euery persone doo all for hym self yf it pleseth hym. Now late euerych doo as hym good shal seme, and take whiche that he wylle ; for he may wynne by doyng well, and also lese by doyng euyll.

[* fo. 9] * Wherfor God made not the man suche as he myght not synne. capitulo iiii°.[2]

Whan Our Lord God created the man, he gaf to hym power to doo his fre wille, that is to wete to doo good or euyll, whiche he wolde. Ffor yf God had made the man suche as he myght not haue synned ne to haue don nothing but well, he shold haue take from hym somwhat of his power ; ffor he myght not thenne haue don euyll whan it had plesyd hym, and thenne it shold haue folowed that, wold he or not, he shold alway haue doon weel withoute reson ; and thus he shold not haue ben cause of the good that he shold haue doon, but it

---

[1] ewrous : O.F. beneüré (happy, blessed).
[2] O.F. text, Ch IV[1].

sholde haue proceded of another whiche by force sholde
haue caused hym and haue gyuen hym the wylle. And
he by the moyen of that he so shold do shold deserue
the gwerdon, and not only he ; ffor lityl deserueth he
that by force of other doth seruyse.[1] Who that to morow
shold put me in a stronge prison ayenst my wille for to
doo good, I shold not holde hym for wyse, ffor he shold
doo me wronge.

Neuertheles it was wel in Our Lordes power, yf it had
plesed hym, to haue made man suche that he shold not
haue synned ne haue don ony harme ne euyll. But he
had not deseruid yet suche merite ne reward as he now
doth in no tyme of the world. And therfor God gaf to
man playn fre wille to doo weel or euyll to thende that
in weel doyng and leuyng the euyll he myght haue
more merite ; ffor other wise * he myght not deserue so
moche. Yf God had made thangels suche as myght not
haue synned dedly ne haue don euyll, ffor that yet
shold not they deserue so noble a yefte as the men.[2]
And who that wille deserue these hye merytes, he ought
gladly with entier herte and parfyght serue, by grete
loue and grete Reuerence, hym that hath made hym for
to conquere and come to the most hye honour.

And Our Lord God wolde that man were suche that,
by right, he myght deserue as moche good a boute hym
as he hym self hath. And therfore he gaf to hym
witte and reson for to haue entencion[3] to hym ; ffor by
right he ought wel to serue hym.

Thenne is he a moche fool that pourueyeth not to
doo well whilis he is here lyuynge ; ffor alle the good
that euery man shal doo shal be for hym self, and alle
the euyll also ; and eche man shal haue for one good
thinge an hondred good thinges, and for one euyll an
hondred euillis. Ffor he is a moche fool that weneth to
doo to God ony bounte of his goodis in ony maniere that

[* fo. 9, vo.]
b 1

---

[1] "Whan Our Lord God . . . doth seruyse": St. Augustin,
De Libero Arbitrio, II. 1 (Migne's *Patrologia*, t. 32, col. 1221).
[2] O.F. text (p. 64): If God has made the angels such that they
cannot commit a deadly sin nor do evil, at the same time they
cannot deserve the same rewards as men.
[3] entencion : heed.

it be; and whan he absteyneth hym fro doyng euyll, so moche Our Lord holdeth hym the derrer and loueth hym the better. Ffor yf he loste alle the world, Our Lord shold neuer be the lasse worth, ne none of the goodis that ben in his power.

Yf alle the sayntes that euer here[1] to fore in the world or euer shal be had neuer don good, and that alle by her[2] demerytes were perpetuelly dampned in helle, yet for alle that Our Lord God shold neuer haue the lasse joye ne consolacion, and shold not be the lasse worth, ne noo thinge that is in heuen.[3]

[* fo. 10] But the sayntes were wyse, *prudent and constaunt for to doo weel and prouffyt, as they that playnly knewe that this world is not but a vayn thinge and transi- toire; and had moche leuer to suffre paynes and trauaylles, and offre their bodyes to tourment and martirdom, and to haue shames, blasphemies and other iniuries for the loue of Our Lord in this myserable world that so litil while endureth, and to haue the goodes of heuen euer lastyng, than to haue ease chaungeable to the body for to haue payne perdurable. They retched[4] not ne had no charge of suche goodis that atte laste shold be of no value, but they toke the bridle by the teeth for to gete the right hye witte and vnderstandyng of heuen. And ther ben many of them that holde them for foolis in this world, the whiche now at this tyme haue their neckis charged of whiche the other be deliueryd; ffor they ben herberowed in heuen. And yet holde they many a wise man for fool that preyse not moche their wordes.

Ther ben plente of wise peple in heuen now, that, yf they had preysed the folissh dictes or sayengis and the folissh werkis of the peple that so moche coueyte the nauoir and loos of this world for the worde of foles, that they had lefte the commandemens of God. In whiche the sayntes in heuen dyde gretely their deuoyr[5]; ffor they lefte not, for the delytes of the world, to serue their

---

[1] here = were.   [2] her : their.
[3] O.F. (p. 64): And neither He nor anything that is in Heaven would be worth any the less.
[4] retched : cared.   [5] deuoyr : duty.

maker and creatour for to gete heue*n* where they haue
joye and alle honour, as they that ben lordes and shal
ben withoute ende. And yf they had don otherwise,
they shold haue perpetuelly shame, fylthe and tour-
mentis of helle where as ben alle the euyllys that *man
can deuise.   [fo. 10, vo.]
                                                              b 2

It is moche grete meruaylle of this world how that
it is so, that ther ben so moche peple that will suffre
payne and trauaylle more for to gete loos of the peple
or for to amasse grete tresours the whiche so lytil
tyme abide with hem that in an only hour they faylle,
than they wille doo for to conquere the goodes of Our
Lord, the whiche shal neuer faylle, whiche the blessid
sayntes haue goten by a lytil hard lyf that they haue
endured in this world, that ne semeth but a right
delyte to them that of good herte doo it. And in thende
it semeth to them that for lytil or nought they haue
goten heuen.

And alle thus may euery persone gete it, and be
comyn of ¹ the goodes of Our Lord and haue the joyes
and glorye of heuen, yf the defaulte be not in hym
self. But they that desire the joyes, the glorye and
honours of this world, they empayre them self so moche
that they may not lerne no good ne entende to their
sauacion. And had moche lieuer the ease and consola-
cions of the body, of whiche they ben so sone put out
and brought to sorow and payne, than they doo the
ease of the sowle whiche endureth without ende. Ne
they preyse not the wytte ne entendement of the man,
yf he can not wel haue hym in the world and haue
plente of temporel goodes by whiche he may be enhaunsed and lyft vp in the world ; but saye he is nyce ²
and folissh by cause he can not their malices and cawteles.

But alle they ben cursed of God by the mouth of Dauid
the prophete, that so payne them to plese the world by alle
the wayes that they can doo ; ffor suche pryde is vayne
thynge by whiche *the soule is eupayred.³ Of whom   [* fo. 11]
Dauid saith in the psaulter : Acursid be alle they and

---

¹ be comyn of : participate in.
² nyce (O.F. nice) : silly.   ³ eupayred : harmed.

confused as peple of exyle, that playse the world; ffor of alle goodes they extende them[1] and discorde fro God and fro his loue, syth they haue gyuen them and that they acorde them to the world, to his vanytees and delytes; ffor God hath them alle in despyte, and put them fro his grace, by cause they seche the loos and the glorye of the world in whiche he was put out and sette aback and in thende crucyfyed and holden for a fool.

Thus saith Our Lord God in his gospell, that alle they shal be blessyd that haue the world in despyte and shal be as peple hated, defowled and cast out as foles for the loue of me and of my name; ffor they shall haue in heuen their reward and guerdoun. And this may euery man, yf God hym self lye not, and trouthe may not be false, that they whiche plese the world and wille haue and take the loos and glorye of the world, it may not be but they after haue sorowe. Therfor he is a fool that secheth to haue it, by cause alle they that weeshe or pourchace it by euyl connceylled[2]; ffor alle suche maner of peple ben by the deuyl ledde in to helle where they haue a right soroufull guerdoun. And ther is nowher so valiaunt a kynge ne so puissaunte prince, duc, erle, knyght or noble man to whom the deuyl hath regard, but that he doo to hym as moche grief to his power as to the most vyle and most poure that cometh in to helle, whan he hath so vsed his dayes and lyf that he is fallen in his hondes; ffor alle they that ben dampned for to goo theder, of what estat that they be, ben alle called Rybauldis; ffor he mocht haue conquerd in heuen
*[fo. 11, vo.]
b 3
more noble and more worthy * Royamme than is in this world; ffor who that in this world serueth Our Lord vnto the deth, he is more honoured in heuen than alle the kynges that euer were in this world that so litil erídureth with vs. Now serue we hym thenne and leue we the euyll, the glorye and the vanyte of this world.

Syth thenne that hereto fore we haue deuised how and wherfor God hath created the world and wherfore

---

[1] extende them : deprive themselves.
[2] by = be (2nd ed. : be euyl counseyled).

he made man, we shal deuise to yow herafter the fourme
of the world and the facyon after that it conteyneth and
compriseth, and how it is made and composed rounde
aboute. But it is expedyent that to fore this we speke
of the vii Artes liberals and of theyr resons, and how
they were founden by them that apperceyued the
sciences and vertues ; ffor by the vii Artes ben knowen
the faytes of the world and how it is sette. And therfore
we owe now to speke therof for to vnderstonde the
better that we shal saye here after.

Wherfor and how the vii Artes liberal were founden
and of their ordre. capitulo v°.[1]

N ow declareth this book whiche is drawen out of
Astronomye how somtyme the notable and wyse
philosophres wold enquere of the maner of the world,
and how hit had ben created and made of God, wherof
moche peple meruaylled.

And thenne whan the world was made and compassed,
ther was peple ynowhe of whiche many behelde the
firmament that torned round aboute the world and
meuyd. They had grete meruaylle how it myght be
made, *and they waked and studyed many nyghtes and   [*fo. 12]
many dayes. Thenne began they to beholde the sterres
that roos in the eest, and meued aboute ouer their hedes.

Certaynly thise philosophres apetyted not these grete
mangeries ne delicyous wynes, ne for to fille their belyes
as don beestis that seche nothinge but their pasture,
like as this day doo they that retche of nothinge but to
fylle their paunche with good wyncs and good vitailles
and after to haue a fair bedde, white shetes and softe,
and there to slepe as the swyne.[2] But those were
wakyng and studyeng many nyghtes, and it greued
them not ; but they were embelisshid moche of that they
sawe the firmament thus torne and so nobly to holde his
cours and termes.

Thus sawe they the sterres meue til they went doun in

---

[1] O.F. text, Ch. V [1].

[2] "And thenne whan . . . as the swyne" : Neckam, *De Naturis
Rerum*, II. 173 ; *De Laudibus Divinae Sapientiae*, 10. (ed.
T. Wright, London, 1863.)

the weste, somme on that one side, and somme on the
other side, and somme sonner than the other. Thus
behelde the prudent men, philosophres and other, aboute
the firmament til it was day, that they sawe the sonne
shewe and ryse in the mornyng rede and clere, whiche
ascended and mounted half the day, and that other
half descended so longe til he wente vnder, whiche
made the nyght tapproche. And thenne cam agayn
the sterres in the nyght in their cours til the sonne
cam agayn and enlumyned the day, and helde his way
and cours til that he repayred on the morn in to his
pryncypal place.

After they behelde the mone whiche was a comune
thynge and appered to the world dyuersely. One tyme
she was rounde, another tyme half and after horned,
and so wente and becam such as no man myght see her.
And after she appered horned and syth half as she had
ben to fore, and * also round and full. Thenne knewe
they well by their entendement that she approched
the sonne til she was euen ayenst hym, and after
departed. And after she withdrew her more and more
til that she was vnder the sonne as she had ben
to fore. And thenne she wente and cam agayn euery
nyght and day tornyng and makyng her cours aboute
the firmament, right as she now doth wyth out ony
thyng changyng the contrarye.

But now as said is, the peple that ben now thynke
more and ben moche more curyous of their grete and
fatte paunches for to fylle, and to make them fatte, by
whiche they come the sonner to their ende and to
carayn, and by their ouermoche nourisshyng and vylay-
nous, whiche delyuereth them first to trauaylle and after
to shame and dampnacion.

The auncyent faders gouerned them not in this wyse;
ffor they setted not of mete and drynke but for talegge
their hungre and thurste for to susteyne their bodyes
and to holde hem in helthe in suche wyse as they myght
helpe them self by their wittes, as they ought to doo
for to come to the glorye of Our Lord. And that tyme
they lyued xx or xxx yere lenger than they doo now

[*fo. 2, vo.]
      b 4

of an honderd one ; and that procedeth of theyr folissh
and outrageous gouernaunce. Certaynly such peple
vnderstande not wel the worde of Our Lord whan he
said to the deuyll whan he cam to tempte hym and saide
that he shold make of the stones brede and that he
shold ete. Thenne Jhesu Cryst answerd that man lyued
not only by brede, but by the worde that procedeth fro
the mouth of God.[1]

Yf the men in thise dayes vnderstode wel this
worde, they wolde reteyne more gladly the doctrynes
* that procede and come fro the mouth of our creatour   [* fo. 13]
and maker. But the grete rentes that they haue, and
the grete tresours of their coffres ben cause of
shortyng and abreggyng of their dayes, by their
disordinat mangeries that ouermoche noye and greue
them, so that nature may not wel bere ne susteyne,
wherof they muste nedes the sonner rendre their soule
and dye. Thus their Rentes, their tresours or other
thinge wherin they delyte them, take a way theyr lyf,
their herte and their wytte alle att ones, in suche wyse
than whan deth cometh and muste nedes dye, they haue
loste wytte and vnderstondyng ; of whom many ben
deed and dampned, whiche at their nede may not be
counseilled ne can not helpe them self whan they haue
moste nede.

They lyue not lyke them that, for to kepe them fro
peryllis, studyed in sciences and vsed their lyf in suche
manere that they wold but susteyne their body only as
longe as they shold be in this world, as they that wel
knewe that this lyf shold not to them longe endure.
And had enuye at none other thinge, but only for to
lerne suche science by whiche they myght knowe the
souerayn kynge allmyghty that alle had created of
nought and made it with his hand.

Thenne they thought in their entendement, as peple
that was of noble and vertuous entencion, that they
shold neuer haue knowleche of Our Lord God, ne of so
hye myght, but yf they entended and serched in his

---

[1] "Thenne Jhesu . . . of God": *St. Matthew* iv. 4.

werkes whiche they fonde so excellente and as grete as
they myght enquere and knowe ; ffor men shal neuer wel
knowe the maistre, but yf byfore men knowe parfightly
his estate and what his werkes been ; ffor by the werkys
[*fo. 13, vo.] is the werkeman * knowen, and how he may be suche
one. And therfor the auncyent faders wold employe
them and assaye the werkis of Our Lorde, and first for
to haue knowleche of his power and his vertue, considering that they myght not ocupye them self in a more digne
ne worthy science ne more diffycile. And whan the
more that they knewe of his werkis and of his wisedom,
so moche more had they the better wille to loue her
creatour and maker, and to honoure hym, considering
that he had made so noble a thinge and so worthy as is
the heuen in whiche ben the sterres that shyne bright
therin, and his other meruayllous vertues whiche they
preysed moche ; ffor, how moche more they preysed hym,
so moche with good wille they seruyd hym ; ffor it was
all their affeccion, intencion and reson to knowe God,
ffor as moche as they knewe certainly that God had gyuen
to them, with nature, witte and raison for to serche and
compryse of thinges of therthe and of them of heuen as
moche as they myght knowe ; ffor otherwyse they myght
neuer haue thought it.

Thus a man, be he neuer so wise ne discrete, may
neuer come for to vnderstande the hye secretes of God
ne of his myracles, but by hym ; ffor by right he
knoweth all. But of them that by nature be made
and ordeyned in heuen and in erthe, man may wel
enquere somme resouns, yf it be gyuen hym and that
he be garnysshid of good quyk witte, and that he
haue sette and employed his tyme to studye and to
lerne.

And sith they had goten vnderstandyng and raison by
their grete estudye, labour and trauayll, so moche that
they myght comprise wherfore and how alle the world
[* fo. 14] was made and * compassed, as ye haue herd here to fore,
so thought they thenne that they myght wel knowe and
haue reson of somme thinges, sith they had the vnderstandyng of hym that is almyghty to knowe in partie, or

atte leste of suche as they myght see with their eyen,
how wel that they were ferre.[1]

Thus wold they knowe the reson of that that they
sawe so meue the sterres of the firmament, and of them
that shone so clere. Certainly this was the pryncipal
cause why first they put them to studye for tenquere the
science that they knewe not; and knewe wel that they
shold enquere sonner of thinges that they sawe than of
them that they sawe not. And therfore were they meuyd
for to knowe and tenquere the science whiche they knewe
not of that they had ofte seen the firmament to meue,
and wolde knowe the trouthe. And saide it was right
good to knowe it, yf it pleasid God, and to knowe of
his naturel werkis, ffor the more parfightly to bileue and
knowe how he was God alle myghty; ffor men coude
not knowe ne fynde no resons of God but only by his
werkis.

The good Auncyent wise men, wiche diligently wolde
vnderstonde this mater, had noo cure for to amasse none
other goodes, but only to lerne the pure science. They
were nothing couetous, ne sette not to gadre tresours.
And ther were plente of them that apperceyued, as wise
men, that it was a grete charge to them oftymes as wel
to kepe it as to spende it by mesure, as in other wayes
to gete it and bringe it to gedre, and that all this was a
letting to them for to lerne.[2]

And they deliberid emong them and concluded that
somme caste and threwe their tresour in to the see.
The other * gaf it away and abandonned to them that   [*fo. 14, vo.]
wold take it, and wente as hermytes. And the other
departed it to poure peple. And other ther were that
lefte their good in suche wyse as them semed that they
shold haue lasse cause to thynke theron, and reteyned
nothyng but only for their vse. And helde with hem
certayn folke to serue them, to thende only that they

---

[1] "how wel that they were ferre": although they were so far
away from them.

[2] "And ther were . . . to lerne": And many of them, as wise
men, saw that it was often as much a burden to keep their treasures,
and to spend them, as to gather them; and that all this was a
hindrance to learning.

shold entende to nothyng but to studye and to lerne.
They dyde do edefye their houses fro the peple like as
religious peple, and sette them in suche places that
thries or foure tymes the weke they myght assemble
and come to gydre for to solace them and sporte. And
there eche rendred his reson of that he had founde and
lerned. And so longe dyde they thus til they had
experimented whiche was trewe and who knewe most,
and that they had founden who had moste grettest
entendement; and hym they chose by consent of them
alle for maistre. And he recorded their resons, heeryng
alle the felawys, and reherced to them alle to gydre
that euery man had said. In this manere were the
clergies first founden, contryued and auaunced.

And somoche trauaylled and studyed that they knewe,
by the helpe of Our Lord of whom alle science groweth
and haboundeth, grete partye of that it is. But this was
not in lytel tyme, ffor they were longe in studye and
vnderstode moche. And they that were first, alle that they
vnderstode and knewe, they put it in wrytyng the best
wise they coude, to thende that they that shold come
after them and wold entremete in [1] connyng, myght haue
their wrytyngis and trauaylle alway in the science, as
they had don byfore. Alle that they fonde and sawe,
[* fo. 15] they sette in compilacions. * And dide so moche, eche in
his tyme, that they were more than .ii.M. and .CCCC.
yere er they, by their labours and continuel studyes, had
goten the vii Artes or sciences liberal and put to gydre.

But they helde their labour wel employed, and the
payne that they put therto; ffor they knew, by their
witte and by their clergye, alle that was come on erthe
by nature, whan they wold sette their cure theron.
And also were not abasshed whan a merueyllous
caas happed on heuen or on erthe; ffor they coude wel
enquere the reson wherfore it was, and sith that it
happed by nature. And so loued God moche the more,
whan they sawe suche meruayllous werkis.

And watched many nyghtes with right grete joye and
grete studye of this that they sawe; and fonde so hye

---

[1] entremete in : busy one's self with, cultivate.

werkes, by whiche they amended them self ayenst Our
Lord, that they knewe trouthe and lefte the vanyte of
this world that so litil is worth, for to come to the joye
that neuer shall faylle. Of whom plente of wyse philosophres that were in the world deyde wrongfully and
without reson, by cause they shewde rightfully to the
grete lordes, and gaf them fair examples in repreuyng
and myspreysing their euil tyrannyes and thextorsiouns
that they dyde to moche peple ; and preched to them
right and trouthe. And they that wold not bileue them
and had shame of that they were of them blamed, they
made them to be put in their prisons, where they made
them to deye by greuous tourmentes, by cause they
shewd to them the trouth wherof they were certayn,
like as was don to holy sayntes that suffred deth and
passion for the loue of Ihesu Cryste whom they wold
enhaunse.

So were ther suche philosophres that by their witte
*and vnderstandyng prephecyed the holy tyme of the   [*fo. 15, vo.]
comyng of Ihesu Cryste ; lyke as Virgyle saide whiche
was in the tyme of Cezar at Rome, by whiche plente of
peple haue ben better syth than they were bifore ; ffor
he saide that a newe lignage was enioyed[1] fro heuen
on hygh, that shold do vertues in erthe, by whom the
deuyl shold be ouercome. Vpon whiche saynt Poul that
sawe this escripture whiche he moche preysed, saide
with a sorouful herte, for so moche as he had not ben
crysten : Ha! that i shold haue rendred and yelden the
to God, yf thou haddest lyued and that i had come
to the.

Other philosophres ther were of whome euerich saide
good wordes and meruayllous. But we may not now
reherce alle the good thinges that they saide, ffor they
were prudent alle and valyant, seen that they set to fore
alle other thynges clergye ; ffor yf it were not by clergye,
men shold not knowe that God were ; and yf they had
not ben so prudent men as they were, ther had neuer

---

[1] enioyed : O.F. text (p. 73) has *eslessiée* (from "s'eslessier,"
to rush). Caxton has probably mistaken this verb. for the past
part. of *s'esleecier*, to rejoice.

be so grete clergye as is now ; and yf ther were now
suche as they were thenne that fonde first clergye,
it shold be other wyse than it now is.   But clergye
goth now al to nought, that almost it is perisshid ; ffor
in thise dayes the peple seeth not by cause that they
that ought wnderstande vertues and to teche other and
enseyne and gyue example to doo well, they ben they that
recule and withdrawe fro it.[1] And alle this procedeth
by their folye ; ffor noma*n* holdeth clergye for vertue,
ne he loueth it not ne applyeth it in all poyntes.   But
many ther ben that sechen the lyes and drestis,[2] and
leue the clere wyn*n* ; ffor noman lerneth ne secheth
now, but for to conne so moche that he myght conquere

[* fo. 16]   and * gete the moneye. And whan they haue goten and
largely assemblid therof, thenne ben they werse than
they were a fore ; ffor the money hath so surprysed
them that they may entende to none other thinge.

Ther ben plente of pour clerkes that gladly wold lerne
yf they had the power.   But they may not entende
therto, by cause they haue not wherof for to furnisshe
them of their necessitees as wel for to haue bookes as
mete, drinke and clothes, but ben constrayned for to
gete their liuyng other wise ; ffor the riche haue now
in thise dayes seased so moche that the poure abide
naked and must suffre.

Yet ben ther plente of Riche clerkis that haue bookes
without nombre of one and other, richely adoubed and
couerd, to thende that they ben holden for wise and
good clerkes ; ffor they seche to haue nomore, but only
the loos and preysing of the peple. And doo in lyke
wyse as the Cock that shrapeth in the duste for to fynde
pasture ; he shrapeth so longe in the duste and mulle til
he fynde a gemme riche and precyous whiche shyneth
clere ; thenne he begynneth to loke theron and beholdeth
it, and doth no more but late it lye, ffor he demandeth
not after the ouche[3] or gemme, but had leuir haue

---

[1] "ffor in thise . . . fro it" : For nowadays people do not see
that those who ought to be virtuous and to set an example to
others are the very people who abstain from doing good.

[2] lyes and drestis : dregs of wine.

[3] ouche : O.F. *noche*, necklace. Here "ouche" is evidently
synonymous with "gemme."

somme corn to ete. In like wise is it of many of thise not wise clerkis couetous that haue the precyous bookes richely lymined, storyed and wel adoubed, that doo nothinge but loke and beholde them without forth, while they be newe, by cause them seme that they ben fair; and so they beholde them gladly and passe ther with; and after they torne on that other side and thinke for to fylle their belyes and to come to their folyssh desyres.

And they myght lerne ynoughe yf they * wolde [*fo. 16, vo.] entende it; ffor they haue wel the power, and myght doo as the wise men dyde herto fore, the whiche by their trauayl, studye and diligence fonde first the clergyes; but they haue their entendement folissh and out of the waye. And therfor the sciences and artes perisshe in suche wise that vnneth and with grete payne knowe they their partes of reson, whiche is the first book of gramaire, the whiche is the first of the seuen sciences, but put their artes in their males, and goo lerne anon the lawes or decretals, and become aduocates and iuristes for to amasse and gadre alway money wherin the deuyl conforteth hem; and yet doo they not somoche for to lerne as they doo for to fylle their purses.

In Parys, Oxenford and Cambrige is ther suche maner of clerkes that ben acustomed to wille haue the Renomme and fame to be called maistres for to be the more preysed and honoured. And haue leuer to conne lytil and to haue the name of maistre, than they shold be good clerkes without hauyng the degree and name of maistre. But they be called maistres wrongfully, ffor vanyte maistryeth them in suche wise that they can but lytil trouthe; bicause that they haue so soone the name of maistre, they leue the clergye and take them to the wynnyng, lyke as marchants doo and brokers.[1]

And in this wise ben many in the world that haue the name of maistre, that knowe right lytil of good and reson; ffor they that now desire this ben not maistres

---

[1] "bicause that . . . brokers": For as soon as they have the name of master they give up the pursuit of knowledge and take to making money like merchants or brokers.

[² fo. 17]

after right, ffor they ordeyne them otherwise to the sciences than they dyde that fonde them first. They entred first in to gramayre for to drawe reson in their ordynaunce; and after, logyque * for to preue and shewe the trouth fro the false. After they fonde rethoryque for to speke fair in iugement and right whiche they moche loued; and after, arsmetryque for to expert in alle thinges; after they fonde geometrie for to mesure and compasse alle maistrye; and after they fonde the science of musyque for to sette alle thinges in concordaunce; after, they had the vnderstandyng of astronomye, ffor therby were they meuid to haue science and vertue.

In this manere ye may vnderstande how they that first fonde science ordeyned the vii artes or vii sciences. And they ben in suche wise entrelaced that they may not be auctorised that one without that other ne entrerly preysed; and also the first may not be perfightly conned withoute the laste, ne the laste wythout the firste; and he that wille lerne one a right and vnderstonde it, hym behoueth to lerne alle the other; ffor otherwise may not be knowen appertly the certayn ne the incertayn, ffor that one is so comune to that other that it behoueth to knowe of alle.

But now men seche to lerne no more but the arte for to gete þe moneye, and ben to blame of that the other were preysed that first so trauaylled of whiche it is to vs so grete nede; ffor litil shold we haue knowen yf we had not seen it by writing[1]; ffor, as it is tofore said, yf clergye had be loste, we had knowen nothing ne who had be God, ne men shold neuer haue knowen what thing had ben best to doo: and so shold alle the world haue ben dampned. Thenne had we ben born in an euyll houre, ffor the men had knowen nomore than do dombe beestis.

And alle the good thinges ben now knowen, and alle comen of the vii sciences that the philosophres fonde

---

[1] "But now men . . . by writing": But now men only try to learn the art of making money, and people who do work are blamed; while the Ancients were praised for doing what is so necessary to us: for without their writings we should have known but little.

somtyme by their wyttes ; ffor therby * had they vnder-   [*fo. 17, vo.]
stondyng to loue God and his vertues, and that God is   c 1
alway and shal be withouten ende. And so bileued they
in grete faith truly in the auncyent lawe. But in thise
dayes the sciences perisshe by our enuyes, detracconns
and other euylles, in suche wise that right lityl is
reteyned of one and other ; ffor now dar no man entende
but for rychesse, ffor myssayers, felons and enuyous
men that wil lerne no good ; and yf they see ony
entende to sciences and clergyes, and they be not riche
and myghty for to furnysse hem, the Ryche men wil
anon scorne and mocque them.

And thus wil the deuil exhorte them, that is their
maister and their lord and to whom it pleseth that they
messaye, in so moche as he shal reward them with grete
hyre that they shal be sure to haue alle euyl aduentures
in helle that stynketh, where they shal mocke them self
and shal saye that they were born in an euyl houre,
whan they haue not lerned that they ought to lerne.

There shal they haue more prouffyt of their sciences,
that loued better to conquere clergye, than the fool to
conne knowe to assemble the grete tresours and the
grete richesses. And knowe ye that alle they that, for
to gete worldly goodes, lefte their tyme for to lerne
good, ben alle assured to haue euyl and payne after their
deth ; ffor by their auarice and cheuaunce the sciences
come to nought, so that almost they be perisshyd ; and
that whiche now is knowen cometh and groweth of the
vnyuersitees of Parys, Oxenford and Cambrige and
other, etc.

Of thre maner of peple and how clergye cam first in
to the Royamme of Fraunce. capitulo vi°.[1]

Now regneth clergye moche strongly in Ffraunce in
the cyte of Parys as somtyme was in the cyte of
Athe*-nes whiche thenne was moche noble and puissaunt.   [* fo. 18]
The philosophres that thenne were, and whiche that
oughte to teche and lerne other, acompted but thre
maner of peple in the world after their vnderstandyng :
and that were clerkes, knyghtes, and labourers. The

---

[1] O.F. text, Ch. VI[1]

labourers ought to pourueye for the clerkes and
knyghtes suche thinges as were nedeful for them to lyue
by in the world honestly ; and the knyghtes ought to
defende the clerkis and the labourers, that ther were no
wronge don to them ; and the clerkis ought to enseigne
and teche these ii maner of peple, and to adresse them
in their werkis in suche wise that none doo thinge by
whiche he sholde displese God ne lese his grace.

Thus setted somtyme the wise philosophres thre maner
of peple in the world,[1] as they that knewe that no man
myght sette his corage in that he myght be wise a right
in ii maners or thre ; ffor it happed neuer day of the
world that clergye, cheualrye and labourers of therthe
myght be well knowen by one only man in alle his lyf,
ne lerned, ne reteyned. Therfore he that wold lerne
byhoueth hym only to lerne one of the thre ; and therfore the philosophres sette thre maner of peple without
moo in the erthe, ffor they wold seche the very trouthe.

And sought a cyte in the world, where they myght
best be and dwelle for tenquere thestate of the clergye.
And thus the better for tadresse them and to teche
other, they chees the cyte of Athenes whiche was
noble and somtyme one where they had their comyn
residence and assemblee. And there regned first
chyualrye with clergye. And after fro thens it wente to
Rome whiche now is of grete Renommee ; and there
cheualrye contynued long. And frothens after it
remeuid in to Ffraunce, * where chyualrye hath more
power than ony other place in the world. And thus
haboundeth there that one and that other, ffor cheualrye
sieweth alway clergye where she goth.

Thenne the kynge of Ffraunce and of Englonde may be
ioyous that there is in his Royammes suche seignourye as
is science of clergye where euery man may drawe out
wytte and connyng humayn, and ther abydeth neuer the
lasse [2] ; ffor it is as a fontayn that contynuelly sourdeth

---

[1] "The philosophres that thenne . . . in the world" : *Neckam*,
II. 21.
[2] "where euery . . . lasse ;" O.F. text (p. 78) : "ou chascuns
puis sens humains, ne pour ce mains n'en i remist il pas," *i. e.* from
which every man could draw human wisdom, and yet the supply
would be no smaller.

and spryngeth, and the more it renneth and the ferther, the more it is holsom ; and how more the sprynge of the fontayn renneth and ferther, somoche is the more of the water and the more may be taken fro it for nede.   In lyke wyse may I saye to yow that Parys, Oxenford and Cambryge ben the fontayns where men may drawe out most science, and more in Parys than in other places. And sith it is soo that clergye is somoche auaunced in Ffraunce, thenne ought we knowe by reson, in especyal yf the heyres of Fraunce daigne to conne it ; ffor like as the sonne is most fair of alle the sterres and causeth moste good thinges to growe in the world by the bounte that haboundeth in hym, so ought the kyng be of more valewe than ony other, and to haue more vnderstandyng and clergye, so that by his valyaunce and suffysaunce he myght shyne emonge other peple, and, by thexemple of his wel doyng that they see in hym, they myght by right condůyte drawe them to Our Lord.   And in suche wise shold he be kynge by right in this world and in heuen.

So thenne shold it be wel right and raison þat they doo their diligence to lerne suche clergye and science, that after this mortal lyf they lese not the seignourye of heuen ; ffor by nature and lignage ought they alle to loue clergye and alway to * lerne it.   [*fo. 19]

Certes themperour of Almaygne [1] louid with al his herte clergye, and auanced it to his power in Ffraunce. And alle the good clerkis that he coude fynde, he reteyned them to his courte, and sente for them oueral where he knewe ony.   He had in his tyme many a trauayll, many a payne, and many a danngier and ennoye for to mayntene and enhaunce crysten faith.   And therfore he neuer lefte, but helde the clerkes in right grete reuerence [2] ; ffor gladly he lerned alway, as is founden by his dedes.   He was a good Astronomyer, and was moche louid in Lorayn ; ffor gladly he dwellid there.   And yet ben ther many of his iewellis fair and riche that he gaf vnto chirches as a good blessid man as he was.   Truly he louid God aboue alle other thyng, and dyde moche

---

[1] "themperour of Almaygne" : O.F. text (p. 79) gives "*Charlemaine*," i. e. Charles the Great.
[2] "Certes themperour . . . reuerence" : *Neckam*, II. 174.

dyligence in his tyme for to brynge the sciences and the
clergye in to Fraunce; and yet they abyde there and
regne by his prowesse. And hath moche taught and
gyuen ensample to kynges that come after hym; ffor
euermore he hath in Parys conquerd science and
clergye.

Now thenne Almyghty God holde it, and that it may
in the cyte be alway mayntened. Ffor yf the studye
wente out of Ffraunce, knyghthode wold goo after, as it
hath alway don; ffor contynuelly that one is by that
other. Therfor late the kynge of Ffraunce for his weel
reteyne it yf he may; ffor he may wel lose his
Royamme, yf clergye departe out of Ffraunce.

Also ther ben in Ffraunce an other peple whiche ben
late come; and they ben ffreris mynours and iacobyns,
whiche haue take on them relygion for the loue of God for
to lerne and entende to serue God; of whom Our Lord
hath don to vs so grete honour and Reuerence that they
[*fo. 19, vo.]
c 3 reteyne alle the flour of * clergye in their ordres for
tadresse and enhaunce our moder holy chirche by their
estudye and trauaylle; ffor they haue good wille for to
serue Our Lord and to lerne sciences and the holy scripture,
as they that haue gyuen ouer the world and habandonned.
And me semeth that they doo as dyde they that setted
them by hynde the hutyns [1] in theyr cloyster vnder the
peple for the better to gete the merite of heuen in leuyng worldly possessions. And Our Lord hath don grete
bounte to them that haue them in their cytees, in their
castels and townes; ffor they serue not for tricherye and
barat, but trauaylle in prechyng and makyng sermones
for to brynge the peple to good lyf and to the waye of
trouthe. And oftymes suffre grete disease for to brynge
other in ease; ffor I bileue wel that, yf ne were theyre
bounte and good prechynge and techyng, Cristente
shold be exyled by errour and euyl byleue.

Yf they holde hem and kepe that they haue emprised,

[1] hutyns: The meaning of this word is doubtful. The whole
passage is a free translation of the O.F. text (p. 79), in which the
word corresponding to "hutyns" does not occur. Dr. Bradley, in
a kind reply to our inquiry on the subject, suggests that "hutyns"
is a misprint for *lutryns*, i.e. reading-desks.

as they that haue leyd doun vnder them alle the richesses
of the worlde, without retornyng agayn therto, thenne
haue they a moche good manere[1]; ffor they haue taken
on them for the loue of Our Lord the lyf of pouerte;
and plente of other that be in the world don in like wise,
that take ensample at them, that see that they weel doo.[2]

Therfor ought we to yeue[3] thankynges to God, and
adresse our hertes to doo well, in suche wise that by
right we myght goo to the joye of heuen by our good
deedis, of whiche God gyue vs myght to deserue that
therof we may be partoners.

But for as moche as ye haue herde reherce how the
vii artes or sciences liberall were founde and by whom,
I passe and deporte; but wille reherce what they be
and wherfore they serue; ffor fro them * procedeth
sens or wytte humayn and alle maner werke that is
made with hondes, alle prowesses, and all habilitees,
alle goodes and alle humylitees. And therfore I wil
descriue in mater and substance couenable the vertues
of eche of them, and wherof they procede particulerly
and of their nature; and after we shal speke of the
world, and how it is composed alle rounde. But byfore
alle other werkes we shal speke of the vii sciences
whiche ought not to be forgeten.[4] And first we shal
touche of the science or arte of gramaire whiche is the
first of the seuen and without whom the other syxe may
haue no perfeccion.

[*fo. 20]

Gramaire. capitulo vii°.[5]

The first of the vii sciences is gramaire of whiche, for
the tyme that is now, is not knowen the fourth
parte; wythout whiche science sikerly alle other sciences
in especial ben of lytil recommendacion, by cause without gramaire ther may none prouffyte; ffor gramaire is
the fondement and the begynnyng of clergye; and it is

[1] "Yf they . . manere": If they persist in what they have
undertaken, after giving up all the goods of this world for ever,
then they deserve much praise.
[2] "and plente . . . weel doo": and many others in the world
act likewise, and follow their example, as they see that such
people are doing what is right. [3] yeue: give.
[4] The description of the VII Arts is found in *Neckam*, II. 173;
De Laudibus, 10. [5] O.F. text, Ch. VII [1] (a).

the yate by the whiche in thenfancye is bygonne, and in
contynnyng, men* comeand atteyne to sapye*n*ce of clergye.
This is the scyence to fourme the speche, be it in latyn,
ffrenshe or englisshe, or in ony other langage that men

Fig. 5.

speke with. And who that coude alle gramaire, he coude
make and construe euery worde and pronounce it by
example. God made the world by worde, and the
worde is to the world sentence.

Here foloweth of logyke.   capitulo viii°.[1]

The seco*n*de science is logyke whyche is called dyale-
tyque. This science proueth the 'pro' and the
'contra': that is to saye the verite or trouthe, and
otherwyse. And it preueth wherby shal be knowen the
trewe fro the fals and the good fro the euyll, so veryly
that for the good was created heuen and maa , and
on the contrarye wyse, for the euyll was helle maad
and establisshyd, whiche is horryble, stynkyng and
redoutable.

[1] O.F. text, Ch. VII [1] (*b*).

FIG. 6.

Hier speketh of Rethoryque.   capitulo ix°.[1]

The therde of the vii sciences is callyd Rethoryque,
whyche conteyneth in substaunce rightwisnes,
Rayson and ordynaunce of wordes. And ought not to * be [*fo. 21

FIG. 7.
[1] O.F. text, Ch. VII [1] (c).

holden for folye; ffor the droytes and lawes by whiche
the iugements be made, and that by rayson and after
right ben kept and mayntened in the court of kynges, of
princes and of barons, come and procede of Rethoryque·
Of this science were extrayt and drawen the lawes and
decrees whiche by nede serue in alle causes and in alle
rightes and droytes.

Who wel knewe the scyence of Rethoryque, he shold
knowe the right and the wronge; ffor to doo wronge to
another, who so doth it is loste and dampned, and for
to doo right and reson to euery man, he is saued and
geteth the loue of God his creatour.

Here foloweth Arsmetryque and wherof it procedeth.
ca. x°.[1]

Fig. 8.

[*fo. 21 vo.]   The fourth scye*n*ce is called arsmetri*-que. This
science cometh after rethoryque, ande is sette in the
myddle of the vii sciences. And without her may none
of the vii sciences parfyghtly ne weel and entierly

[1] O.F. text, Ch. VII [1] (*d*).

be knowen. Wherfor it is expedyent that it be weel knowen and conned; ffor alle the sciences take of it their substaunce in suche wise that without her they may not be. And for this reson was she sette in the myddle of the vii sciences, and there holdeth her nombre; ffor fro her procede alle maners of nombres, and in alle thynges renne, come and goo.[1] And no thyng is without nombre. But fewe perceyue how this may be, but yf he haue be maistre of the vii artes so longe that he can truly saye the trouthe. But we may not now recompte ne declare alle the causes wherfore; ffor who that wolde dispute vpon suche werkes, hym behoued despute and knowe many thynges and moche of the glose.

Who that knewe wel the science of arsmetrique he myght see thordynance of alle thynges. By ordynance was the world made and created, and by ordynance of the Souerayn it shal be deffeted.

Fig. 9.

[1] "ffor fro her . . . and goo.": Caxton translates literally an obscure passage of MS. Roy. 19 A IX., which follows the Paris MS. A (p. 81): "par toutes choses querent et vont et viennent." The correct reading is: From Arithmetic proceed all numbers; by means of *numbers* all things run, come and go.

Next foloweth the scyence of Geometrye.   capitulo xi°.[1]

The fyfthe is called geometrye, the * whiche more auaylleth to Astronomye than ony of the vii other ; ffor by her is compassed and mesured Astronomye. Thus is by geometrye mesured alle thingis where ther is mesure. By geometrye may be knowen þe cours of the sterres whiche alleway go and meue, and the gretenes of the firmament, of the sonne, of the mone and of the erthe. By geometrye may be knowen alle thynges, and also the quantyte ; they may not be so ferre, yf they may be seen or espyed with eye, but it may be knowen.[2]

Who wel vnderstode geometrie, he myght mesure in alle maistryes ; ffor by mesure was the world made, and alle thinges hye, lowe and deep.

Here foloweth of musyque.   capi-.[3]

The sixthe of the vii sciences is called musyque, the whiche fourmeth hym of Arsmetryque.

Of this science of musyque cometh alle attemperaunce, and of this arte procedeth somme phisyque ; ffor like as musyque accordeth alle thinges that dyscorde in them, and remayne them to concordaunce, right so in lyke wyse trauaylleth phisyque to brynge Nature to poynt that disnatureth in mannes body, whan ony maladye or sekenes encombreth hit.   But * phisyque is not of the nombre of the vii sciences of philosophye.   But it is a mestier or a crafte that entendeth to the helthe of mannes body, and for to preserue it fro alle maladyes and sekenesses as longe as the lyf is in the body.   And therfor it is not liberal, ffor it serueth to hele mannes body whiche ellis oftentymes myght lightly perysshe.   And ther is nothyng liberal ne free that groweth of therthe ; and for as moche as science that serueth to mannes body leseth his franchise, but science that serueth to the soule deserueth

---

[1] O.F. text, Ch. VII[1] (*e*).

[2] "they may not . . . knowen" : However far they may be, if they can be seen with the eye they can be measured (*it*, i. e. their *quantity* may be known.)

[3] "capi*tulo xii*°" is missing in Caxton (correct in 2nd edit.). O.F. text, Ch. VII[1] (*f*).

in the world to haue name liberal [1]; ffor the sowle ought
to be liberal as thyng that is of noble beyng, as she that
cometh of God, and to God wille and ought retorne; and
therfor ben the vii sciences liberall, ffor they make the
soule all free.　And on that other part they teche and

FIG. 10.

enseygne alle that in euery thyng ought proprely to be
don.　And this is the very reson why thise artes alle vii
ben called vii sciences liberall, ffor they make the soule
liberall and delyuer it fro alle euyll.

Of this arte is musyque thus comune that she accordeth her to euerich so well that by her the vii sciences
were sette in concorde that they yet endure.　By this
science of musyque ben extrayt and drawen alle the
songes that ben songen in holy chirche, and alle the
accordaunces of alle the instruments that haue dyuerse
accordes and dyuerse sownes.　And where ther is reson
and entendement of somme thinges, certes who can

---

[1] "and for as . . . name liberal": Wherefore the science
which has for its object the healing of man's body is devoid of
freedom; but the sciences which have for their object man's soul
deserve in this world the name of "liberal."

wel the science of musyque, he knoweth the accordance
of alle thinges. And alle the creatures that payne them
to doo wel remayne them to concordance.

* Hier speketh of Astronomye.   capitulo xiii°.[1]

FIG. 11.

The vii and the laste of the vii scyences liberal is
astronomye whiche is of alle clergye the ende. By
this scyence may and ought to be enquyred of thinges of
heuen and of therthe, and in especyal of them that ben
made by nature, how ferre that they bee. And who
knoweth wel and vnderstandeth astronomye, he can
sette reson in alle thinges; ffor Our Creatour made alle
thynges by reson and gaf his name to euery thyng.

By this Arte and science were first emprysed and goten
alle other sciences of decrees and of dyuinyte, by whiche
alle Cristiante is conuerted to the right faith of Our Lord
God to loue hym, and to serue the Kynge Almyghty ffro
whom alle goodes come and to whom they retorne,
which made alle astronomye and heuen and erthe, the
sonne, the mone and the sterres, as he that is the very

[1] O.F. text, Ch. VII[1] (*g*).

rewler and gouernour of alle the world, and he that is
the very reffuge of alle creatures ; ffor without his
playsir nothyng may endure.

Certes he is the very Astronomyer, ffor he knoweth
all, the good and the badde, as he hym self that
composed astronomye, that * somtyme was so strongly [*fo. 23, vo.]
frequented and was holden for a right hye werke ; ffor
it is a science of so noble beyng that, who that myght
haue the parfayt scyence therof, he myght wel knowe
how the world was compassed and plente of other
parcyal sciences ; ffor it is the science aboue alle other
by whiche alle maner of thynges ben knowen the
better.

By the science of Astronomye only were founden alle
the other . vi . to fore named ; and without them maye
none knowe a right Astronomye, be he neuer so sage ne
myghty.   In like wise as an hamer or an other tool of a
mason ben the instruments by whyche he formeth his
werke and by whiche he doth his crafte, in like wise
by right maistrye ben the other the instruments and
fondements of Astronomye.

And the auncyent wisemen, as kynges, prynces, dukes,
erles, knyghtes and other grete lordes, by their vnderstondyng, grete trauayll, estudye, and by the hye
conduyte that was in them, sette by good manere alle
their payne and labour to lerne and knowe the sciences
and artes of clergye for to vnderstond the science of
astronomye.   And so longe they trauaylled that, by
the wille of Our Lord, they lerned and knewe ynough.
Ffor they knewe plente of grete affaires and werkes that
happened in the world.   And they preysed nothing tho
thinges that were erthely, as they that knewe wel the
resons therof.

And that tyme was the custome that yf a man
were bonde to one or moo, or yf he were comen
of lytyl extraccion and were riche and ful of grete
goodes, yet durste he not estudye in the vii sciences
liberall for the nobles and hye men that in alle poyntes
wolde reteyne * them princypal, and to thende that they [* fo. 24]
were free and liberall.   And by this reson they put

therto for name the vii artes or sciences liberall; ffor
they ben so free that they rendre to God the soule alle
free. And they ben so wel to poynt that ther may
nothyng be taken away ne nothyng put to, how well yf
ony wold or coude medle ther wyt¹, thaugh he were a
good clerke and experte; ffor yf they were torned or
chaunged ony thyng that myght be, alle shold be dis-
fygured; by cause they ben so resonably and truly
composed that ther is noman lyuyng in the world, be he
neuer of so moche and perfounde science, be he paynem,
Jewe or Crysten, that may ony thyng or can change,
torne, ne take away, ne defowle it in ony maner.

And who that parfyghtly knewe the vii artes, he shold
be byleuid in alle lawes; ffor ther is noman that coude
interrupte hym of ony thing that he wolde preue, were
it true or otherwyse, by cause he shold preue by quyck
reson alle that he wolde, were it wronge or right.
Thenne is he a fool that thynketh to knowe perfyghtly
ony thyng that apperteyneth to clergye, by what mystere
or crafte that may come to hym, but yf it be by myracle
of God that alle may doo, yf he can none of the vii
sciences. Ffor otherwise alle his trauaylle shold be of
no valewe, ne he shold not conne shewe thynge of
Recommendacion, ne preue by right the pro and contra.

Therfore the vii sciences ben byleued in alle the
lawes, there as they ben red. And ther is noman,
be he neuer of so dyuerse a lawe ne of so diuerse
langage, that, yf he conuerse with peple that can
nothyng of the vii sciences ne preue of their vsages ne
[* fo.24,vo.] of their partes, that *shal be bileuid for experte and
wise. Ne ther shal neuer be paynem ne sarrasyn so
moche diuerse, that a Cristen man or a Jewe may with-
saye hym of thinges that he wil alegge or preue. And
the decretals ne the lawes be not euyl, thaugh somme
peple holde euyl the constitucions that ben emonge them,
bicause that other doo them and holden; ffor alle the
lawes depende of the vii sciences, and alle men byleue
them and reteyne them there where as peple knowe
them. And alle resons that procede of the vii sciences
ben trewe in alle causes and in alle places. Thus ben

not the sciences muable,[1] but alleway ben establc and trewe.

Herwith I deporte me to speke more to you herof, ffor ther is ynough here of tofore made ample mencion.[2]

And now I shal reherce to you here after of thaccidentes and of the faites of nature; and that shal be short. Ffor God created nature altherfirst, and tofore he created ony other thinge that apperteyned to the world. And we ought to fore alle other werke saye and declare what she is, for to deuyse after and descryue of the world. Ffor the firmament torneth and meueth by nature, and in like wise doo alle the thinges that haue meuyng. Nature meueth the sterres and maketh them to shyne and growe, and also may anoye and greue as moche as she wille. And by cause alle men vnderstonde not wel what this foloweth in substaunce, we shal declare a litil our matere a longe ffor to gyue the better vnderstondyng what nature is and how she werketh, to thende that more fully ye may compryse the facion of the world by this that herafter shal be to you declared, yf ye will wel vnderstande the resons. And therfore gyue *ye dyligence for to comprise them and wel to reteyne them. [* fo. 25]

Here foloweth of Nature, how she werketh and what she is. capitulo xiiii°.[3]

Ovre Lord God created alther first nature, ffor she is the thynge by whiche alle creatures and other werkes haue dured and lyue, what someuer they bee ordeyned of God vnder the heuen. Without nature may nothinge growe, and by her haue alle thinges created lyf. And therfor behoueth nature to be firste, ffor she noryssheth and entertieneth alle creatures, and habandonneth her self where it pleseth the creator or maker. Nature werkyth in lyke wyse, whan she is employed, as

[1] In one of the B. M. copies, the word muable has a *t* written above it. It would read: mu*t*able. 2nd ed. "muable."
[2] "Herwith . . . mencion": Now I shall refrain from saying any more to you about this; for I have made sufficient mention of it so far.
[3] O.F. text, Ch. viii.[1]

doth the axe of a carpenter whan he employeth it in his werke ; ffor the axe doeth nothynge but cutte. And he that holdeth it addressith it to what parte he wylle, so that in thende by the axe the werke is achieuid and made after thentente of the werker. Ryght so nature maketh redy and habandonneth where as God wylle ; for alle thinges ben made by her and entiertiened as God wille make them ; and she werketh after this in suche manere that, yf she lacke on one syde, she recouerith it on that other.

Nature fourmeth nothing in vayn, but she werketh in suche maner that she taketh away fro nothyng his playn ; ffor her werke is alway hool after that she fyndeth matere, be it in persones or in bestes. Thenne ben her werkes aboue alle other to be recomended, as she that doth nothyng that in ony wise may be con- trarye to God. But where as mater lacketh, she leueth [* fo. 25, vo.] to werke ; and alleway sòmoche ther is more of * mater, *d 1* somoche more she werketh ; as men see of somme beestis, of whiche somme haue two heedes and vi feet, or it hath a membre lasse than he ought to haue, of whiche he abydeth without veray fourme naturell and may be called therfor a monstre. Also men see otherwhile somme that almost lacke alle, and other that haue plente and habondaunce in their faites. Alle in like wise falleth ofte and is seen happen vpon somme men the whiche, whan they ben born, they haue vi fyngres on one hand, and other that haue one or ii or iii lasse than they shold haue ; or them lacketh an hole membre, by whiche they be of lasse valewe of that that apperteyneth to the world. And in an other shal be so grete habundaunce of nature or matere in body or in membre that he hath other thing than fourme humayn setteth ; ffor hym lacketh a foot or a honde, or he shal be born somtyme more or lasse, or he shal haue a legge more lenger or shorter, or an arme, than the other.

Yet ther is another thyng whiche ought not to be forgoten : ffor that one shal be born black or broun, and that other whyte, one grete, and another lytil ; that one shal happen to be wyse and discrete, and that other folissh

or shrewyssh; somme be wise and sadde in their yongthe,
and in their age ben ofte folissh; somme be foles yong
and olde, and other ben wise alle their lyue, yong and
olde; somme be fatte and somme be lene; somme be
seek and somme ben hool; somme be sklendre and
somme be thyck; somme be harde and rude, and somme
be softe and tendre; somme be slowe and somme be
hasty; somme be hardy and somme be cowardis; somme
be lame, haltyng and croked; somme ben wel fourmed
in alle rightis and poyntes. A grete man is ofte euyl
made, and a lytil man is ofte * wel made and auenaunt, [*fo. 26]
ffor ther is no membre but it be wel made and apper-
teynyng to his body. A fair childe oftymes in his
growyng becometh fowl. Somme wil haue their willes,
and other desyre it but lytyl. Euerich hath his talente
and his appetyte. A litil man engendreth ofte a grete
man, and a grete man ofte getyth a lytil one; a litil
man otherwhile empriseth to doo a grete thing that
right a grete man wil not emprise. Somme deye lightly,
and other lye longe; and somme lyue aslonge til age make
them to gyue ouer the world, after that that nature
endureth to them by the wille of God.

Also it is seen ofte emonge men that somme entende
to clergye, and other gyue them to other style of science
and crafte, as of carpenter, mason, smyth or ony other
crafte in whiche he employeth his tyme; ffor euery man
gyueth hym self gladly to that whiche his entendement is
enclyned to; and to other crafte or science than nature and
vnderstondyng gyueth hym to, he shal neuer perfightly
vnderstonde, ne so well meddle with all as he shold to
that whiche his propre nature gyueth hym to. Ther ben
yet other maner of peple that sette and gyue them self to
do many thinges þat other may not ne can not do, for
asmoche as their nature hath not gyuen it to them; ffor
somme pretende to hye estates and grete richesses, and
other ben content with lytil estate. And it happeth ofte
that a man cometh to that where he pretendeth, and
other can not come therto, but torneth contrarye to them
and to their dommage; and ofte with grete payne may
they come to their aboue of þat thing þat they wolde

accom*p*lysshe[1]; and other doo and make plente of thinges
that so*m*me can not ne may not doo ne make. Ffor in
the persones ben so many dyue*r*sitees and * facions not
lyke, and of willes, that men shal not fynde in ony
contree of the worlde two men that parfyghtly be lyke,
who ferre they can seche, but that they be dyuerse in
so*m*me caas or of body, or of membres, or of entendement, or of the visage, or of their sayengis, or of their
faytes or dedes; ffor the puissaunce of nature is so
dyuerse that ther is nothyng that hath growyng but
that she hath vpon it myght, in suche wyse that she
gyueth to one so*m*me thyng that another hath not in
hym, how be it that noman can perceyue ony distaunce.[2]
Suche is the vertue of Nature, where plente of clerkes
haue so*m*tyme sette their entendeme*n*t and cure, and
haue strongly laboured to thende that they myghte
better declare the fayte and puissaunce of nature. And
first of alle saith Plato, whiche was a man of grete
renommee, that nature is an ouer puissaunce or myght
in thinges that she maketh to growe lyke by lyke after
that that euerych may bee.[3] And this may be vnder-
standed by one man that engendreth another, and by
bestes, by plantes and by seedes the whiche after their
semblaunces growe, and after their facion. And lo this
is that that the wise Platon saith whiche was a grete
clerke.

After hym saith Aristotle, that this was a yefte
comen fro the hye prynce, whan he gaf vertu to the
firmament and to the sterres for to meue and to be,
and that without God suche power ne myght not be
gyuen, as the thynges that haue power to remeue, to bee

---

[1] "and ofte with . . . accom*p*lysshe": O.F. text (p. 88):
"Si qu'a painnes peut venir a chief de chose que il vueille mener
a fin," *i. e.* and only with much trouble can he carry out what he
wishes to accomplish.
[2] "distaunce": O.F. (p. 88) *dessevrance*, i. e. distinctive
feature, difference.
[3] "And first . . . may bee." Cf. Homer, *Odyssey*, 17,218:
ὡς αἰεὶ τὸν ὁμοῖον ἄγει θεὸς ὡς τὸν ὁμοῖον; Proverb in Plato's
Gorgias: ὁμοῖος ὁμοίῳ; Boethius, quoted by Albertus Magnus,
Summa Theologiae (Opera Omnia, vol. 31, p. 307, Paris 1895),
VII. 30.6: "*Natura est vis insita rebus ex similibus similia
procreans.*"

and to meue.[1] Aristotle that saith this studyed in many
a book treatyng of nature. Many other philosophres
ther were that said that nature proceded of vertues of
hete whiche causeth alle thinges to growe and nourisshe.
* But for this present tyme I passe ouer for to speke of [* fo. 27]
other matere. Tho philosophres ensieweth better Plato
than Aristotle; thus said they that them semeth. And
they spack so hye, lyke as afore is sayd, that fewe
clerkes myght atteyne to come therto. And for to
abregge it, he is not that myght parfyghtly knowe what
it is, sauf God that alle knoweth & that alle seeth, and
that first wold establisshe for taccomplyssh alle thinges.
Herby may wel be knowen that God is of moche grete
puissaunce; and it is of hym a right grete thinge
whan he of nought and without trauayll created &
fourmed so excellent a thinge, & so hye and noble a
werke. And therfore wold he hym self create & make
man to the ende that he myght be so myghty & haue
suche witte & vnderstandyng in hym self, that he knewe
by nature that whiche myght greue hym in his sowle,
and lyue vnto Our Lord [2]; ffor yf he wille iustely and
rightfully conduyte hym self, he may well brynge his
herte to that, that nature shal not mowe greue hym
in no manere.

And therfore were founden the vii sciences or artes
for to take away the euyl thoughtes that myghte brynge
a man to the deth, whiche they may destroye by the
sciences. And thus may one chaunge his euyl estate
by the techynges of a good maistre; and therfore it is

[1] "After hym . . . and to meue." Aristotle, *Physics* (Teub-
ner, Leipzig, 1879) 2. 1. 192 B. 14 : Things which exist by nature
have in themselves a principle of movement and rest : τούτων
μὲν γὰρ ἕκαστον ἐν ἑαυτῷ ἀρχὴν ἔχει κινήσεως καὶ στάσεως.
2. 1. 193 A. 28 : Nature is the primary substratum of all things
which have within themselves a principle of movement and
change : ἕνα μὲν οὖν τρόπον οὕτως ἡ φύσις λέγεται, ἡ πρώτη
ἑκάστῳ ὑποκειμένη ὕλη τῶν ἐχόντων ἐν αὐτοῖς ἀρχὴν κινήσεως καὶ
μεταβολῆς, ἄλλον δὲ τρόπον ἡ μορφὴ καὶ τὸ εἶδος τὸ κατὰ τὸν λόγον.
   Metaphysics, 11. 3. 1070 A. 6 : Nature is a principle within
itself ; *e.g.* man begets man : ἡ γὰρ τέχνη ἢ φύσει γίγνεται ἢ τύχῃ
ἢ τῷ αὐτομάτῳ. ἡ μὲν οὖν τέχνη ἀρχὴ ἐν ἄλλῳ, ἡ δὲ φύσις ἀρχὴ
ἐν αὐτῷ, ἄνθρωπος γὰρ ἄνθρωπον γεννᾷ.
   [2] "that which myght . . . Our Lord" : O.F. text (p. 89) :
"ce qui grever li porroit a l'ame et nuire envers Dieu" : what
might harm his soul and do him harm before God.

good for to haunte emonge the vertuous men, ffor ther
men may lerne and prouffyte in dyuerse maners. Thus
thenne is he wyse that is prudent in suche manere that
after his deth he hath the better and that God receyueth
hym in gree. Thus than he shal haue doon more for his
owen prouffye than for an other. This knowe alle men

[*fo. 27, vo.]
d 3 certaynly. * Ffor he shal resseyue alle the weel.

And moche is he a fool that somoche louyth his body
that he forgeteth to saue his sowle whiche God hath
lente to hym pure and clene to thende that he shold
rendre it suche agayn at his deth, and that he gouerne
hym not in suche wise that by his culpe & defawte
defowle hym in synnes. He that so conduyteth hym
self doth in lyke wise as the euyll seruaunt dyde to
whom the maistre delyuerd his besauntes for to multeplye
in good ; but he dyde not iustly, as he that was of euyl
faith. Wherfor the maistre, seeyng the vntrouth of
hym, chaced hym away fro hym. And euer after he had
shame and reproche, like as the gospel witnesseth and
to vs reherceth.[1] Alle in lyke wyse shal it be of them
that leue the good grayn for the chaff ; these ben they
that suffre their sowles to perisshe for the playsance of
their bodyes, of whiche alle euylles come to them.

Herwith for this present I leue the declaracion of the
vii sciences and of nature, and purpose by the grace of
God to deuyse the facion of the world, how it is by
nature made & pourtrayed of God whiche of one only
wille created and fourmed the world and alle that is
therof apendaunt. Now entende ye to this that we saye
to yow.

Of the fourme of the firmament. capitulo xv°.[2]

God fourmed the world alle rounde, lyke as is a pelette
the whiche is al round ; and he made the heuen al
rounde whiche enuyronneth and goth round aboute the
erthe on alle parties hooly without ony defaulte, * alle
[* fo. 28] in lyke wise as the shelle of an egge that enuyronneth

---

[1] "He that so . . . reherceth" : *St. Matthew* xv. 14 ; *St. Luke* xix. 12.
[2] O.F. text, Ch. IX[1].

the white al aboute. And so the heuen goth rouud[1] aboute
an ayer whiche is aboue thayer, the whiche in latyn is
called hester, this is as moche to saye as pure ayer and
clene, ffor it was made of pure and of clere purete.[2]

This ayer shyneth nyght and day of resplenduer perpetuel, and is so clere & shynyng that, yf a man were
abydyng in that parte, he shold see alle, one thinge and
other, and alle that is, fro on ende to the other, also
lightly, or more, as a man shold doo here bynethe vpon
the erthe the only lengthe of a foot or lasse yet, yf he
had nede.[3] Alle in lyke wyse I saye to yow, who that
were there he myght see al aboute hym as well ferre as
nyghe, the ayer is so clere and nette.

Of this hester thangels taken their bodyes & their
wynges, whan Our Lord God sendeth them in message
hether lowe in to therthe to his frendes, whan he wyll
shewe to them ony thynge. And therfor seme they
to be so clere to synful men in this world, that their
eyen may not suffre the resplendour ne beholde the grete
clerenes, as they that ben ful of obscurte and derknes,
that is to saye of synnes and of inyquytees of whiche
they ben resplenesshid. And it happeth oftymes that,
whan thangels ben comen to ony man in ony place by
the wyll of God for to saye & shewe their message, that,
whiles thangele speketh to hym, he falleth to grounde
as he were a slepe or in a traunce. And hym semeth he
hereth not the worde of thangele but as he dremed. And
is muet without spekyng, vnto the tyme that thangele
repayred agayu.[4] Thenne whan he was awaked and

---

[1] rouud : round. 2nd ed. "rounde."

[2] "God fourmed . . . purete" :. *Neckam*, I. 3 ; *De Laud.*, 5.

[3] "yf a man . . . nede": if a man lived there, he could see
to the very end of all things, if need be, as easily as a man on
this earth can see an object at a distance of a foot or even less.

[4] "Of this hester . . . repayred agayn": Gregory the Great,
Moralia (Migne, *Patrologia*, t. 76, col. 450), 28, 1: Nisi enim
Angeli quaedam nobis interna nuntiantes ad tempus ex aere corpora sumerent, exterioribus profecto nostris obtutibus non appare-
rent ; nec cibos cum Abraham caperent, nisi propter nos solidum
aliquid ex cœlesti elemento gestarent.

Baeda, *Liber variorum quaestiones* (Migne, *Patrologia*, t. 93,
col. 463), 9 : Angeli corpora in quibus hominibus apparent, in
superno aere sumunt, solidamque speciem ex cœlesti elemento
inducunt, per quam humanis obtutibus manifestius demonstrentur.

Neckam, I. 3.—Honorius Augustodunensis, *Imago Mundi* (Migne,
Patrologia, t. 172), I. 67 and 53.

[* fo. 28, vo.]
d 4 comen agayn to hymself, he remembrid wel * the sayeng
of thangele, and what he hadde shewd to hym.

Thus I saye you for trouthe that no bodyly man may
not susteyne for to see hym in no manere,[1] for so moche
as a man is made of heuy matere. Ne no byrde ne fowle,
be he neuer so stronge ne so well .fleyng, may not suffre
to be there, but that hym behoueth to come doun as sone
as a stone, tyl that he come in to thayer where he may
repryse his fleyng, yf he were not abasshid to descende.
Ffor there may nothing abyde but yf it be thinge espiri-
tuel, ne may not lyue there; ffor nomore than the ffysshe
may lyue in this ayer where we ben in, ne susteyne hym,
but right soone muste dye and shortly perisshe, but yf
he be contynuelly nourisshid in the water, all in like
wyse I say you of vs; ffor we may not meue in this
ayer perpetuel, ne lyue, ne dwelle there as longe as we
haue the body mortall.

How the four Elementes ben sette. capitulo xvi°.[2]

This clerenesse of whiche we haue spoken, whiche is
callyd ayer spyrituel, and where the angels take
their araye and atourement, enuyronneth al aboute the
worlde the foure elementis whiche God created and sette
that one with in that other. Of whiche that one is the
ffyre, the seconde is thayer, the therde is the water, and
the fourthe is therthe; of whiche that one is fastned in
that other, and that one susteyned that other in suche
manere as therthe holdeth hym in the myddle.[3] The
ffyre, whiche is the firste, encloseth this ayer in whiche
we bee. And this ayer encloseth the water after, the
[* fo. 29] whiche hol*-deth hym al aboute the erthe: Alle in liche

---

[1] Between "in no manere" and "for so moche" Caxton omits
a passage which occurs in O.F. MSS. A and Roy. 19 A IX., in a
corrupt form, and which he therefore did not attempt to translate.
The amended passage runs as follows, the words in italics, which
make the sense clear, being taken from other MSS.: "*De cele
clarté est la lumiere* qui est près du saint ciel la sus, dont nous
sommes si en sus mis" (O. F. text, p. 91): the light of Heaven,
which is so far above us, is made up of this brightness.

[2] O.F. text, Ch. X[1].

[3] "This clerenesse . . . myddle": *Neckam*, I. 16; *Honorius
Aug.* I. 3.

wise as is seen of an egge, and as the whyte encloseth
the yolke, and in the myddle of the yolke is also as it
were a drope of grece, whiche holdeth on no parte ; and
the drope of grece, whiche is in the myddle, holdeth on
neyther parte.[1]

By such and semblable regard is the erthe sette in the
myddle of heuen so iuste and so egally that as fer is the
erthe fro heuen fro aboue as fro bynethe ; ffor, whersom-
euer thou be vpon therth, thou art liche fer fro heuen,
lyke as ye may see the poynt of a compas whiche is
sette in the myddle of the cercle ; that is to saye that
it is sette in the lowest place. Ffor, of alle fourmes
that be made in the compaas, alle way the poynt is
lowest in the myddle. And thus ben the foure elementes
sette that one within that other, so that the erthe is
alway in the myddle ; ffor as moche space is alway the
heuen from vnder therthe as it appiereth from a boue.
This fygure folowyng on that other side of the leef
sheweth the vnderstandyng therof, and denyseth it
playnly ; and therfore ye may take hede therto.[2]

How the erthe holdeth her right in the myddle of the
world. capitulo xvii°.[3]

For as moche as therthe is heuy more than ony
other of thelementis, therfore she holdeth her more
in the myddle ; and that whiche is most heuy abydeth
aboute her [4]; ffor the thynge whiche most weyeth draweth
most lowest, and alle that is heuy draweth therto.
And therfore behoueth vs to joyne to the erthe, and
alle that *is extrait of therthe. [*fo. 29, vo.]

Yf so were and myght so happene that ther were
nothing vpon therthe, watre ne other thinge that letted
& troubled the waye what someuer parte that a man
wold, he might goo round aboute therthe, were it man
or beste, aboue and vnder, whiche parte that he wolde,

[1] "Alle in liche . . . neyther parte": *Honorius Aug.* I. 1 ;
Philosophia Mundi, IV. 1 (*Patrologia*, t. 172) ; Abelard, *Hexæm-
eron*, V. 1367 (*Patrologia*, t. 178, col. 735 D, 736 A) ; Gervase of
Tilbury, *Otia Imperialia*, I. 1 (ed. Leibnitz, Hanover, 1707).
[2] Cf. *Fig. 12*, p. 52. [3] O.F. text, Ch. XI[1].
[4] "For as moche . . . her": *Neckam*, II. 48.

lyke as a flye goth round aboute a round apple. In like
wyse myght a man goo rounde aboute therthe as ferre
as therthe dureth by nature, alle aboute, so that he
shold come vnder vs.[1] And it shold seme to hym that
we were vnder hym, lyke as to vs he shold seme vnder
vs, ffor he shold holde his feet ayenst oures and the

FIG. 12.

heed to ward heuen, no more ne lasse as we doo here,
and the feet toward therthe. And yf he wente alway
forth his way to fore hym, he shold goo so ferre that
he shold come agayn to the place fro whens he first
departed.

And yf it were so that by aduenture two men departed that one fro that other, and that one went alle
way to ward the eest and that other to ward the weste,
so that bothe two wente egally, it behoued that they
shold mete agayn in the opposite place fro where as they
departed, & bothe two * shold come agayn to the place
fro whens they meuyd first; ffor thenne had that one
and that other goon rounde aboute the erthe aboue and

[* fo. 30]

¹ "lyke as a flye . . . vnder vs": *Neckam*, II. 48; *Honorius
Aug.* I. 5.

vnder, lyke as rounde aboute a whele that were stylle
on therthe.[1]

In lyke wise shold they goo aboute therthe, as they
that contynuelly drewe them right to ward the myddle of
therthe; for she fastneth alle heuy thyng to ward her.
And that most weyeth, moste draweth and most ner
holdeth to ward the myddle; ffor who[2] moche depper
one delueth in therthe, somoche heuyer shal he fynde it.

And for to vnderstonde this that I haue deuysed to
you here to fore of the goynges of the flyes aboute
thapple & of the men aboute therthe, in lyke wyse
maye ye see alle the manere & facion by thyse two
fygures the whiche ben here to you represented and
shewde alle entierly.[3]

FIG. 13.

Bvt for to vnderstonde the bettre, and more clerly
conceyue, ye may vnderstande by another ensample:
Yf the erthe were departed right in the myddle, in suche

---

[1] "And yf it were . . . therthe": *Neckam*, II. 48; *Philosophia Mundi*, IV. 3.   [2] who: how. 2nd ed "who."
[3] Cf. *Fig. 13*, p. 53, and *Fig. 14*, p. 54.

wyse that the heuen myght be seen thurgh, and yf one
threwe a stone or an heuy plomette[1] * of leed that wel

Fig. 14.

weyed, whan it shold come in to the myddle and half
waye thurgh of therthe, there ryght shold it abyde and
holde hym ; for it myght nether go lower ne arise hyer,
but yf it were that by the force of the grete heyght it
myght, by the myght of the weight in fallyng, falle
more depper than the myddle.[2]   But anon it shold arise
agayn in suche wise that it shold abyde in the myddle of
therthe, ne neuer after shold meue thens ; ffor thenne
shold it be egally ouerall vnder the firmament whiche
torneth nyght and daye.   And by the vertue and myght
of his tornyng nothyng may approche to it that is
poysant and heuy, but withdraweth alway vnder it ;

[1] plomette : O.F. plomée, a club, a ring of lead or iron, a
weight.

[2] "yf the erthe . . . myddle" : Vincentius Bellovacensis, *Speculum Naturale* (Douai 1624, vol. I.), VI. 7 (who quotes as his
authority Adelard of Bath) : Quorsum injectus lapis erit casurus,
si perforatus sit ei terrae globus.—Vincent's quotation is taken
from Adelard's *Quaestiones Naturales* (Louvain, 1480), Quaest. 49.
Neckam, I. 16 : Si terra in centro suo intelligatur esse perforata,
ita quod magnus sit ibi hiatus, et descenderet maximum plumbi
pondus sine omni obstaculo, quiesceret motus ejus in terrae centro.

of whiche ye may see the nature and vnderstondyng
by this present figure, on that other side.[1]

And yf the erthe were perced thurgh in two places,
of whiche that on hole were cutte in to that other
lyke a crosse, and foure men stoden right at the foure
heedes of thise ii hooles, on aboue and another bynethe,
and *in lyke wyse on bothe sides, and that eche of them [* fo. 31]

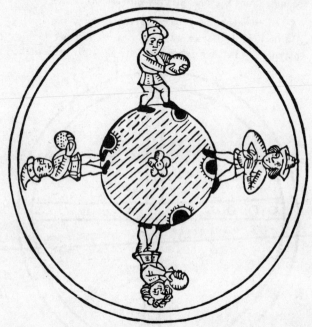

Fig. 15.

threwe a stone in to the hoole, whether it were grete or
lytyl eche stone shold come in to myddle of therthe
wythout euer to be remeuid fro thens, but yf it were
drawen away by force. And they shold holden them
one aboute another for to take place eueriche in the
myddle of therthe.[2]

And yf the stones were of like weight, they shold
come therto alle at one tyme, as sone that one as that

---

[1] Caxton has omitted the figure to which he refers here, and also
another diagram of the O.F. MSS. illustrating the last paragraph
of this chapter (p. 56, 'And so moche . . . playn trouthe.").
[2] Cf. *Fig. 15.* This figure does not occur in the O.F. text.

F

other; ffor nature wold suffre it none other wise. And
that one shold come ayenst another as ye may playnly
see by this fygure.[1]

And yf their weyght and powers were not egall fro
the place fro whens they shold falle, that whiche
were most heuy, that sholde sonnest come to the myddle
of therthe, and the other shold be al aboute her, as this
seconde figure sheweth playnly on that other side.[2]

And so moche may be caste therin that the hooles
may be full lyke as they were to fore, as ye may
[* fo.31, vo.] *playnly see in thys fygure whiche sheweth to you the

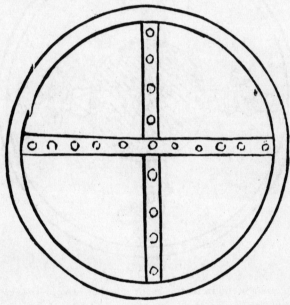

Fig. 16.

playn trouthe. Now thys suffyseth ynowh herof, & here
after we shal speke of other thynges.

What the roundenes of the erthe is.   ca. xviii°.[3]

Now thenne plese it you to here for to deuyse
playnly to you how the erthe is rounde.

Who that myghte mounte on hye in thayr and who

---

[1] Cf. *Fig. 16.*   [2] Cf. *Fig. 17.*   [3] O.F. text, Ch. XII[1].

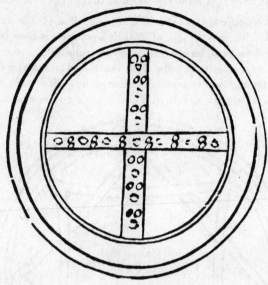

Fig. 17.

that myght beholde by valeyes & by playnes the hyenes
of the grete montaynes and the grete and depe valeyes,
the grete *wawes of the See and the grete flodes, they   [* fo. 32]
shold seme lasse tappere vnto the gretnes of the erthe
than sholde an heer of a man doo vpon an apple or vnder
his fyngre. Ffor neyther montayne ne valeys, how
someuer hye ne depe it be, taketh not away fro therthe
his roundenesse,[1] no more than the galle[2] leueth to be
rounde for his prickis; ffor it behoueth the erthe to
be rounde ffor to amasse the more peple; and we shal
saye to you here after how the world muste nedes be
round.

---

[1] "Who that . . . roundenesse": Ne·kam, *De Laudibus,* 5;
Honorius Aug. I. 5: "Si enim quis in aere positus eam (terram)
desuper inspiceret, tota enormitas montium, et concavitas vallium
minus in ea appareret, quam digitus alicujus, si pilam praegrandem
in manu teneret." This passage, which comes originally from
Seneca (*Quaest. Nat.* IV. 11), has been rendered rather freely in
the O.F. text, perhaps, as Fritsche suggests, owing to a confusion
between "pilam," a ball, and "pilum," a hair. Yet, as a rule,
Gossouin is sufficiently independent from his sources in the choice
of similes to be credited with an original idea.
[2] galle: O.F. *gale,* a chestnut.

Wherfor God made the world al round.   ca.   xix°.[1]

G od fourmed the world al round; ffor of alle the
    fourmes that be, of what dyuerse maners they be,
may none be so plenere ne resseyue somoche by nature
as may the figure rounde.   Ffor that is the most ample of
alle figures that ye may take example by.   Ffor ther is
none so wise ne so subtyl in alle thinges, ne somoche can

Fig. 18.

vnderstande, that may for ony thynge make a vessel, be
it of woode or of stone or of metall, that may be so
ample, ne that may holde within it so moche in right
quantite as shal do the rounde.

   Ne fygure that ony may make may so sone meue ne so
lyghtly make his torne to goo aboute, that ony man
can vnderstande, but that it muste take other place than
this to fore, sauf only the Rounde whiche may meue
round without takyng other place; ffor she may haue

¹ O.F. text, Ch. XIII.¹

non other than the firste, ne passe one only ligne or
Ray fro the place where she holdeth her in.   Wherof ye
may see the nature by a fygure squared sette withiu a
rounde or another * whiche is not round, and make them   [*.o. 32,vo.]
bothe to torne; the corners of them that ben not rounde
shal take dyuerce places that the rounde secheth not.
And that may ye see by thise iii figures in one, whiche
ben here ; of whiche that one is rounde alle aboute, and
the other tweyne ye may see squared.[1]

Yet is ther another thynge : that ther is nothyng
vnder heuen enclosed, of what dyuerse facion it
be, that may so lightly meue by nature as may the
rounde.   And therfore God made the world round to
this ende that it myght best be filled on alle partyes ;
ffor he wil leue nothyng voyde, and wille that it torne
day and nyght ; ffor it behoueth to haue meuyng on the
heuen whiche maketh all to meue, ffor alle meuynges
come fro heuen ; therfore it behoueth lightly and swyftly
to meue ; and without it ther is nothyng may meue.

Of the meuynges of heuen and of the vii planetes, and
        of the lytilnes of therthe vnto the Regarde of heuen.   [fo. 33]
        capitulo xxº.[2]

Owr Lord God gaf meuyng vnto the heuen whiche
goth so swyftly & so appertly that noman can
comprise in his thought ; but it semeth not to vs for his
gretenes, nomore than it sholde seme to a man, yf he
saw fro ferre an horse renne vpon a grete mountayne, it
shold not seme to hym that he wente an only paas ; and
for somoche as he sholde be most ferre fro hym, somoche
the lasse sholde he seme to goo.

And the heuen is somoche hye and ferre aboue vs that,
yf a stone were in thayer as hye as the sterres be, and
were the most heuyest of alle the world, of leed or of metall,
and began to falle fro an hye aboue, this thyng is proued
and knowen that it shold not come to therthe tyl thende of
an hondred yere, so moche and ferre is the heuen fro vs,

---

[1] Cf. *Fig. 18*.   [2] O.F. text, Ch. xiv[1].

the whiche is so grete that alle the erthe round a boute
hath nothyng of gretenes ayenst the heue*n*, nomore than
hath the poynt or pricke in the myddle of the most grete
compaas that may be, ne to the grettest cercle that may
be made ori therthe. And yf a man were aboue in
heuen, and behelde and loked here doun in the erthe, &
that alle the erthe were brennynge alle in cooles flam*m*yng
& lighted, it shold seme to hym more lytil than the lest
sterre that is aboue semeth to vs here in therthe, thawh
we were on a montayne or in a valeye.[1]

& therfor it may wel be knowen that the heuen muste
lyghtly meue, whan it maketh his torne and goth round
aboute therthe in a day and a nyght, lyke as we may
apperceyue by * the sonne that men see in the mornyng
arise in thoryent or in the eest, and goth doun in the
west; and on the morn erly we see hym come agayn in
the eest. Ffor thenne he hath perfourmed his cours
round aboute therthe, whiche we calle a day naturel, the
whiche conteyneth in hym day and nyght.[2] Thus gooth
and cometh the sonne, the whiche neuer shal haue reste
ne neuer shal fynysshe to goo wyth the heuen, lyke as
the nayle that is fixed in the whele, the whiche torneth
whan she torneth.

But by cause that it hath meuyng ayenst the cours
or tornyng of the firmament, we shal saye to yow
another reson: Yf a flye wente rounde aboute a whele
that wente rounde it self, and that the flye wente ayenst
it, the whele shold brynge the flye with her; and so
shold it falle that the whele shold haue made many
tornes whilis that the flye shold make one torne, and er
she had gon round aboute the whele vnto the first poynt.[3]
So ye muste vnderstonde that in suche manere goon the
mone and the sonne by a way that is comune to the vii
planetes that ben on the heuen, whiche alle goo by the

fo. 33, vo.]
e 1

---

[1] "And yf a man . . . valeye": *Neckam*, I. 5: Tanta est firma-
menti quantitas, ut ipsi totalis terra collata quasi punctum esse
videatur.

[2] "Ffor thenne . . . nyght": *Neckam*, I. 10; *Philosophia
Mundi*, II. 28.

[3] "Yf a flye . . . poynt": *Neckam*, I. 9: Simile autem inducere
videntur in musca quae a rota defertur, motu tamen suo contra
rotae impetum agitatur.

same way, alleway to ward the eest. And the heuen
torneth to ward the weste, lyke as nature ledeth hym.[1]
Thus and herwith the first partie taketh his ende of this
present booke ; and shal folowe for to deuyse of the
seconde partye, of therthe and of the fourme of the
firmament.

Thus endeth the first partye of this present book.
* Here after bygynneth the seconde partye of this   [* fo. 34]
present book, and declareth how therthe is deuyded and
what partye she is enhabyted.   capitulo p'o.[2]

Syth that the erthe is so lytil as ye haue herd here
to fore deuised, lytil maye we preyse the goodes
therof vnto the regard of heuen, lasse than men do
donge ayenst fyn gold or ayenst precyous stones ; how
wel that in thende that one and that other shal be of
no valewe. But for somoche as we, beyng in this
world, vs semeth that the erthe is moche grete, we haue
declared to yow as wel the roundenesse as the gretenes
to our power, and that shortly.

Syth we haue vnderstande how the erthe is rounde
on all partes as an apple, neuertheles it is not enhabited
in alle partyes, whiche is wel knowen, of no peple of
the world. And it is not enhabited but in one quarter
only, lyke as the philosophres haue enserched, whiche
put for to knowe it grete trauayll and estudye. And
therfore we shal deuyse it al aboute in foure partyes.
Of whiche ye may take ensample by an Apple whiche
shal be parted by the myddle in foure parties right
of lengthe and of brede by the core. And pare a
quarter and stratche the parell,[3] for to see and vnderstonde the facion, in playn erthe or in your hande.[4]

---

[1] "So ye muste . . . ledeth hym": *Neckam,* I. 9 ; *Honorius
Aug.* I. 68.

[2] p'o is of course the abbreviation for *primo.*   O.F. text, Ch. I[2].

[3] parell : O.F. text (p. 103) "*la peleüre,*" i.e. the peel

[4] "And pare . . . hande": pare a quarter of the apple, and
then stretch the peel on the ground or on your hand in order to
see the shape of it.

In the MS. Roy. 19 A IX., several lines of the O.F. text have
been omitted. These lines are also missing in the English translation ; thus providing us with an additional proof that Caxton
must have used MS. Roy. 19 A IX.   This passage completes

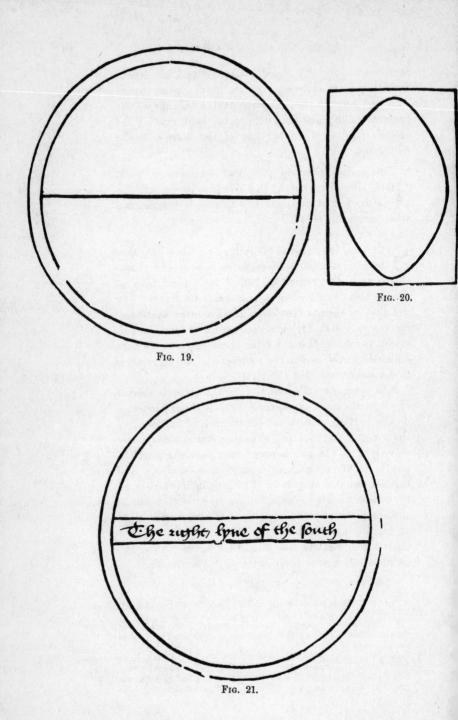

FIG. 19.

FIG. 20.

The right lyne of the south

FIG. 21.

[* fo. 34, vo.]
e 2

* **A** nd in the ende of this lyne, lyke as she gooth right by lyne, we may see a cyte whiche is callyd Aaron. It is sette in the myddle of the world and was made all rounde.[1] There was founden first Astronomye by grete studye, by grete maistrye, and by grete dilygence.

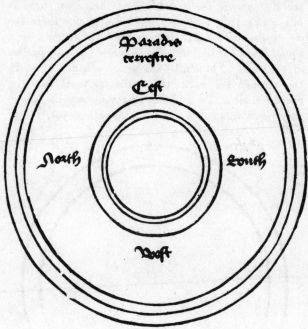

FIG. 22.

[*fo. 35]

This place Aaron is named the ryght * mydday, as she that is sette in the myddle of the worlde. That other heed of this lyne whiche gooth right to ward the lyfte syde is callyd septentryon, that is to saye north; and taketh his name of the vii sterres,[2] and torneth to ward another sterre that ledeth the maronners by the see.[3]

---

fo. 34: "*Only one quarter of the earth is inhabited. One half of the earth is called 'east,' the other half 'west.' The line which divides them is called 'the straight line of the south.' All this you can see by these three figures. And in the ende . . .*" The three figures referred to are *Nos. 19, 20, 21* (p. 62).

[1] "And in the ende . . . rounde": See *Introduction*, p. xv.

[2] "That other heed . . . sterres": Isidore of Seville *Etymologiae, (Patrologia,* t. 81–84). XIII. 11, 11; XIII. 1, 6.

[3] "and torneth . . . see": O.F. text (p. 105): "et tourne vers l'autre *montaingne* qui mainne les mariniers par la mer." It

In that other lyne that is in the myddle, whiche the south cutteth, in the ende to ward the eest, as the Auctours saye, is paradys terrestre where Adam was in somtyme. This place is callyd Oryent, that is to saye eest, ffor fro thens cometh the sonne whiche maketh the day aboute the world.[1] And that other heed is callyd Occydent, that is to saye weste; ffor there the day faylleth and wexith derke whan the sonne goth doun there. Thus and by this reson be named the foure parties [*fo. 35, vo.] of the world; * of whiche the first conteyneth the eest, the seconde the weste, the therde the south, and the fourthe the north. And this that we enseygne you, ye may see by this figure to fore on that other syde.[2]

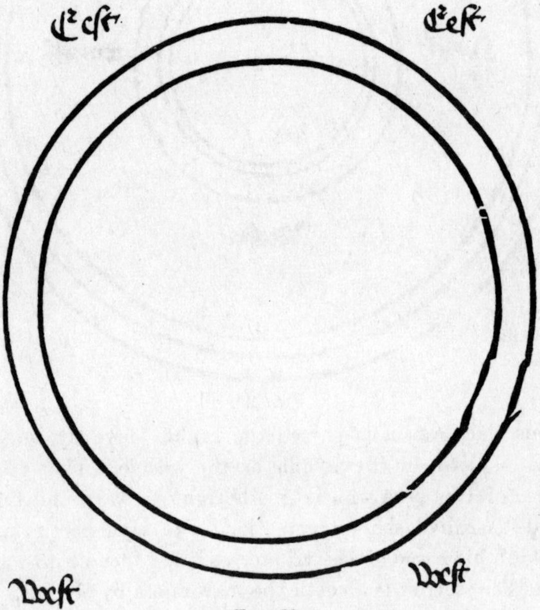

FIG. 23.

is impossible to say for certain what "mountain" Gossouin is alluding to. Caxton's emendation ("star" for "mountain") is certainly a way out of the difficulty.

[1] "In that other . . . world": *Genesis* ii. 8; *Isidore*, XIII. 1, 4.

[2] Cf. *Fig. 22*, p. 63. For the *Figs. 19, 20, 21*, p. 62, see note 4 p. 61.

Thise iiii parties that I haue declared to you, whiche ben sette in a quarter of alle the erthe of the world, o ught to haue a round fourme; ffor Raison and nature gyue that alle the world be rounde. And therfore vnderstande ye of this quarter as it were alle rounde. Now make we thenne of this quarter a cercle that is al round & al hool, and late vs sette in the myddle of this lyne that sheweth the eest and the weste, for to sette the parties in her right, as this presente figure that here is represented sheweth to you playnly.[1]

Affter late eche partye be torned to ward his name in therthe, of whiche eche shal be the fourth parte,

Fig. 24.

and * this present fygure is enseygnement and demon- [* fo. 36] straunce certayne and trewe, without ony variacion ne doubtaunce.[2]

[1] Cf. *Fig. 23*, p. 64.   [2] Cf. *Fig. 24.*

A lle the erthe that is in the world enhabited is
deuided in to thre parties [2]; and therfor it behoueth
by this reson to make an other dyuision. Of whiche
the partye to ward orient is callyd Asia the grete, and

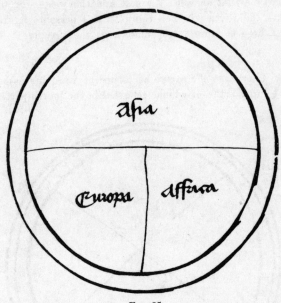

Fig. 25.

[*fo. 36, vo.]
¢ 4
taketh the name of a quene that somtyme was lady of this
regyon and was * callid Asia. This partie named Asia
holdeth and conteyneth as moche space as doo the other
tweyne; and therfor it is callyd Asia the grete; and
dureth fro the north vnto the south [3] lyke as this figure
sheweth.[4]

    [1] O.F. text has no separate chapter here. The text goes on
without interruption.
    [2] O.F. MSS. A and Roy. 19 A IX., both have "iiii. parties."
Caxton corrects here an obvious mistake.
    [3] "Of whiche . . . south": *Isidore*, XIV. 3. 1; *Honorius
Aug.* I. 8.
    [4] Cf. *Fig. 25*.

THAT other part is called Europe & taketh his name of a kynge callyd Europes the whiche was lord of this contre ; & therfor it was so callyd. And it endureth fro the weste vnto the north,[1] & marcheth vnto

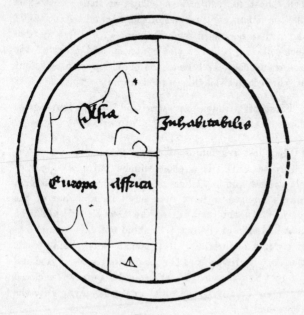

FIG. 26.

Asie the grete. That other parte is Affryque whiche stratcheth fro the south vnto the weste. And Affryque hath his name of helle, and is as moche to saye as born a way.[2] Like as this figure deuyseth, in iii partyes, of whiche figure this is the demonstrance.[3]

---

[1] "That other part . . . north": *Isidore*, XIV. 4. 1 ; *Honorius Aug.* I. 22.

[2] "That other parte . . . a way": *Isidore*, XIV. 5. 2 ; Vincentius Bellovacensis, *Speculum Hist.* I. 76 ; *Honorius Aug.* I. 32.

[3] "Like as . . . demonstrance": O.F. text, p. 108 : "*Ainsi est la terre devisée* en iii. parties. Dont ceste figure est devisement sanz nulle doute." The words in italics have been omitted by Caxton. They complete his sentence, which is otherwise obscure, and which ought to read: "Thus is the earth divided, like as this figure . . ." Cf. *Fig. 26.*

Off thise thre parties of the world here tofore named holden euerych many regyons and many contrees, of whiche, or at the leste of the most noble partye, we shal declare the names, arid how the bestes that ben there ben *most comynly called. Thus we shal saye to you the condicions and fourmes of somme, and in especial of them that ben most seen by men. And first we shal speke of the peple of the contrees, and after of the bestes and ffisshes; lyke as the book deuyseth to vs out of which is drawen this Mappa mundi.

Ffirst of paradys terrestre and of the foure grete fflodes that departe fro thens.   capitulo iii°.[1]

The first regyon of Asia the grete is paradys terrestre. This is a place whiche is ful of solace, of playsances and of delices, so that none that is therin may be greuyd ne haue none euyll in no maner of the world.[2] In this paradys is the tree of lyf; and who that had eten of the fruyt, he shold not deye as longe as the world endureth.[3] But noman liuyng may come theder, but yf Our Lord God or his angele conduyted and brought hym theder; ffor alle round aboute it is enclosed wyth fyre brennyng, the whiche goth flammyng vnto the clowdes.[4]

Ther withinne sourdeth and spryngeth a fontayne or welle whiche is deuyded in to four flodes; of whom that one is called Vngages[5] that renneth a longe thurgh the Royame of Ynde, and departeth in to many armes or braces.[6] It sourdeth of the monnt that is called

---

[1] O.F. text, Ch. II [2] (a).

[2] "The first . . . world": *Genesis* iii. ; *Isidore*, XIV. 3. 2 ; *Honorius Aug.* I. 9.

[3] "In this . . . endureth": *Genesis* ii. 9 ; *Isidore*, XIV. 3. 2 ; *Honorius Aug.* I. 9.

[4] "But noman . . . clowdes": *Genesis* iii. 24 ; *Isidore*, XIV. 3. 2 ; *Honorius Aug* I. 8.

[5] Ungages: O.F. text (p. 109), "*Phisons ou* Ganges." Caxton copied the name "Ungages" from Roy. 19 A IX. MS. A gives "Ongages." The mistake is evidently due to a scribe's carelessness, who left out the name "Phisons." In later copies "ou Ganges" was contracted into all the strange forms which we find in the various MSS. : Ouganges, Ongages, Onagagez, Ungages.

[6] "Ther withinne . . . braces": *Genesis* ii. 10. 13 ; *Isidore*, XIV. 3. 3, XIII. 21. 8 : *Neckam*, II. 2 ; *Honorius Aug.* I. 9. 10.

Ortobares, the whiche is to ward thorient, and falleth in
to the see Occian.[1]

The second of the four flodes is named Gyon or
Nylus, whiche entreth in to therthe by an hool, and
renneth vnder the erthe so ferre that it resourdeth
in to the Longe See whiche enuyron*-neth alle Ethiope, [*fo. 37, vo.]
so that it departeth in to vii parties, & goth rennyng
by Egypte so longe that it cometh and falleth in to
the Grete See.[2]

The other ii flodes, of whiche that one is callyd Tygris
and that other Eufrates, sourden in Hermenye nygh vnto
a moche grete montayne whiche is named Partheacus.
And thise two flodes trauerse many grete contrees so
longe tyl they mete in the see Moyen where bothe two
falle inne, lyke as theyr nature requyreth.[3]

On this side paradys terrestre alle aboute ben many
dyuerse places withoute ony resorte ; ffor none may
dwelle there ne fynde place to lyue in ; but there be
plente of euyl beestis whiche ben fiers and crymynel
and of many guyses ther ben. Ther ben geannts rowh
and heery[4] whiche deuoure & ete alle thyng as wulues
don, and many other wylde beestes.[5]

Here speketh of Ynde & of thynges that be found
therin. capitulo iiii°.[6]

Affter comen the contrees of Yndes whiche take their
name of a water that is called Ynde, which
sourdeth in the north. The Yndes ben closed with the
Grete See that enuyronneth them round aboute.[7]

[1] "It sourdeth . . . Occian": Orosius, *Histor.* (*Patrologia*,
t. 31), I. 2 : *Mons Oscobares; Honorius Aug.* I. 10.
[2] "The second . . . Grete See": *Genesis* ii. 13 ; *Neckam*, II. 2 ;
Isidore, XIII. 21. 7 ; *Honorius Aug.* I. 10.
[3] "The other ii . . . requyreth": *Orosius*, I. 2 : *Parchoatras;
Isidore*, XIII. 21. 10 ; *Honorius Aug.* I. 10.
[4] "geannts rowh and heery": O.F. text (p. 110): *li jaiant
et li chenillieu*, giants and Canaanites. The O.F. word *chenillieu*
(L. *Chananœum*) is evidently used in a disparaging sense by
Gossouin. Caxton's rendering (rough and hairy) seems to be
fairly correct.
[5] "ffor none . . . beestes": *Honorius Aug.* I. 10.
[6] O.F. text, Ch. II [2] (*b*).
[7] "Affter comen . . . aboute": *Isidore*, XIV. 3. 5 ; Neckam,
De Laud. III. 1021 ; *Honorius Aug.* I. 11.

In Ynde is an yle named Probane,[1] wherin ben founded ten cytees and plente of other townes, where as euery yere ben two somers & two wynters; and ben so attemprid that there is alway verdure,[2] and vpon the trees ben contynuelly flowres, leeuis and fruyt. And it is moche plenteuous of gold and syluer, and moche fertyle of other thynges.

[* fo. 38]
There be the * grete montaynes of gold and of precyous stones and of other richesses plente. But noman dar approche it for the dragons and for the gryffons wylde whiche haue bodyes of lyouns fleyng, whiche easily bere a man away armed and syttyng vpon his hors, whan he may sease hym with his clawes and vngles.[3]

Ther ben yet plente of other places so delectable, so swete and so spyrytuel that, yf a man were therin, he shold saye that it were a very paradys.

Here foloweth the dyuersitees beyng in the lande of Ynde.   capitulo v°.[4]

There is in the lande of Ynde a right grete montayne that men calle mount Capien, and it is a moche grete regyon. Ther ben a maner of peple without wytte & without discrescion, whiche the kyng Alysaundre enclosed therin. And ben named Goths and Magoths, or Gog or Magog. They ete flessh all rawe, be it men or wymmen or bestes, as men wood, mad or demonyacks.[5]

This Ynde of whiche I you reherce conteyneth xiiii Regyons, and in euerich of thise regyons ben moche peple.

And also ther is therin grete trees and so hye that they towche the cloudes. And there dwelleth peple that ben horned, and ar but ii cubites hye. And they goon to gydre in grete companyes; ffor ofte they fighte

---

[1] Probane : Taprobane, *i. e.* Ceylon.

[2] "In Ynde . . . verdure" : *Honorius Aug.* I. 11.

[3] "There be . . . vngles" : *Isidore*, XIV. 3. 9 ; *Gervase of Tilbury*, II. 3 ; *Honorius Aug.* I. 11.

[4] O.F. text, Ch. II [2] (*c*).

[5] "There is . . . demonyacks" : *Honorius Aug.* I. 11.

ayenst the Cranes whiche them assaylle. But within vii
yere they become aged and olde that they deye for age.
This peple is callyd Pygmans, & ben as lytil as dwarfes.

Ryght nygh vnto this contree groweth pepre alle
whytte. But the vermyne is there so * grete that,   *fo. 38, vo.]
whan they wold gadre and take it, they muste sette
fyre therin for to dryue away the vermyne; and whan
it is so brent, the pepre is founden al blacke scorchid
and cryspe.

Yet ben there other peple whiche ben callyd Groyne
& Bragman, whiche ben fayrer than they to fore
named, that, for to saue anothers lyf, wyll put them
in to a brennyng fyre.

Ther is yet another maner of peple the whiche, whan
their fadres and modres or their other frendes ben
passyng olde and eaged, they slee them and sacryfye
them, be it wrong or right, and eten their flesshe[1]; and
holden them for meschan*n*t and nygardis that so doo
not to their frendes; ffor they holde this maner emong
them for grete wele, grete worship and for grete largesse;
and therfor eche of them vse it.

Toward the eest is another maner of peple that
worshyppe the sonne only, and taketh it for their
god for the grete goodes that come therby. And by
cause that in alle the world they see none so fayr a
thyng to theyr semyng, they byleue in hit as their god.[2]

Yet ben ther other peple that ben al rough, whiche
eten fysshe al Rawe and drynke water of the salt see.[3]

Toward this same contre is a maner of peple that ben
half bestes and half men. Yet ben ther in that partye
other peple whiche haue on one foot viii toes.

In thise contrees is grete nombre of bestes right
dredful and terryble, whiche haue bodyes of men and
heedes of dogges; and haue so grete vngles or clawes
that areste alle that they can holde; and clothe them
with the hydes and skynnes of bestes; and haue suche
maner of voys as barkyng of dogges.

---

[1] "And also ther is . . . flesshe": *Honorius Aug.* I. 11.
[2] "Toward the eest . . . their god": *Isidore*, XIV. 3. 12.
[3] "Yet ben ther . . . salt see": *Honorius Aug.* I. 11.

Yet ben ther other called Cyclopyens[1] whiche passe by rennyng the wynde; * & haue only but one fote of whiche the plante[2] is so right longe and so brode that they couere them therwith fro the shadowe whan the hete cometh ouer sharp on them.[3]

Another maner peple ther is whiche haue only but one eye, and that standeth right in the myddys of the fronte or forhede, whiche is so reed and so clere that it semeth properly fyre brennyng[4].

And there also ben founde another maner of peple that haue the visage and the mouth in the myddle of their breste, and haue one eye in euery sholdre, and their nose hangeth doun to their mouth; & haue brestles aboute their mosell lyke swyne.[5]

Yet ben ther founden toward the ryuer of Ganges a maner of strange peple and curtoys whiche haue the right fygure of a man, whiche lyue only by the odour and smellyng of an apple only. And yf they goo ferre in to ony place, they haue nede to haue thapple wyth them; ffor yf they fele ony stenche euyll & stynckyng and haue not thapple, they deye incontynent.[6]

Of the serpentes and of the bestes of Ynde.   ca. vi°.[7]

IN Ynde ben plente of serpentes whiche ben of suche force and myght that they deuoure and take by strengthe the hertes and buckes.[8]

Yet ther is an other maner beste whiche is callyd Centycore, whiche hath the horne of an herte in the

[1] The description of the Sceinopodae, erroneously called by Gossouin "Cyclopien," is taken from Honorius, who merely mentions the name "Cyclops" in his next paragraph without adding any further details.

[2] plante: O.F. plante, the sole of the foot.

[3] "Toward this same contre . . . sharp on them": *Honorius Aug.* I. 12.

[4] "Another maner . . . brennyng": *Isidore*, XI. 3. 16, XIV. 6. 33; *Honorius Aug.* I. 12 (Cyclopes).

[5] "And there also . . . swyne": *Isidore*, XI. 3. 9; *Honorius Aug.* I. 12.

[6] "Yet ben ther founden . . . incontynent": Jacobus de Vitriaco: *Historia Hierosolomitana* (Douai, 1597), 92; *Honorius Aug.* I. 12.

[7] O.F. text, Ch. II[2] (d).

[8] "In Ynde . . . buckes": *Honorius Aug.* I. 13.

myddle of his face, and hath the breste and thyes lyke a lyon, and hath grete eeris and feet lyke an hors, and hath a round mouth.   His mosell is lyke the heed of a Bere,[1] and his eyen ben nyghe that one that other,[2] and his voys is moche lyke the voys of a man.[3]

*Another beste men fynde there moche fyers, whiche [*fo. 39, vo.] hath the body of an hors, the heed of wylde boor, and the tayll of an Olyphaunt.   And he hath two hornes whiche eueriche is as longe as a Cubyte, of whiche he sette that one vpon his back whylis he fyghteth wyth that other.   He is black and a moche terryble beste & merueyllous delyure; and is both in watre and on the londe.[4]

There ben also seen bullys which ben alle whyte. They haue grete hedes, and their throte is as wyde & brode that it endureth from that one eere to that other ; and haue hornes that remeue aboute hym so that noman may tame ne danute[5] them.

Another maner of bestes ther is in Ynde that ben callyd manticora ; and hath visage of a man, & thre huge grete teeth[6] in his throte . He hath eyen lyke a ghoot and body of a lyon,[7] tayll of a Scorpyon and voys of a serpente, in suche wyse that by his swete songe he draweth to hym the peple and deuoureth them.[8]   And is more delyuerer to goo than is fowle to flee.

Ther is also a maner of Oxen or buefs that haue their

---

[1] "Yet ther is . . . Bere": O.F. text (p. 113) has "comme le chief d'un *tuel*" (like the top of a *spout*) instead of "heed of a Bere" (bear).—*Honorius Aug.* I. 13.

[2] "and his eyen . . . that other": This passage is apparently taken from Solinus.   It does not occur in any of Gossouin's usual sources, Honorius, Neckam, Jacobus de Vitriaco.   The full description of the *Centycore*, as given in the *Image du Monde*, is found in Solinus, *Polyhistor* (Biponti, 1794), 52.

[3] "and his voys . . . man": *Honorius Aug.* I. 13.

[4] "and is both in watre and on the londe": O.F. text, p. 113: "et est moult penible en eaue et en terre": and is most indefatigable both on land and in water.

[5] danute = daunte, *i. e.* tame.

[6] "thre huge grete teeth": O.F. text, p. 113: iii. ordenées de denz: three *rows* of teeth.

[7] "Another beste . . . lyon": *Honorius Aug.* I. 13.

[8] "tayll of . . . deuoureth them": *Solinus*, 52.

feet all round, and haue in the myddle of their fronte
iii hornes.[1]

Yet is ther there another beste of moche fayr
corsage or shappe of body whiche is called monotheros, whiche hath the body of an hors and feet of an
Olyfant, heed of an herte and voys clere and hye & a
grete tayle.   And hath but one horne whiche is in the
myddle of his forhede, whiche is four foot longe, ryght
& sharpe lyke a swerd and cuttyng lyke a Rasour.   And
alle that he atteyneth to fore hym and towcheth is
broken and cutte.   And for trouthe this beste is of suche
condicion that, by what someuer engyne he is taken, of
[fo. 40] grete desdayn * he suffreth to be slayn and deye.   But
he may not be taken but by a pure virgyne whiche is
sette to fore hym where as he shal passe, the whiche
muste be well and gentylly arayed.   Thenne cometh the
beste vnto the mayde moche symply, & slepeth in her
lappe.   And so he is taken slepyng.[2]

In Ynde ben ther other bestes grete and fyrs
whiche ben of blew colowr, and haue clere spottes on
the body ; & ben so right stronge and crymynell that
noman dar approche them ; and ben named Tygris.
And they renne so swyftly and by so grete myght
that the hunters may not escape fro them in no wyse
but yf they take myrrours of glasse and caste them
in the waye where they shal renne ; ffor the tygris
ben of suche nature that, whan they see their
semblaunce, they wene that it be their fawnes.   Thenne
goon they aboute the myrrours so longe til they
breke the glasse and see nomore ; in whiche while
the hunters escape fro them that ben there.   And
somtyme it happeth so of thise tygres that they
thynke so longe and beholde their figures, that
otherwhyle they ben taken so lokyng all quyck and
liuyng.[3]

[1] " Ther is also . . . hornes ": *Honorius Aug.* I. 13.
[2] " Yet is ther there . . . slepyng ": The full description of
the rhinoceros is found in *Isidore*, XII. 2. 12 ; *Neckam*, II. 103,
104, and *Jacobus*, 88.
[3] " In Ynde ben . . . liuyng ": Neckam, *De Laud.* IX. ; *Jacobus*,
86, 88.

Yet ben ther other beestes whiche ben called Castours, whiche haue this nature in them that, whan they ben honted far to be taken, they byte wyth their teeth their owne genytoirs or ballocks aud [1] lete them falle ; and thus they ghelde them self.[2] Ffor they wel knowe that for none other thyng they be hunted.

Also there groweth another beste lyke a Mous, & hath a lytill mouthe, and is named Muske or mus-kaliet.[3]

In this contree ben the drye trees that spake to Alysaundre, the puissaunt kynge.[4]

Another beste ther is that men calle Salemandre, * whiche is fedde and nourysshed in the fyre. This [*fo. 40, vo.] Salemandre berith wulle of whiche is made cloth and gyrdles that may not brenne in the fyre.[5]

There ben yet myes [6] the whiche ben as grete as cattes & also swyft in rennyng.

Toward thoryent ben the lyons whiche haue more strength and myght in their brestes to fore and in alle their membres than ony other beste haue. And they come to fede their fawnes the iii day after they haue fawned, as they that were deed and ben as reysed agayn from deth ; & whan they slepe they holde their eyen open ; and whan the hunters hunte them they couer the traas of theyr feet wyth their taylle. They shal neuer do harme ne grief to man but yf they ben angred. And whan they be assaylled they deffende them. And whan he that kepeth them bete and chastyseth a lytil dogge to fore them, they fere and doubte hym lyke as they knewe hym wel. And the lyonnesse hath the first yere fyue fawnes, and euery yere after folowyng one lasse, vnto her ende so declynyng.

Ther is another beste whiche is lytil, and is so terryble and redoubted that no beste dar approche it. And by

---

[1] aud = and.

[2] "Yet ben ther . . . ghelde them self": *Neckam*, II. 140 ; *Jacobus*, 88.

[3] "Also there groweth . . . muskaliet": *Isidore*, XII. 3. 4 (musaraneus).

[4] "In this contree . . . kynge": *Jacobus*, 85.

[5] "Another beste . . . fyre": *Neckam*, I. 7 ; *Jacobus*, 89.

[6] myes : mice.

nature the lyon doubteth and fleeth from it ; ffor ofte it
sleeth the lyon.[1]

In this partye conuerseth & repayreth another beste
whiche is of dyuerse colours by spottes white, black,
grene, blewe and yelow, lyke as it were paynted ; and
is moche propre, and is called panthere. And ther
cometh out of his mouth so swete a sauour and breeth
that the beestes goo folowyng after it for the swetnes
of his body, sauf the serpent to whom this swete smelle
greueth in suche wyse that ofte the serpent deyeth.
And whan this beeste is otherwhile * so fylled and full
of venyson that he hath taken and eten, he slepeth iii
dayes hool wythout awakyng. And whan he awaketh,
he gyueth oute of his mouth so swete a sauour and
smelle that anon the beestes that fele it seche hym.

[* fo. 41]

This beest hath but ones yong fawnes. And whan she
shal fawne, she hath suche destresse and anguyssh that
she breketh with her naylles and renteth her matryce
in suche wyse that her fawnes come out. And neuer
after, whan the matryce is rente and broken, they
engendre ne brynge forth fawnes.[2]

Ther is a maner of Mares that conceyue of the wynde,
and ben in a contre that is named Capadoce ; but they
endure not but iii yere.[3]

In this contre ben the Olyphauns whiche is a beste
grete, strong and fyghtyng. And whan they see their
blood shedde to fore them, they be most corageous and
most stronge, and fnght [4] in alle places & alle bataylles.
Vpon this olyphaunts were wonte to fyghte the peple of
Ynde and of Perse ; ffor an olyphaunt bereth wel a tour
of woode vpon his back, fulle of men of Armes, whan it is
wel sette on & fermly. And they haue to fore them in
maner of boyell grete and large, whiche they ete by,
whiche they renne on men, & haue anon deuoured them.[5]

---

[1] "Toward thoryent ben the lyons . . . sleeth the lyon":
Jacobus, 88.
[2] "In this partye . . . fawnes": *Neckam*, II. 133 ; *Jacobus*,
88.
[3] "Ther is a maner . . . yere": *Neckam*, II. 158 ; *Jacobus*,
88.
[4] fnght = fight ; 2nd ed. fyghte.
[5] "And they haue to fore . . . deuoured them.": O.F. text, p.

Kynge Alysaundre whiche was a good clerke & prynce
of grete recommendacion, & that wente in to many contrees for to serche & enquyre the aduentures more than
he dyde to conquere, thenne whan he shold fyght ayenst
them that had taught & lerned tholyfauntes to fyghte
in playn londe, he dyde do make vessels of copper in
fourme of men, & dyde do fylle them with fyre
*brennyng, and sette them to fore hym to fyght ayenst
them that were vpon tholyfauntes. And whan tholyfauntes caste their boyel by whiche they slewe the peple,
vpon tho men of copper, feelyng that they were so hoot
that they brenned them, thenne they that were so taught
wolde nomore approche tho men for doubte of the fyre;
ffor they thoughte that alle men had ben as hoot as they
were of copper, whiche were ful of fyre. And thus
kynge Alysaundre, as a sage prynce, eschewed the parell
and daunger of thise olyfauntes, and conquerd this
wylde peple, and in suche wyse dompted tholyfauntes
that they durst doo nomore harme vnto the men.

[* fo. 41, vo.]
ƒ 1

The olyfauntes goo moche symply and accordyngly to
gydre. And whan they mete and encountre eche other,
they bowe their heedes that one to that other lyke as
they entresalewed eche other.

They be right colde of nature; wherof it is so that,
whan one putteth vpon the tooth of yuorye a lynnen
cloth and brennyng cooles ther vpon, the lynnen cloth
shal not brenne; ffor, assone as the coole feleth the
cold, he quencheth, the yuorye is so colde. The tooth of
an olyfaunt is yuorye.

Tholyfauns haue neuer yong fawnes but ones in longe
tyme; and they bere them ii yere in their flankes.

An olyfaunt lyueth ccc yere. He doubteth & fereth
the wesell and the culeuure & dredeth vermyne. Yf the
culeuure clyue & be on tholyfaunt, it departeth not tyl
it hath slayn hym. She fawneth her fawnes & hydeth

116: "Si ont. i. bouel par devant, grant et large, dont il menjuent.
Et en prennent bien .i. houme et deveurent en poi d'eure." And
they have a kind of large bowel in front with which they eat.
By means of it they can catch a man and devour him in a short
time.

them where is no woode ¹ and fawneth in the water ; ffor
yf she laye on therthe, she sholde neuer aryse ne releue,
ffor as moche their bones ben al *hool without joyntes
from the bely vnto the feet.

And whan tholyphaunt wylle slepe, he leneth vnto a
tree and there slepeth stondyng. And the hunters that
seche them and knowe the trees to whiche they lene ²
whan they slepe, thenne whan they haue founden them,
they sawe them lowe by the ground almost a sondre that
whan tholyfaunt cometh and knoweth nothyng therof and
wold slepe and leneth to the tree, and anon he falleth with
the tree vnto the grounde and may not releue hym self. ³
Thenne he begynneth for to braye, crye and waylle, that
somtyme ther come many olyfauntes to hym for to helpe
hym. And whan they may not redresse and reyse hym,
they crye and braye and make a meueyllous⁴ sorowe.
And they that ben most lytil and smale goo aboute for
to lyfte and reyse hym to theyr power in suche wyse that
other whyle they lyfte and reyse hym vp. But whan
they may not reyse ne releue hym, they goon theyr way
wayllyng and makyng grete sorowe and leue hym. And
the hunters that ben embusshed by, come ; & by their
engyns that they haue propice for the same take hym ;
thus by this subtylte ben tholyfateuns ⁵ taken. ⁶

Wythin the ryuer & flode of Ynde named Ganges
goon the eeles by grete renges, whiche ben ccc feet long,
& ben good mete to ete at nede. ⁷

Many other bestes peryllous and terryble ben ther in
Ynde, as dragons, serpentes & other dyuerse beestes
whiche haue feet, heedes and taylles dyuerse.

---

¹ "She fawneth . . . woode" : O.F. text, p. 117 : "Ele repont
ses faons es illes ou il n'a *boz* ne couluevres." She brings forth
her young on islands where there are neither *toads* nor adders.—
Caxton mistook "boz," toad, for "bois" or "bos," wood.
  ² There is a blot on "lene," which makes the *l* look like a *b*.
There is no doubt as to the true reading ; 2nd ed. "lene."
  ³ O.F. text, p. 118 : "et ne se puet sus relever" (and may not
releue hymself) : and cannot rise up again.
  ⁴ meueyllous = merueyllous, marvellous ; 2nd ed. merueyllous.
  ⁵ "tholyfateuns" : this is evidently a misprint for "tholyfauntes."
  ⁶ "In this contre ben the Olyphauns . . . tholyfateuns taken" :
The whole description of the elephant is taken from *Jacobus*, 88.
  ⁷ "Wythin . . . nede" : *Honorius Aug.* I. 13.

Ther ben the basylicocks whiche haue the sight so venymous that they sle all men ; and in lyke wyse doo they alle fowles and beestes. *He hath the heed lyke a cocke and body of a serpent. He is kynge of alle serpents, lyke as the lyon is kynge aboue alle beestes. He is whyte rayed here and there. Ther is neyther herbe ne fruyt on the erthe wherby he shal passe, ne the trees that ben planted, but they shal perisshe. Yf he haue byte or slayn beste or other thynge, neuer other beeste dar approche it.[1]

Ther is in this Regyon another maner of serpents that haue hornes lyke a shepe.[2]

Ther groweth a beest named Aspis that may not be deceyuyd ne taken but by charmyng, ffor he heerith gladly the sowne.[3] But assone as he heerith the charme, he putteth his taylle in his one eere. And that other he leyeth to the ground doubtyng to be deceyuyd by the charme.[4]

Other serpentes ther be whiche be named Tygris, whiche ben taken alle quyck by force of engyns. And of them men make tryacle whiche deffeteth and taketh away other venym.[5]

Other wormes ther growe there, whiche haue two armes so longe and so dyuerse that they bete and slee the Olyphaunts. This worme lyueth right longe. And whan he is olde and feleth hym feble, he consumeth hym self by fastynge ; aud [6] suffreth to be enfamyned so ouermoche that lytil abydeth of his body. Thenne he goth in to a lytil hool of somme stone, whiche is wel strayt, and thenne he putteth hym self out with so right

[*fo. 42, vo.] ƒ2

---

[1] "Ther ben . . . approche it": *Solinus*, 27, *Isidore*, XII. 4, 6, 7, *Neckam*, II. 120, 153, and *Jacobus*, 89, give a full description of the basilisk ; but none of them describe it as having "the heed like a cocke and body of a serpent."

[2] "Ther is . . . shepe": *Jacobus*, 89.

[3] "that may not be . . . sowne": O.F. text, p. 119 : "Qui ne puet estre pris ne enchantez, *se n'est pur douz chant ;* car il en ot trop volentiers le son": which cannot be taken nor enchanted *except by sweet singing,* the sound of which he hears with delight.

[4] "Ther groweth . . . charme": *Neckam*, II. 114 ; *De Laud.* IX. 289 ; *Jacobus,* 89.

[5] "Other serpentes . . . venym": *Neckam*, II. 108 (De tiria) ; *Jacobus,* 89.

[6] aud = and.

grete distresse, that his skynne remayneth al hool.
And ther groweth & cometh on hym another skynne.
And thus reneweth his age as a wyse best that he is.[1]

[* fo. 43] Ther ben plente of other serpents that haue many
precyous stones in the heedes *and in the eyen, the which
ben of right grete vertue for them that myght haue
them and bere them.[2]

Now we shal deuyse to yow of stones that growe in
Ynde and ben there founden.

Here foloweth of precyous stones and of their vertue,
whiche growe in Ynde. capitulo vii°.[3]

IN Ynde groweth the Admont stone, whiche is a
stone charged with many grete vertues. She by
her nature draweth to her yron, and maketh it to cleue
to it so fast that it may vnneth be taken fro it for the
vertue that is in it.[4]

The dyamont groweth also in Ynde alle hool, and it
may not be broken in pieces ne vsed, but it be by the
vertue of the blood of a ghoot alle hoot.[5]

Yet growe there other stones of many dyuerse facions
and vertues, the whiche ben of moche noble recomenda-
cion, renommee, and of moche fayr vertue. And first I
shal speke of the Emerawde whiche is so playsaunt to
the eye that it reconforteth all the sight of hym that
beholdeth it.[6]

In lyke wyse groweth in Ynde an other stone the
whiche is callyd Carboncle; the whiche, by nyght or
yf it be in derke place and obscure, it shyneth as a cole
brennyng.[7]

---

[1] "Other wormes . . . that he is": *Jacobus*, 89.
[2] "Ther ben plente . . . bere them": *Neckam*, II. 146 ; *Jacobus*, 89.
[3] O. F. text, Ch. II². (*e*)
[4] "In Ynde . . . is in it": *Neckam*, II. 94, 98 ; *Jacobus*, 91.
[5] "The dyamont . . . hoot": *Neckam*, II. 92: *Jacobus*, 91.
[6] "And first . . . it": *Neckam*, II. 90, 91 (De beryllo); *De Laud.* VI. 153 ; *Jacobus*, 91.
[7] "In lyke . . . brennyng": Neckam, *De Laud.* VI. 241 ; *Jacobus*, 91.

Also ther growe Saphyres whyche by theyr vertue take away the swellyng and redenes of the eyen.[1]

Ther groweth also a stone callyd Topace whiche is of colour lyke vnto fyn golde and also is of hye vertue. Yet also ther growe there Rubyes, whiche is a stone moche preysed & loued emong the peple, and is also of right more grete valewre and * vertue than is the toupace. She reioyseth the sight and comforteth it moche, and specyally to them that bere it.[2]

[* fo. 43, vo.]
f 3

Yet ben ther also in Ynde plente of other maner stones whiche haue in them moche fair vertues and bountees. And who that wil more knowe of their vertues and bountees maye rede in the book called lapydayre, in whiche he shal knowe the names and vertues ; ffor now at this tyme we shal make an ende of this mater for to recounte yow the contrees and Royames of Ynde.

Here foloweth of the contrees and Royammes of Ynde. capitulo viii°.[3]

IN Ynde is plente of grete contrees merueyllously whiche ben peopled with dyuerse maners of peple & of grete plente of bestes of many dyuerse facions and condicions. Emonge alle other ther is a contree named Perse, and conteyneth xxxiii regyons ; of whiche the first is the Royame of Perse, where as a science called Nygromancie was first founden ; whiche science constrayneth the enemye, the fende, to be taken and holde prisonner.

In this contree groweth a pese[4] whiche is so hoot that it skaldeth the handes of them that holde it ; and it growyth with encresyng of the mone, and wyth

---

[1] "Also ther . . . eyen" : Neckam, *De Laud.* VI. 135 ; *Jacobus*, 91.
[2] "Ther groweth . . . bere it" : Neckam, *De Laud.* VI. 192, 241 ; *Jacobus*, 91.
[3] O.F. text, Ch. II[2] (*f*).
[4] O.F. text, p. 121 : "En cele contrée croist *une poiz* qui est si chaude . . ." Caxton mistakes "la poiz" (pitch) for "le pois" (the pea).

wanyng it discreceth at eche tyme of his cours. It
helpeth wel to them that ben nygromanciers.[1]

After this Royame is another whiche is called Meso-
potamye, wherin Nynyue, a Cyte of grete seynourye
and myghty, is sette and establissnid, whiche is iii
daye journeyes of lengthe and is moche large and
* brood.[2]

[* fo. 44]

In Babylone is a tour that somtyme was made by
grete pride, qf whiche the wallis ben meruayllously
grete, stronge and hye, and is called the towr of Babel;
it is of heyght round aboute iiii. M. paas vnto the
hyest.[3]

In the Regyon of Caldee was first founden Astronomye.[4]

In this Regyon is the lande of Saba, and therby is
the Regyon of Tharse, and after is that of Arabe.
Of thise iii Regyons were lordes and prynces the
thre kynges that offryd to Our Lord Sauyour Jhesu
Cryste gold, encence and Myrre, that tyme whan he laye
in the Crybbe aftyr his blessyd Natyuyte, as he that
was the sone of God. And this knewe they by their
grete witte and vnderstandyng of astronomye in whiche
they were endowed and founded. In this Regyon of
Arabe groweth thencence and the myrre. And ther
ben therin many peples and dyuerse folke.[5]

Ther is also in Egypte a Regyon whiche is called
Assyrie.[6]

And the Regyon of Ffenyce is there, whiche taketh his
name of a byrde callyd ffenyx of whiche in alle the world
is on this day but only one a lyue; and whan he deyeth,
anone groweth another of hym self. He is grete and
moche fair of Corsage, and hath a creste on his heed,
lyke as the pecok hath. The breste and the gorge of
hym shyneth and draweth toward the propre colour of

[1] "of whiche the first . . . nygromanciers": *Gervase of T.* II.
3 (t. II. p. 756, ed. Leibnitz); *Honorius Aug.* I. 14.

[2] "After this . . . brood": *Jonah* iii. 3; *Gervase of T.* (t. II.
p. 756) II. 3; *Honorius Aug.* I. 15.

[3] "In Babylone . . . hyest": *Gervase of T.* II. 3; *Honorius
Aug.* I. 15.

[4] "In the Regyon . . . Astronomye": *Honorius Aug.* I. 15.

[5] "In this Regyon . . . folke": *Psalm* lxxii. *Honorius Aug.*
I. 15.

[6] "Ther is also . . . Assyrie": *Honorius Aug.* I. 16.

fyn golde. And he is alonge on the back also reed as a
rose. And toward the tayll he is of the colour of Asure,
lyke vnto the heuen whan it is pure and clere. And
whan he is olde and eaged, he withdraweth hym vnto
an hye and meruayllous fair place or montaygne, where
as sourdeth a fontayne right grete and large, and the
water *fair and clere. And ouer the welle groweth a   [* fo. 44,vo.]
fair tree and grete, whiche may be seen fro ferre. And   *f* 4
he maketh vpon this tree his neste and his sepulture
right in the myddle of the tree. But he maketh it of
spices of so right grete odour that ther may be founden
no better. And after he adressyth hym in his neste whan
he hath all perfourmed it ; he thenne begynneth to meue
and to bete his wynges ayenst the sonne so faste and so
longe that a grete hete cometh in his fethers, in suche wyse
that it quykeneth of fyre and brenneth al rounde aboute
his body that he is on a clere fyre. And thus the fyre
brenneth and consumeth hym alle in to asshes ; and out
of thise asshes and pouldre groweth agayn another
byrde alle lyuyng semblable to hym.[1]

After this regyon of Fenyce is the Royame of Damas
where as good fruytes growe.[2] And after Damas is
founden the Regyon of Anthyoche where as be founden
grete plente of Camels.

After cometh the contre of Palatyne, and after that
Samarye, thenne Sebaste,[3] and thenne Penthapolye where
somtyme were founded two myghty cytees, that one
callyd Sodome and that other Gomor, the which God
wolde they shold perisshe for the grete and enorme
synnes that they commysed. On this parte is the Dede
See in whiche is nothing that bereth lyf. There is
a contree that men calle Ysmaelite, whiche is enhabyted

[1] "And the Regyon of Ffenyce . . . to hym": This account of
the phenix seems to be taken from *Neckam* I. 34, 35, where all
the details given by Gossouin are found. *Solinus* (33), *Isidore*
(XIV. 3. 17 ; XII. 7. 22), *Jacobus* (90), and *Honorius* (I. 16)
give a much shorter description.

[2] "After this . . . growe": *Honorius Aug.* I. 16, 17.

[3] From Isidore we learn that Samaria and Sebaste are two
names for the same town. Sebaste is not a separate country.
Etym. XIV. 3.22 : "Samaria regio Palæstinæ ab oppido quodam
nomen accepit, quod vocabatur Samaria, civitas quondam regalis
in Israel, quæ nunc ab Augusti nomine Sebastia nuncupatur."

by xii maner of peple[1]; & after this thenne is Egypte the grete where it neuer reyneth, & conteyneth xxiiii peoples.[2]

Another Regyon ther is the whiche cometh toward the north, in whiche ther dwelleth noman, but wymmen whiche ben as fyers as lyons. And whan

[* fo. 45]

nede is, they fyghte *frely ayenst the men. They go armed as knyghtes in bataylle, and brynge doun their enemyes withoute sparynge. They haue fair tresses of their heer whiche hange doun byhynde them, and they be garnysshed with grete prowesses in alle their werkes and affayres, and ben called Amazones. But they haue men nyghe to their contre dwellyng, whom they euery yere fetche for to be in their companye viii or xv dayes longe, and suffre them to knowe them carnelly so longe that they suppose that they haue conceyuyd. And thenne departe the men fro that contre and goon agayn thedyr that they come fro. And whan thise wymmen haue childed, yf it be a doughter they reteyne her with them. And yf it be a sone they nourysshe it fyue or vi yere, and after sende it out of the contre.[3]

Yet in other places ben many fayr ladyes whiche in betaylles & in estowrs vse alle their Armes of syluer for lacke of yron and of steel of whiche they haue not.

In the woodes of Ynde ben other wymmen the whiche haue their berdes so longe that they come doun to theyr pappes. They lyue by wylde beestis, and clothe them with the skynnes of the same beestis.

And ther ben men and wymmen alle naked and also Rowhe as beeres, & ben dwellyng in caues[4] in the erthe; & whan they see other men they hyde them in the caues[5] so that they appere not oute. Other peple ther ben that ben also Rowhe as swyne & why-nyng. And ther ben other wymmen Rowh also lyke vnto the men; but they ben moche bestyall and whyte

---

[1] "After cometh . . . peple": *Honorius Aug.* I. 16. 17.
[2] "& after this . . . peoples": *Honorius Aug.* I. 18.
[3] "Another Regyon . . . contre": *Isidore* (IX. 2. 64) and *Jacobus* (92) both give the same details as Gossouin about the Amazons.
[4] caues: caves. O.F. text (p. 123) has "yaue," *i. e.* water.
[5] caues: ,,   ,,   ,, (p. 123)   ,,   ,,   ,,

as snowe. Their teeth ben more lyke vnto houndes than
to other. And dwelle and abyde wel in the water.[1]

Another grete regyon ther is in whiche * dwelle xliii   [*fo 45, vo.]
peoples. Ther ben the byrdes whiche ben ful of deduyte,
of whom the pennes shyne by nyght like vnto fyre.[2]

There ben popengayes whiche ben grene & shynyng
lyke pecoks, whiche ben but lytil more than a jaye ; of
whom, as men saye, they that haue on eche foot fyue
clawes ben gentyl, and the vylayns haue but thre. He
hath a tayll lengre than a foot, and a becke courbed &
a grete tongue and forked. Who that myght haue one,
he myght wel lerne hym to speke[3] in the space of two
yere.

Another byrde ther is in this contre, whiche is named
pellicane, and alle hoor. Whan he leueth his chekens, &
cometh agayn to fede them as is of nede, hym semeth
that they ben al deed, thenne he smyteth hym self with
his bylle in his breste tyl that the blood sprynge out ;
wherof he reyseth agayn to lyf his birdes.[4]

In Armenye is a maner of peple that haue al their
heer whyte.[5] In thise parties is a moche hye mountayne where vpon the Arke of Noe abood and rested
after the flood was passed.[6]

After cometh the prouynce of Ynde the lasse[7] whiche
is alle enuyronned wyth the see, wherin ben many regions
of whom for this present tyme we wil not declare the
names.[8] In this prouynce of Asie is the Regyon of Dar-
dane, and the contre of Ffrygye in to whiche Parys,
whan he had rauisshed Helayne, brought her to ; wherfor the puissaunte cyte of Troye the grete was, at

---

[1] "Yet in other places . . . water" : *Jacobus*, 92.
[2] "Another grete . . . fyre" : *Honorius Aug.* I. 19.
[3] O.F. text, p. 124 : "Qui l'a *joene*, il le puet faire parler . . ." :
whoever takes it *young* can teach it to speak . . .
[4] "There ben . . . birdes" : *Neckam* (I. 36, 38, 73 ; *De Laud.*
II. 657) and *Jacobus* (90) give a similar account of the popinjay
and the pelican.
[5] "In Armenye . . . whyte" : *Honorius Aug.* I. 19 (Albania).
[6] "In thise parties . . . was passed" : *Honorius Aug.* I. 19.
[7] O.F. text, p. 124 : "Après vient Aise la menour" : Caxton
gives "Ynde the lasse" instead of "Asia Minor."
[8] "After cometh the prouynce . . . names" : *Honorius Aug.*
I. 20.

thempryse of the Grekes, destroyed by fyre and glayue. This Cyte was sette at one of thendes of Grece. In thise partye is sette the noble Cyte of Lychaonie. And nyghe to the same stondeth another Cyte called Cayer,[1] by whiche renneth the grete flood name Herme, of whiche the grauel * is of gold all shynyng.[2] Ffro this parte toward thende of Egypte cometh to vs the paillole whiche is of fyn golde.[3]

[* fo. 46]

Ther. is toward thoryent on that other syde a maner of peple that somtyme descended fro the Jewes ; and ben peple of .their condicion vyle, fowl and stynkyng. They haue no wyues wedded, ne holde no concubynes ne other, for as moche as they may not byleue that wymmen may holde them to one man only, withoute to double them with other. And therfore they sette no store by wymmen, but only that they may haue generacion.[4]

Another maner of peple ther ben in this prouynce, whiche ben callyd Barbaryns, & ben also called Jacobyns, ffor Jacob was auncyently their maistre. And ben crysten men corrumped by the mariages and Alyaunces that they doo and make wyth the sarasyns whiche on that one syde marche on them. Thise Barbaryns pourpryse wel xl Royammes. In no wyse they byleue that confession be vayllable to shewe it to ony man sauf to God only.[5] Whan they confesse them to God they sette by them fyre and encence, and they wene certaynly that their thoughtes goo vp vnto Our Lord in this fumee ; but it is not so as they byleue, but they mysbyleue saynt Johan Baptiste the whiche first baptysed them ; ffor to fore all thinges they behoued to saye their synnes to hym self,

---

[1] O.F. text, p. 124 : "une autre cité qui *Charie* a non." "Cayer" stands therefore for "Caria."

[2] "In this prouynce . . . shynyng" : *Honorius Aug.* I. 21.

[3] O.F. text, p. 124 : "De cele part devers la fin nous vient la paillole qui est de fin or" : From the borders of that country comes the dust of fine gold.—There is no mention of Egypt in the O.F. text.

[4] "Ther it toward . . . generacion" : This is translated from *Jacobus*, (82), who adds : ". . . dicuntur Essæi, de genere Judæorum descendentes."

[5] O.F. text, p. 125 : "Il ne croient pas confession a nul autre houme fors que a Dieu" : They do not believe in confession to other men, but only to God.

and after they receyued of hym baptesme. Ffor seynt
Johan Baptest sayth hym self that, whan one telleth his
synnes to another that may be a synner as he is, this
shame that he hath to saye his synnes is torned to hym
in stede of penytence and is to hym allegeance[1] of his
synnes ; & hym ought by reson the sonner to absteyne
hym fro syn*-nyng, seen that he muste shewe them to [*fo. 46, vo.]
another man, by whiche he may haue of Our Lorde
remyssion and pardon of his synnes and inyquytees.
This witnesseth to vs saynt John Baptyst the whiche,
by the holy & blessyd sacrament of baptesme, rendreth
vs quyte[2] ayenst Our Lord God of our synnes, & that we
may be purged by very confession, good contricion &
ful satisfacion, euerych after his power. Ther for thise
Jacobyns ben gretly deceyued, ffor they haue euyl
reteyned the holsome doctryne that seynt Johan Baptyst
taught them.

In this regyon is another maner of peple Crysten
that byleue a lytil better in God, and ben stronge
and myghty in bataylle. The sarasyns doubte them
moche and dar not mysdoo them, but ben to them
swete and amyable. Thise peple be named Georgiens
and ben good crysten men, and ben enclosed round
aboute with feloun and mysbyleuyd peple. And they
ben called, as afore is said, Georgiens, bycause they crye
alle way on seynt George in batayll, in estours and in
Recountres ayenst the sarasyns. And also they wor-
shype and loue hym aboue alle other seyntes. They
haue alle crownes shauen on their heedes ; but the
clerkes haue them round and the laye peple haue them
square. Whan they goo to Jherusalem for to worshipe
the holy sepulcre of Our Lord Jhesus, the sarrasyns dar
not take of them ony tolle ne nothyng hurte them, by
cause they doubte that, whan they come and repaire
agayn, they sholde abye it dere. The gentyl ladyes of
the contre Arme them and ride vpon good horses rennyng and swyfte, and fyghte asprely in the companye
of the knyghtes of Georgie ayenst the sarasyns. They

---

[1] allegeance : alleviation.
[2] quyte : O.F. "quites," quit, clear.

H

vse *lyke lawes & lyke termes of speche as don the
Grekes.[1]

Hier speketh of the ffysshes that be founden in Ynde.
ca. ix°.[2]

IN the see of Ynde is a maner of ffysshes that on
their skynnes growe heer so longe that the peple
make therof robes, mantellis and other vestementis
whiche they were whan they haue taken and made
them.[3]

Yet ther is another maner of ffysshe in this see, whiche
ben named escimuz,[4] whiche ben no lengre that a foot
longe; but they haue suche strengthe that, in contynent
that they touche a ship, one of them only reteyneth
hym stylle that he may not goo forward ne afterward.[5]

Ther is also another maner of ffysshe that be comynly
callyd dolphyns; they haue a custome that, whan they
fele that the tempest shal come and that the shippes ben
in daunger for to be lost and perisshid, they warne them
out of the watre and shewe and playe on the wawes of
the see in suche wyse that somtyme they be playnly
seen.[6]

In this see of Ynde is another fysshe so huge and grete
that on his backe groweth erth and grasse; and semeth
proprely that it is a grete Ile. Wherof it happeth somtyme that the maronners sayllyng by this see ben gretly
deceyued and abused; ffor they wene certaynly that it
be ferme londe; wherfor they goo out of their shippes
theron. And whan they haue made their preparacions
and their logys theron, and lyghted their fyre and

---

[1] "Another maner of peple . . . Grekes": This account of
Jacobins and Georgians is translated from *Jacobus* (76 and 80).
Sir John Maundeville, who owes much to the O.F. original of
the *Mirror*, gives an almost literal translation of these two passages.

[2] O.F. text. Ch. II [2] (*g*).

[3] "In the see . . . made them": *Jacobus*, 90.

[4] escimuz: O.F. "eschinuz," prickly. As a substantive this
word denotes the sucking-fish or remora.

[5] "Yet ther is . . . afterward": *Neckam*, II. 34, 43; *Jacobus*,
90.

[6] "Ther is also . . . playnly seen": *Neckam*, II. 27, 28;
Jacobus, 90.

made it to brenne after their nede, wenyng to be on a
ferme londe, but incontynent as this merueyllous fysshe
feleth the hete of the fyre,[1] he meuyth hym * sodenly   [*fo. 47, vo.]
and deualeth doun in to the water as depe as he may.
And thus alle that is vpon hym is lost in the see.   And
by this moyen,[2] many shippes ben drowned and perisshid,
and the peple, whan they supposed to haue be in sauete.[3]

Ther is in this see plente of other ffysshe the whiche
haue heedes and bodyes lyke vnto a mayde, and haue
fair tresses made of their heer.   The shapp of their
bodyes vnto the nauel is lyke a mayde, and the reme-
naunt is lyke the body and tayll of a fysshe.   And
somme haue wynges lyke fowles ; and their songe is so
swete and so melodyous that it is meruaylle to here ;
and they be called seraynes or mermaydens.   Of whom
somme saye that they be fysshis, and other saye that
they be fowles whiche flee by the see.   But take it
aworth, ffor at this tyme I shall deporte to speke more
of this mater ffor to telle & recounte to yow of the
meruayllous trees that growe in Ynde, of whiche ben
many dyuerse and bere soudrely fruyt, as here after
al a longe shal be declared to yow.

Hero[4] foloweth of the trees that ben in Ynde and of
theyr fruytes.[5]   capitulo. x°.[6]

I N Ynde groweth a tree moche grete and right fayr,
     and is moche swete smellyng and is called
palmyer, and bereth dates.   This fruyt is good and
holsom.   Ther ben also apple trees the whiche ben ful
of longe apples whiche ben of merueyllous good sauour.

---

[1] "and lyghted . . . the fyre" : O. F. text, p. 126 : "si alument
lor feu et font leur cuisine. Mais quant li poissons sent le feu . . ." :
then they light their fire and do their cooking. But when the fish
feels the fire . . .—Caxton's sentence is quite clear if "but" is
omitted before "incontynent."
[2] moyen : means
[3] "In this see . . . sauete" : The description of the whale is
taken from *Jacobus*, 90.
[4] Hero : sic. 2nd ed. "Here."
[5] This chapter, as a whole, is translated from *Jacobus*, 86, 87.
[6] O. F. text, Ch. II[2] (h).

And they entretiene and cleue to gydre wel an hondred
in a clustre.   And the leues that growe on this apple

[* fo. 48] trees ben wel two * fote longe & a foot brode.   Other
apples ther growe moche grete, wherin appiereth the
bytte of a man with his teeth.   And ben called thapples
of Adam by cause of the bytte that appiereth in them.
Ther ben other trees whiche bere apples that ben right
fair without forth.   And within it is as it were asshes.

The vygnes bere there grapes of whiche wynn is maad.
They ben so habondaunt of fruyt, and the clustres of
grapes ben so grete and so full of Muste, that two men
ben gretly charged to bere one of them only vpon a
colestaff.   Also ther growe lytil smale trees that be
remeuyd euery yere, the whiche bere cotoun.   Also ther
growe in many places canes grete and longe, whiche ben
within forth ful of sugre, so moche and especial that
ther growe none lyke in alle the worlde.

At one of the hedes of the Royame of Babylone
groweth the bame whiche is moche dere; and crysten
men that ben prisonners there delue and laboure the
erthe.   And the sarasyns saye that they haue ofte
preuyd it that, whan they doo delue and laboure that
erthe with peple of other nacions than crysten men,
that it bereth no fruyt ne bame that yere.   And vpon
the felde where the bame groweth, somme saye that
there spryngeth a fontayne where the blessyd virgyne
Marie bayned her sone Jhesus.   And wyth the watre
of this fontayne is the bame watred; and of this water
may not be employed ne born in to other place, ffor
in substaunce it doth nomore than other water.

In this contre ben other trees the whiche in stede
of leues bere wulle of whiche is made cloth right fair
& subtyle, of whiche thynhabitauns of the contre make

[*fo. 48, vc.] them robes and mantellis * for their weryng.

Yet ben ther other trees that bere a fruyt right swete
smellyng.   But this tree takyth his fruyt by nyght in
hym, and in the mornyng it cometh out agayn when
the sonne is rysen.

Ther growe there plente of other trees of whom the
cooles, whan they be afyre, duren in their asshes an

hole yer without goyng out, or quenchyng, or mynuyssyng.[1] Also ther growe plente of Cedres and of lybans,[2] the whiche, as men saye, may not rote. Other trees there growe moche gloryous and right good whiche bere clowes, and other that bere notemygges. And of the rynde and scorce [3] is the canell or synamom*n*; and also ther groweth gynger. In this partye growe the good espyces of alle maner habou*n*dantly. Also there growe notes grete plente whiche ben also grete as grete Apples, and other that ben as grete as the hede of a man.

To the Regard of the trees that ben in paradys terrestre we knowe not what fruyt they brynge forth. But it is wel knowen of the tree that Eue had so grete desire to ete aboue the commandement of Our Lord God, & of whiche she deceyued Adam our first fader; and in lyke wyse is there the tree of lyf, of whiche we haue spoken to fore more largely. Ther ben in this right noble paradys so many other trees beryng fruyt so good and so delicyous that it semeth that the glorye of Our Lord be therin ouerall. But ther is a meruayllous watche and kepar; ffor the Angele of God is kepar of thentree with a naked swerd in his hande contynuelly brennyng, to thende that nomen ne bestes ne euyll spirytes approche ne Auaunce them for to take in ony wyse there their delytes and playsaunces, and *taccom- [* fo. 49] plissh them ther within.[4]

And here wyth we make an ende of this purpoos for to speke of the contrees of Europe and of the condicions.

---

[1] "Ther growe . . . mynuyssyng": The usual sources of Gossouin do not mention this tree. "mynuyssyng:" O.F. amenuisier, to diminish.

[2] lybans: O.F. ebanus, ebony-tree. There seems to be a confusion between "ebanus" or "ebenus" and "lybans" (F. for "Mount Lebanon"), probably caused by the mention of "cedars" immediately before.

[3] scorce: bark.

[4] "To the regard . . . ther within": *Genesis* iii.

Now foloweth of Europe and of his contrees.   ca. xi°.[1]

SYTH we haue deuysed to you of Asye and of his contrees and regyons, I shal saye to you of Europe and his condicions shortly, ffor as moche as we may ofte here speke therof.

The first partye of Europe is Romanye and a parte of Constantynoble, Trapesonde,[2] Macedone, Thesalye, Boheme, Sapronye,[3] Pyrre,[4] & a moche holsom contre named Archade. In this contre sourdeth & spryngeth a fontayne in whiche men may not quenche brennyng brondes, ne cooles on fire and brennyng.[5]

In Archade is a stone whiche in no wyse may be quenchyd after it is sette a fire tyl it be alle brent in to asshes.[6]

After Archade is the Royame of Denemarke, and thenne Hongrye, & sythe Hosterich ; and thenne foloweth Germanye, whiche we calle Almayne, whiche conteyneth a grete pourprys toward thoccident, in whiche pourprys ben many grete & puissaunt Royames.

In Allemayne sourdeth a grete flood & ryuere named Dunoe, the whiche stratcheth vnto in Constantynople, and there entreth in to the see ; but erst it trauerseth vii grete floodes by his radour & rennyng, &, as I haue herd saye, the hede of this Dunoe begynneth on one side of a montayne, & that other side of the same montayne[7] sourdeth another grete ryuer which is named the Riin[8] and renneth thurgh Almayne by

[*fo 49, vo.] g 1] Basyle, Strawsburgh,[9] * Magounce, Couelence, Coleyn, & Nemyng where fast by it departeth in to iiii ryuers

---

[1] O.F. text, Ch. III [2].

[2] Instead of "Trapesonde," O.F. text has "Rete, Corinte."

[3] 2nd ed. "Saxonye."

[4] Pyrre : O.F. text, p. 129, " Espire," Epirus, Albania.

[5] "In this contre . . . brennyng" : According to Gossouin and *Honorius Aug.* (I. 27, "In Epiro est fons . . ."), this spring rises in Epirus. *Neckam*, II. 6.

[6] "In Archade . . . asshes" : *Neckam*, II. 86 (De asbesto) ; *Honorius Aug.* I. 27.

[7] Caxton probably refers here to Mount St. Gothard, where both the Rhine and the Rhône have their sources.

[8] Riin : 2nd ed. "Ryn," the Rhine.

[9] Strawsburgh : 2nd ed. "Strasburgh."

& renneth thurgh the londes of Ghelres, Cleue and
Holande, and so in to the see. And yet er this ryuer
entre in to the see, he entreth in to another ryuer
named the Mase, & than loseth he his name and is
called the Mase, & Masedepe xl myle longe in the see.[1]

In Europe is also Swauen, Basse[2] Almayn, Ffraunce,
Englonde, Scotland and Irlonde, and aboue this many
other contrees whiche endure vnto the mount Jus[3]; &
thus moche space holdeth the partye of Europe.

Now shal we deuyse to yow how moche Affryke
conteyneth.

Here foloweth of Affryke and of his regyons and
contrees. capitulo xii°.[4]

AFTER Europe is Affryke of whiche the regyon of
Lybe is the firste. This is londe moche riche,
wel peopled and strongly garnysshid. After cometh
the royamme of Surrye, Jherusalem and the contrey
aboute. This is the holy londe where Our Lord Jhesu
Cryst receyuid our humanyte and passyon, and where he
roos fro deth to lyf. After thoppynyon of somme is that
this holy londe longeth to Asye.[5] After thenne cometh
Grece, Cypres, Cecyle, Toscane, Naples, Lombardye,
Gascoyne, Spayne, Cateloyne, Galyce, Nauarre, Portyn-
gal and Aragon.[6] And how be it that the Auctour of
this book saye that thise contrees ben in Affryke, yet, as

[1] The passage from "as I haue herd . . ." to ". . . longe in
the see" is not in the O.F. text.
"& is called . . . in the see": 2nd ed. "and is called the
Mase, and the .xl. myle longe in the see." The word omitted in
the second edition is evidently Caxton's spelling of *Maesdiep*, the
old name of the Channel now called *Oude Maas*, from Dordrecht
to the mouth of the Maas.
[2] Basse: low.
[3] Mount Jus: Mons Jovis, *i. e.* Great St. Bernard.
[4] O.F. text, Ch. IV[2].
[5] "After thoppynyon . . . Asye": This passage is not in the
O.F. text.
[6] "Grece . . . Aragon": Of all the O.F. MSS. which have
been collated, Roy. 19 A IX. is the only one which mentions
"Cypres" (Cyprus), "Secyle" (Sicily), "Naples," "Cateloyne"
(Catalonia), "Galyce" (Galicia), "Nauarre" (Navarra), "Portyn-
gal" (Portugal). Caxton adds "Aragon" and omits from this
list "Alexandrie," Alexandria or Eygpt, which he mentions, however, a few lines farther down.

I vnderstonde, alle thise ben within the lymytes and bou*n*des of Europe.[1]

Also ther ben somme of thise regions & contrees that take their name of somme beestes that dwelle in the same londes, & *the cytees haue taken the fourmes, as Rome hath the fourme of a lyon, and Troye the grete of an hors, &c.[2]

All Barbarye is in Affryke, & Alysandıe. And Ethiope stratcheth vnto thende of Affryke. In this contre of Ethiope the peple ben black for hete of the sonne ; ffor it so hoot in this contre that it semeth that the erthe shold brenne.[3]

Beyonde Ethyope is no londe but deserte & londe withoute bryngyng forth of ony fruyt ; but it is ful of serpentes, of vermyne and of wylde beestis[4] ; whiche londe endeth at the Grete See.

Here shal we speke of dyuerse yles of the see.   ca. xiii°.[5]

SYTH we haue descryuid & deuysed the londe, it is reson that we enquyre of the yles of the see, and in especial of them that we knowe the names, of whiche ther ben plente in the see.

Ther is a moche grete yle called Andos,[6] whiche is to ward Europe ; & syth is the yle of Colchos where the flyes[7] of gold was fou*n*d, lyke as to vs reherceth thystorye of Jason. Ther is another yle called Maron[8] ; in this yle was born the holy man seynt Denys whiche receyuid martyrdom in Frau*n*ce.

Toward Asye the grete ben the nombre of xliiii.[9] There is one yle named Delos ; this yle appiered first after

[1] "And how . . . Europe": This passage is not in the O.F. text (*see Introduction*, p. xvi.).

[2] "Also ther ben . . . hors, &c.": *Gervase of Tilbury*, II. 9 (t. II.); *Honorius Aug.* I. 28.

[3] "In this contre . . . brenne": *Jacobus*, 92.

[4] "Beyonde . . . beestis": *Honorius Aug.* I. 33.

[5] O.F. text, Ch. V[2].

[6] Andos: O.F. text, p. 130, "Avidos," *i. e.* Abydos.

[7] flyes: fleece.

[8] Maron: O.F. text, p. 130, "Naaron," *i. e.* Naxos (*see Introduction*, pp. xvi. and xvii.).

[9] xliii.: O.F. text, p. 130, "cinquante quatre," *i. e.* 54. *Isidore* (XIV. 6. 20) gives the number as *53*.

Noes flood. Ther is another whiche is called Meloth. And
it is so called for the right grete melodye that is herd therin
of swete songe of byrdes that ben in this yle contynuelly.
In this yle groweth plente of whyte marble. Ther is
another yle in this contre that is called Psalmos, in whiche
the quene Sebylle was born, the whiche prophecyed
of many thynges of Our Lord * Jhesu Cryst longe tyme [*fo. 50, vo.
bifore he was born of the virgyne Marie ; and she   g 2
prophecyed thise thinges at Rome where she was sent
fore. In this yle was first founden the maner to make
pottes of erthe, whiche ben yet vsed in many contrees.
In this yle was born a grete philosophre & a good clerke
named Pictogoras, the whiche by his grete entendement
fonde the poyntes and the difference of musyque.[1]

In Affryke is also an yle in the see, whiche is callid
Sardayne, where an herbe groweth whiche is of suche
vertue that, yf one ete of it, he deyeth anon forth with all
lawhyng.[2] Another yle ther is named Bosut,[3] wherin is no
serpent ne vermyne. And ther is another whiche is called
Colombyne,[4] where as is grete plente & foyson of vermyne
and meruayllous serpentes. Yet ther is another yle
that is moche longe and right brode that is called
Alleares. In this yle was first founden the maner of
meltyng of metals.[5] Also ther is the yle of Meroes the
whiche at the myddle of the day hath no shadewe. Yet
ther is pytte in this yle that by right nombre and
mesure is vii foot brode and an hondred foot depe ; and
the sonne shyneth in to the bottom.[6] Also ther is
another yle whiche is called Cylla where the Cyclopiens
were somtyme.[7]

Another yle is in this contre so grete, as the wyse

[1] "Ther is another yle called Maron . . . musyque" : *Honorius Aug.* I. 34.
[2] lawhyng : laughing.
[3] Bosut : Ebusus, now Iviza. (Ptolemy's Ἔβυσσος.)
[4] Colombyne : "Columbina terra" or "Colubraria" in Pliny, may be either "Formentera," one of the Balearic Islands, or the "Columbretes" on the coast of Spain.
[5] "Alleares . . . metals" : *Alleares* : O.F. text, p. 131, "Haleares," the Balearic Islands.—"En cele ylle fu premierement controvée *la fonde*" : "*the sling* was first invented in this island." Caxton confuses *fonde*, a sling, with *fondre*, to melt.
[6] "In Affryke . . . to the bottom" : *Honorius Aug.* I. 36.
[7] "Also ther is another . . . somtyme" : *Honorius Aug.* I. 35.

Plato[1] witnesseth the whiche in his tyme was a
clercke of right grete renommee, whiche hath more of
pourpris & space than alle Europe & Affryke conteynen.
But sith the tyme of Plato it was in suche wyse
destroyed & broken, lyke as it plesid Our Lord, that
it sanke doun in to Abisme for the grete synnes that
they commysed þat were dwellars & inhabitauns * therin.
And is now the see right that is called Bethee.[2]

Another yle is there the whiche may not be seen whan
men wold goo therto; but somme goo thyder, as men saye;
and it is called the yle loste.[3] This yle fonde seynt
Brandon[4] the whiche, beyng therin on ferme londe, sawe
& fonde many meruailles lyke as his legende conteyneth[5];
& who that wil knowe it maye visyte his legende &
rede it.

In the marches hetherward ben fonde many good
yles. The yle of Cypre & of Secyle ther ben, & other
plente that be founden in the see, of whiche I now
speke not.

And be not admeruaylled of suche thinges as ye
haue founden wreton in this present booke, the whiche
may seme to yow moche strange, dyuerse & moche
diffycile to bileue; ffor Our Lord God, whiche is almyghty
maker & creatour of all thynges, & in whom alle
goodes & vertues ben, hath made by His only wille &
playsir in the erthe many meruaylles & many werkes
to be meruaylled on, by cause that noman knoweth by
no waye the raysons wherfore; & therfor we ought not
to mysbileue in no wise that we here redde ne tolde of
the meruaylles of the world vnto the tyme we knowe it
be so or no; ffor the werkes of Our Lord ben so hye & to
the men so difficile & hard that euery[6] man may reporte

[1] Plato's Island is "Atlantis," mentioned in Timæus (25 a) and Critias (113 e).
[2] Bethee: O.F. text, p. 132, "la mer Betéₑ" ("Concretum mare" in *Honorius*).
[3] According to maps of the Middle Ages the "lost island" is situated to the west of Cape Verde Islands.
[4] A long "life of St. Brandan" is given in the second rhymed version of the "Image du Monde."
[5] "Another yle is in this . . . conteyneth": *Honorius Aug.* I. 36.—The rest of the chapter is taken from *Jacobus*, 92.
[6] euery = euery, every.

hym to that that it is, how wel that a man doth not
moche amys somtyme to gyue no bileue to somme thinges,
whan he knoweth not þe trouthe, so that it be not in
erryng ayenst þe faith[1]; ffor it is a good & prouffytable
thing to euery man to vnderstande & reteyne, to thende
that he may lerne of whiche he be not abasshed whan he
heereth speke of suche thinges, & can answere to the
trouthe. Ffor in like wise as to vs seme grete meruaille
of thinges * that I here reherce, in lyke wyse semeth it
to them that ben fro vs, that those thinges of thise
contrees ben moche dyuerse & strange; & meruaylle
gretly by cause they haue litil seen of it; & therfore a
man ought not to meruaylle yf he here somtyme ony
thyng though he can not vnderstonde the rayson; ffor
alleway a man ought to lerne. And ther is noman
that knoweth all, sauf only God whiche all seeth and
alle knoweth.

The geaunts that ben in som place haue right
grete meruaylle of this that we be so lytil ayenst
them ; lyke as we meruaylle of them that ben half
lasse than we be, as it is tofore said : And they ben the
Pygmans whiche ben but iii foot longe. And in lyke
wise meruaylle they of vs of that we ben so grete, &
repute vs also for geaunts. They that haue but one eye
and one foot haue grete meruaylle that we haue tweyne,
lyke as we doo of them that haue but one. And also
as we deuyse their bestis and name them by their
names, in lyke wyse deuyse they oures by theires,
bothe of body and of membres. Yf the centicore haue
an foot of an hors, in lyke wyse hath the hors the foot
of a centicore. Also we may wel saye that the hors
hath the body of monotheros, ffor they ben lyke of
corsaige. And thus their bestes resemble vnto oures,
whiche ben dyuerse of heedes, of bodyes and of men-
bres as oures ben contrarie to theires.

---

[1] "euery man may reporte . . . faith ": Every man may
represent to himself that it is so (*i. e.* may take these works for
granted), though a man does no harm if he disbelieves, sometimes,
things about which he knows nothing, provided that he does not
thereby err against faith.

Of dyuersytees that ben in Europe and in Affryke.[1]
capitulo xiiii°.[2]

[* fo. 52]

We haue in thise parties many thinges that they
of Asye and of Affryke haue none. Ther is
toward * Irlonde on the one syde a maner of byrdes that
flee, and they growen on trees and on olde shipp sides
by the bylles. And whan they be nygh rype, they that
falle in the water lyue, and the other not; they ben
callyd barnacles.[3]

Irland is a grete Ilonde in whiche is no serpent
ne venemous beeste. And who that bereth with hym
the erthe of this yle in to another contre and leyeth
it where as venymous vermyne is, there anon it
deyeth.

Another ylonde is in Irlonde whiche stondeth ferre
in the see, where no wymmen may dwelle; and also
the byrdes that ben femalles may not abyde there.

Ther is another yle wherin nomen may dye in no tyme
of the world. But whan they ben so olde & feble that
their membres faylle and ake and lyue with payne that
they may not helpe ne susteyne them self, and that they
had leuer dye than lyue, they doo them to be born in to
another yle and ouer the water for to dye. And the
trees that ben in this yle kepe their leues grene and in
verdure alle tymes, wynter and somer.

In another yle in Islonde the nyght endureth vi
monethes; and thenne cometh the daye that dureth
other vi monethes shynyng fair and clere.[4]

Another place is in the same ylonde whiche brenneth
nyght and day.

Ther is also in Irlonde a place called seynt Patryks
purgatorye, whiche place is perillous. Yf ony men goon

---

[1] This chapter is almost entirely translated from Giraldus
Cambrensis *Topographia Hibernica* (*Opera*, ed. Dimock, London,
1861–91, 8vo, vol. 5), I. 15, 28–31; II. 4, 5, 7.

[2] O.F. text, Ch. VI [2] (*a*).

[3] barnacles: According to *Jacobus* (92) the barnacle grows in
Flanders (in quibusdam partibus Flandriae).

[4] "And the trees . . . clere": *Jacobus*, 92; *Honorius Aug.*
I. 31. *Isidore* (XIV. 6. 4 and 13) mentions an island, *Tylos*, in
India, where the trees are always green, and another island,
Thyle or *Thule*, near England, where a night lasts six months.

therin and be not confessed and repentaunt of their
synnes, they be anon rauysshed and loste in suche wyse
that noman can telle where they be come. And yf they
be confessyd and repentant, and that they haue don
satisfaccion and penau*n*ce for their synnes, without
that alle be clensed and ful satisfyed, therafter shall
* they suffre payne and greef the tormentis in passing
this crymynel passage. And whan he is retorned agayn
fro this purgatorye, neuer shal no thyng in this world
plese hym that he shal see, ner he shal neuer be Joyous
ne glad, ne shal not be seen lawhe, but shal be contin-
uelly in wayllynges and wepinges for the synnes that he
hath commysed.[1]

Hit may wel be that of auncyent tyme it hath ben
thus as a fore is wreton, as the storye of Tundale & other
witnesse, but I haue spoken with dyuerse men that haue
ben therin. And that one of them was an hye chanon of
Waterford whiche told me that he had ben therin v or
vi tymes. And he sawe ne suffred no suche thynges.
He saith that with procession the Relygious men that
ben there brynge hym in to the hool and shette the dore
after hym; and than he walketh groping in to it,
where, as he said, ben places and maner of cowches to
reste on. And there he was alle the nyght in contem-
placion & prayer, and also slepte there; and on the morn
he cam out agayn. Other while in their shepe[2] somme
men haue meruayllous dremes. & other thyng sawe
he not. And in lyke wyse tolde to me a worshipful
knyght of Bruggis named sir John de Banste that he
had ben therin in lyke wyse and see none other thyng
but as afore is sayd.[3]

In Brytaygne, that now is called Englond, as is said
is a fontayne, and a pyler or a perron[4] therby. And
whan men take water of this welle and caste it vpon the

[margin: [*fo. 52, vo.]
g 4]

---

[1] "but shal be . . . commysed": O.F. text, p. 134: "Mais
adès est en pleur et en gemissement pour les pechiez *que les genz
font et pour les maus qu'il leur voit faire*": . . . for the sins
which *people commit, and for the evil which he sees them do.*

[2] Shepe = slepe, sleep (2nd ed. slepe).

[3] "Hit may wel be . . . is sayd": This passage is not in the
O.F. text (*see Introduction*, pp. xvii. and xviii.).

[4] perron: O.F. "perron," stone, steps.

perron, anon it begynneth to rayne and blowe, thondre
and lyghtne meruayllously.[1]

Also in Ffraunce hath ben seen somtyme a maner of
peple that haue be horned. Toward the mountes of
mount Jus ye * shal fynde plente of wymmen that haue
botches vnder the chyn*n*, whiche hange doun of somme
doun to the pappes; and they that haue grettest ben
holden for fairest. Other folke ther ben that haue
botches on their backes and ben croked as crochettes.[2]
And they that see alle thise thinges ofte meruaylle but
lytyl; also it is ofte seen that in this contre ben born
children deef and dombe, and also of them that haue
bothe nature of man and woman; yet ben ther ofte seen
somme children comen in to this world somme without handes and somme without armes.

Of the maner and condicion of beestes of thise contrees.[3]
capitulo xv°.[4]

The foxe is of suche a condicion that, whan he departeth fro the wode and gooth in to the feldes, there
he lyeth doun & stratcheth hym on the grounde as he
were deed for to take byrdes.

Whan the herte wylle renewe his age he eteth of som
venymous beeste.

Yf the tode, Crapault[5] or spyncop[6] byte a man or
woman, they be in daunger for to dye; it hath be ofte
seen.

The spyttle of a man fastyng sleeth comynly the
spyncoppe & the tode yf it touche them.[7]

Yf a wulf and a man see that one that other fro
ferre, he that is first seen becometh anon aferd.[8]

---

[1] A passage, which is dealt with in the Introduction (cf.
pp. xviii. and xix.), has been omitted by Caxton. In the O.F. text
(p. 134) it precedes the account of horned people in France.

[2] "Also in Ffraunce . . . crochettes": *Jacobus*, 92.

[3] This chapter is translated almost entirely from *Jacobus*, 92.

[4] O.F. text, Ch. VI [2] (*b*).

[5] tode: toad.—Crapault: O.F. "crapaus," Mod. F. "crapaud,"
toad. Caxton uses here, as he often does, two synonymous words.

[6] Spyncop: O.F. text, p. 135, "yraingne," spider.

[7] "The spyttle . . . touche them": The usual sources of Gossouin do not mention this fact.

[8] "he that . . . aferd": O.F. text, p. 135: "Celui qui est
premiers veüz si *enroe*": he who is seen first becomes *hoarse*.

The wulf bereth the sheep without hurtynge or greuyng of hym, doubtyng that he wold crye, and that he shold not be folowed ; and after deuoureth hym whan he hath brought hym to the wode. And yf he be constrayned to leue hym in his berynge, he destrayneth [1] hym with al his myght at his departyng.[2]

   * The spyther or spyncop of his propre nature spynneth   [*fo. 53, vo.] and weueth of his entraylles the threde of whiche he maketh his nettes for to take flyes whiche he eteth.

Whan the sheape hath two whelpes or fawnes, she loueth that one moche better than that other. She berith hym that she loueth best in her armes, and that other she leteth goo, whiche, whan she is hunted, lepeth on the moders backe and holdeth her faste. And that other that she bereth in her armes, she leteth falle and is ofte constrayned to saue her self.[3]

Also it is so that the hounde kepeth the goodes of his lorde and maistre, and ben by hym waranted ayenst men and bestes. And aboue alle other he knoweth his lord and maistre by his smellyng, & loueth hym of so right good loue that ofte it happeth, be it right or wronge, he wyl not forsake his maistre vnto the deth. And also is so sorowful for the deth of his maistre that other whyle he loseth his lyf.

In Englond in som place is ther a maner of houndes that goon & seche out the theuys,[4] and bryngen them fro thens where they fonde them.[5]

The moustele [6] is a right lytil beste & sleeth the basilycock, and in longe fyghtyng byteth hym out of mesure. She of her nature remeueth so ofter her fawnes fro one place to another that wyth grete payne they may vnnethe be founden.

The hyrchon,[7] whan he fyndeth apples beten or blow-

---

  [1] destrayneth : injures.
  [2] "And yf he be constrayned . . . departyng": This passage is not in the O.F. text.
  [3] The passage from "whiche, whan . . ." to ". . . saue her self," is not in the O.F. text.
  [4] theuys : thieves.
  [5] "In Englond . . . fonde them": *Neckam*, ll. 157.
  [6] moustele : O.F. "mustele," weasel.
  [7] hyrchon : O.F. "li heriçons," hedgehog.

en doun of a tree, he woloweth on them tyl he be chargid and laden wyth the fruyt stykyng on his pryckes. And whan he feleth hym self laden as moche as he may bere, he goth his way wyth them syngyng and makyng his deduyt.   And yf he mete ony beste that wold doo hym harm, he reduyseth hym self as rounde * as a bowle, and hydeth his groyne & his feet, and armeth hym wyth his pryckes aboute his skynne in suche wyse that no beste dar approche hym, doubtyng his pryckes.

The lambe, whiche neuer sawe wulf, of his propre nature doubteth and fleeth hym. But, he doubteth nothyng other bestes but goth hardyly emonge them.

Of the maner of birdes of thise forsaid contrees.[1] ca. xvi⁰.[2]

THE egle of his nature taketh his byrdes by the vngles or clawes wyth his bylle.   And hym that holdeth fastest he loueth beste & kepeth them next by hym.   And them that holden but febly, he leteth hem goo, and taketh none hede of them.   Whan the Egle is moche aged, he fleeth so hye that he passeth the clowdes, and holdeth there his sight so longe ayenst the sonne that he hath al loste it and brende alle his fethers. Thenne he falleth doun on a montaygne in a water that he hath to fore chosen, & in this manere he reneweth his lyf.   And whan his bille is ouerlonge he breketh and bruseth it ayenst an hard stone & sharpeth it.

Whan the Turtle hath loste her make [3] whom she hath first knowen, neuer after wyl she haue .make, ne sytte vpon grene tree, but fleeth emonge the trees contynuelly bewayllyng her loue.[4]

The hostryche by his nature eteth well yron, and greueth hym not.

Whan the heyron seeth the tempest come, he fleeth

---

[1] This chapter is translated from *Jacobus*, 92.
[2] O. F. text, Ch. VI [2] (c)
[3] make : mate.
[4] "but fleeth . . . her loue": O.F. text (p. 136) says merely "Ainz s'en vait par les arbres *sés* touz jourz gemissant": flies among *dry* trees always wailing. MS. Roy. 19 A IX., changes *sés* into the possessive *ses* (her), and writes "Ainz s'en vait par les arbres, *ses amours* continuellement gemissant." Caxton translates this last sentence literally.

vp so hye tyl he be aboue the clowdes for teschewe the
rayn & tempeste.

The Chowe [1] whan she fyndeth gold or syluer, of
her nature she hydeth and bereth it away. And who
somtyme * heereth her voys, it semeth proprely that
she speketh. [*fo. 54, vo.]

The crowe weneth that he is the fairest birde of alle
other, and the beste syngyng. Yf her byrdes be whyte
in ony parte, she wil neuer doo them good til they be
all black.

The pecok whan he beholdeth his fethers, he setteth
vp his tayll as Rounde as a wheel al aboute hym, by cause
his beaulte shold be alowed and preysed, and is moche
prowd of his fair fethers and plumage. But whan he
beholdeth to ward his feet, whiche ben fowl to loke on,
thenne he leteth his tayll falle wenyng to couer his feet.

The goshawke and sperhawk taken their prayes by the
ryuers. But they that ben tame and reclaymed brynge
that they take to theyr lord whiche hath so taught them.

The culuer or the dowue is a symple byrde, and of her
nature nourisshith well the pigeons of another douue.
And apperceyuith well in the water by thy [2] shadowe and
seeth therin whan the hawke wold take her.

The huppe [3] or lapwynche is a byrde crested whiche
is moche in mareys [4] & fylthes, and abydeth leuer therin
than out therof. Who someuer ennoynteth hym self
with the blode of the huppe, and happe that after leyde
hym doun to slepe, hym shold seme anon in his slepe
dremyng that alle the deuyllis of helle shold come to
hym and wold strangle hym.

The nyghtyngal of her propre nature syngeth well
and longe, and otherwhyle so longe that she deyeth
syngyng. And the larke in lyke wyse dyeth ofte sing-
yng. The swanne [5] syngeth ofte to fore her deth. In
lyke wyse doo ofte many men.

[1] chowe: O.F. "choé," jackdaw, chough. (*Jacobus*, 92:
monedula.)
[2] thy = the.   [3] huppe: O.F. "hupe," lapwing.
[4] mareys: marshes.
[5] O.F. text (p. 137): "Li cignes est touz blans par dehors, et
par dedenz est touz noirs": The swan is white outside, and black
inside.—This passage has been omitted by Caxton.

I

Of thise thinges and of many other moche peple
meruaylle that neuer herde of suche thinges to fore,
ne knowe not therof as we * doo here that dayly fynde
it ; ffor in this book we fynde many thynges and resons,
wherof men meruaylle strongly that neuer haue seen,
lerned, ne herd of them.

Of dyuersytes of somme comyne thinges.[1]   ca. xvii°.[2]

PLENTE and many thynges ther ben seen at eye, of
whiche the resons ben couuert and hyd fro vs, of
whiche the people meruaylle but lytil, bycause they see
it so ofte.

The quyck syluer is of suche nature and manere that
it susteyneth a stone vpon it, where as water and oyle
may not, ffor the stone in them gooth to the bottom.

The lyme or brent chalke in colde water anon it
chauffeth and is hoot that noman may suffre his hand
on it.[3]

The rayes of the sonne make the heer of a man
abourne or blounde.[4]

And it maketh the flessh of a man broun or black ;
and it whiteth the lynnen cloth ; and the erthe that is
moyst and softe maketh drye and hard ; and waxe that
is drye, it relenteth and maketh softe.   Also it maketh
cold water in a vessel warme.   Also oute of glasse
ayenst the sonne men make fyre, and out of Crystal in
lyke wyse.[5]   Also with smytyng of a stone ayenst yron
cometh fyre, and flammeth.[6]

---

[1] This chapter is translated from *Jacobus*, 93.

[2] O.F. text, Ch. VII [2].

[3] "The lyme . . . hand on it": O.F. text, p. 138: "La chalz
vive a si tost la froide eave eschauffée que l'en n'i porroit
souffrir sa main": Cold water is so quickly heated by lime that
it is impossible to keep one's hand in it.

[4] "The rays of the sun make the hair of a man auburn or
fair": This passage is not in O.F. text.

[5] The passage from "Also it maketh . . ." to ". . . Crystal
in lyke wyse" is unintelligible in the O.F. text.   It is the same
in all the Prose MSS., and reads (p. 138): "Si fait l'en de l'eave
froide en .i. vaissel de voirre le feu encontre le soleill, et du cristal
ausi." *Jacobus* (93) says: "Crystallus licet frigidus sit, aqua
frigida conspersus ad solis radios, ignem ex se producit": Even
if crystal is cold, when covered with water and exposed to the rays
of the sun it produces fire.

[6] Before "The breeth of a man" Caxton has omitted a passage

The breeth of a man, whiche is hoot, coleth hoot thyng; and it chauffeth colde and ayer by meuyng.[1]

The erthe, whiche is peysant and right heuy by nature, holdeth hit in the myddle of thayer without piler and foundement, only by nature. And therfor he is a fool that meruaylleth of thynges that God maketh; ffor noo creature hath the power to shewe reson wherfore they * ben or not; ffor ther is nothyng, how lytil it be, [*fo. 55, vo.] that the glose may be knowen vnto the trouthe, sauf only that whiche pleseth to Our Lord God. Ffor to be wel founded in clergye may men knowe & vnderstande the reson of somme thinges, and also by nature suche thinge as by reson can not be comprehended. Thawh a man enquyre neuer so longe of that is wrought in therthe by nature, he shal not mowe come to the knowelege wherfore ne how they be made. This may noman certaynly knowe, sauf God only whiche knoweth the reson and vnderstondeth it.

Ffor to knowe where helle stondeth, and what thyng it is.[2] capitulo xviii°.[3]

WE haue declared to yow and deuysed the erthe without forth the best wise that we can. But now it is expedyent, after that this that is said, to knowe and enquyre what places and what mansions ther may be within therthe, and whether it be paradys, helle, purgatorye, lymbo or other thynge, and whiche of them is best, and whiche of them alle is worste.

As to the regard of me and as me semeth that that whiche is enfermed and closed in the erthe is helle, I saye this for as moche as helle may in no wyse be in thayer whiche is one so noble a place. Also I may frely mayntene that it is not in heuen; ffor that place is so

---

(O.F. text, p. 138): "Li venz, qui est froiz, esprant le feu et l'enflambe et le fait plus grant": Wind, which is cold, kindles the fire and increases the flames.

[1] "and it chauffeth . . . meuyng": The O.F. text (p. 138) says: *Li airs refroide par mouvemenz, et l'yaue en eschauffe qui est froide:* air is made cool by motion, while cold water is made warm thereby.

[2] Cf. for this chapter *Honorius Aug.* I. 37.

[3] O. F. text, Ch. VIII[2].

right excellent pure and net that helle may not endure
there, ffor as moche as helle is so horryble, stynkyng,
fowl and obscure.   Also it is more poysaunt and heuy

than ony thyng may be; wherfor it may be clerly * vnderstanden that helle hath his beyng in the most lowest place,
moste derke, and moste vyle of the erthe ; and as I haue
here sayd to yow the causes why, in trouthe it may not
be in thayer and yet lasse in heuen, ffor it is in alle
poyntes contrarye to heuen aboue, ffor as moche as thise
two ben contrarye one to another.   Of whiche places,
in that one is founden but alle glorye and consolacion :
that is heuen ; in that other is nothyng but of alle
tribulacion : that is helle.   And therfore it is with-
drawen alle vnder fro that other as ferre as it may, and
that is in the myddle of therthe.

I saye not that helle is not in none other place where
it be, ffor after the deth he hath payne and sorowe that
hath deserued it.   And whan suche one shal haue his
payne aboue, so moche hath he the werse ; alle thus as it
shold be of somme man that had a grete maladye, so
moche that he shold deye, and that he were brought in
to a fair place and plesaunt for to haue Joye and solace ;
of so moche shold he be more heuy & sorowful whan he
sawe that he coude ne myght helpe hym self ne take
therby noo spoort ne releef.   In lyke wyse shal it be of
thise vnhappy caytifs that ben by their demerites
dampned in helle, wherof we shal now herafter to yow
more ample & largely declare ffor to fynysshe the bettre
our booke.

Now yf ye wille take hede and vnderstonde, we
shal deuyse how helle is in the myddle of therthe,
and of what nature it is of, and of the inestymable
tormentis whiche they haue that ben therin put and
condempned.   Ye haue wel vnderstanden how by nature
the iiii elementes holde them, that one within that

other, so that therthe is in the * myddle and holdeth
hym in the myddle of the firmament.   Alle in lyke wyse
is ther in the myddle of therthe a place whiche is called
Abisme or swolowe, and erthe of perdicion.   Thus
moche saye I to yow of this place, that it is ful of

fyre & of brennyng sulfre. And it is ouer hydows, stynkynge, ful of ordure and of alle euyl aduenture; hit is moche large within, and bynethe it is strayt.

Alle that falleth therin anon the sulphre contynuelly brenneth, destroyeth and consumeth. And that thyng that cometh therin shal neuer fynysshe ne haue ende, but alleway shal brenne without ende. Alle way it brenneth, and alle way reneweth. And alle that come therin may neuer deye, ffor this place is of suche náture that the more it brenneth, the lenger it endureth.

This place of helle hath within hym alle the euylles of his partye. There deth holdeth his standard, whiche sendeth out thurgh all the world for to fetche them that ben his, who that hath Joye of heuynesse.[1] Thyder come all euylles and all the euyll apportes.[2] This place is called the erthe of deth, ffor the sowles that ben brought thyder, they abyde and dwelle there without ende. Certaynly they deye lyuyng, and alle way lyue deyeng. The deth is there their lyf and their vyande and mete.

The deth holdeth them there at his commandement. This is the right pytte of fyre that brennyth; & all in lyke wyse as the stone is drowned in the see whan it is throwen and sonken, and neuer shal be after seen, right so ben the sowles sonken in to the bottom whiche contynuelly brenne & be drowned there. But for al that they dymynysshe not ne haue ende, but in suche myserye abye their folyes * nyght and day, and so shall endure perpetuelly and without ende. Ffor what someuer thyng that is spyrituel may neuer dye in suche wyse that it be alle deed; but the deth wold they haue and weesshe after it incessantly.

[* fo. 57]

The sowle may neuer deye after that it is out of the body; but whan it is there, it shall alleway languysshe. And euer after that it is in helle, it shal haue nothing but euyll.[3]

[1] "who that hath Joye *of* heuynesse": O.F. text (p. 140): "qui qu'en ait joie *ne* tristece," whether they await it (death) with joy *or* sorrow.

[2] apportes: O.F. text (p. 140): "viennent a porz," *i. e.* land.

[3] "And euer . . . euyll": Roy. 19 A IX.: "Ne jamaiz de lors

This is the contre & the londe of oblyuion & forgetyng; ffor alle they that ben there shal be forgoten, lyke as they forgate in this world their maker whiche is ful of pyte & of mysericorde. And therfore he hath leyd them there in forgetyng, where they shal neuer haue mercy ne pardon. In this londe so tenebrouse, hydouse and ful of alle stenche and of sorowes, anguysshes, heuynes, hungre and thyrste shal neuer creature haue gladnesse ne Joye. Thise ben the terryble gehynes stynkynge. And there is the fyre so ouer moche ardaunt, hote & anguysshous that our fyre & the hete is nomore vnto the regard of that fyre of helle than a fyre paynted on a walle is in comparison & to the regard of our fyre.

There ben the flodes peryllous whiche ben of fyre and of yce, so hydows, horryble, full of venyme and of fowle beestes that make so grete noyse and so grete grief, payne and ennoye vnto the dolorouse sowles that ben in the sayd abysme, that ther nys creature that can or may recounte or telle the hondred parte.

In this contre ther is plente of other places whiche ben peryllous and horryble. And of them ben somme in the see as wel as wythin therthe. In many yles that ben by the see is terryble stenche of sulphre ardaunt in

[° fo. 57, vo.]
h 1

* grete fyre, whiche is moche paynfull. Ther ben many grete montaynes of sulphre that brenne nyght and daye, where as many sowles ben encombred and brenne contynuelly for to purge their synnes & inyquytees.

This may thenne wel suffyse as touchynge to speke ony more of this matere; ffor ther is no creature that can telle the grete tormentes and inestymable paynes that a man of euyl lyf receyueth for his demerites whan he is departed fro this world; ffor he goth euer from euyl to werse.

Here we shal cesse for this present tyme, and now saye nomore herof. And seen that we haue spoken wel a longe of one of the foure Elementes, whiche is therthe,

---

qu'elle est en enfer n avra si non tout mal." O.F. text (p. 140): "Ne jamais n'avront se mal non," *i. e.* Nor will they (souls) ever have anything else but pain.—Caxton translates Roy. 19 A IX., literally.

we shal now speke of the seconde, and that is of the
water that alway renneth ; and after we shal speke of
thayer, and after of the fyre, euerich in his right ordre.

How the watre renneth by and thurgh therthe. ca. xix°.[1]

THE water that is the depe see the whiche enuyronneth and goth round aboute the world ; and of this
see meuen alle the flodes and Ryuers that renne thurgh
the erthe. And renne so ferre their cours and that
they retorne and come agayn thedyr from whens they
departed, and that is the See. And thus gooth the See
contynuelly tornyng and makyng his cours that, for so
moche as the water is more lyght than the erthe, so
moche is it aboue and is most next to therthe. She
departeth and deuydeth the contrees, and she spredeth
her thurghout alle therthe.

She falleth * agayn in the See, and spredeth agayn by
the flodes and Ryuers, and goth sourdyng and spryng-
yng in the erthe from one place to another by vaynes.
Alle in lyke wyse as the blood of a man gooth and
renneth by the vaynes of the body, and gooth out &
yssueth in somme place, alle in lyke wyse renneth the
water by the vaynes of therthe and sourdeth and
spryngeth out by the fontaynes and welles [2] ; fro whiche
it gooth al aboute that, whan one delueth in therthe depe
in medowe or in montaygne or in valeye, men fynde
water salte or swete or of somme other maner.

[* fo. 53]

How the water swete or salt, hoot or enuenymed
sourdeth out of the erthe. capitulo xx°.[3]

ALLE watres come of the see; as wel the swete as
the salt, what someuer they be, alle come out of
the see and theder agayn alle retorne. Wherupon somme
may demande : "Syth the see is salt, how is it that somme
water is fresshe and swete ?" Herto answerth one of
thauctours and sayth that the water that hath his cours
by the swete erthe is fresshe and swete, and becometh

---

[1] O.F. text: Ch. IX [2].
[2] "She falleth . . . welles": *Honorius Aug.* I. 5.
[3] O.F. text: Ch. X [2].

swete by the swetnes of therthe whiche taketh a way
from it his saltnes and his bytternes by her nature ;
ffor the water whiche is salt & bytter, whan it renneth
thurgh the swete erthe, the swetnes of therthe reteyneth
his bytternes and saltnes.   And thus becometh the
water swete and fresshe whiche to fore was salt and
byttre.[1]

[* fo.58,vo.]
h 2

Other waters sourden and spryngen bytter & black,
whiche somme men drynke * for to be heled of their
maladyes in stede of poyson ; the whiche oftymes make
grete purgacions to somme peple. This is a water
that spryngeth black and clere, and renneth in therthe
whiche is bytter and black ; and it is ful of moche
fylthe ; wherfore men haue grete meruaylle how it may
be holsom to the body of a man.   In another place
sourdeth water whiche is hoot, and that ther myght be
scalded therin a pygge or ghoos,[2] whiche ben called
bathes or baynes naturell.[3] Of suche maner bathes
ben ther in Almayne in the Cyte of Acon,[4] and in
Englond at Bathe[5] ; in Lorayne another atte thabbay
of Plounners[6] ; and at Ays in Gascoygne another.
This procedeth for as moche as within therthe ben
many caues whiche ben hoot and brennyng as fyre.
And therthe hath plente of vaynes whiche ben alle
ful of sulphre.   And ther cometh other while a wynde
grete and stronge, the whiche cometh by the water that
sourdeth.   And that is put forth so strongly that the
sulphre catcheth fyre and brenneth, lyke as a fornayce
alle brennyng shold doo.   And the water that hath his
cours by thyse vaynes become also hoot as fyre.   And
yf it happed that the water ryght there shold sprynge
out of therthe, it sholde yssue sourdyng alle enflamed

1 "Herto answerth . . . byttre" : *Honorius Aug.* I. 46.
2 "and that ther . . ." to ". . . ghoos" is in the O.F.
text.
3 "Other waters . . . naturell" : *Honorius Aug.* I. 48.
4 Acon : O.F. "Ais la Chapele," "Aachen" in German.
5 The O.F. text does not mention "Bathe in Englond."
6 "Thabbay of Plounners" ("Plommieres" in O.F. text, p. 142)
is now "Plombières" in the Département des Vosges. This passage is particularly interesting as it shows Gossouin's intimate
knowledge of the country round Metz, where the O.F. orginal
is supposed to have been written.

and alle boylyng as it were on a fyre.[1]   But fro as ferre
as his cours renneth fro thens, so moche wexeth it lasse
hoot and lasse brennyng ; and it may renne so longe &
so ferre that in thende it becometh agayn alle colde, ffor
ther is nothyng so hoot but that it koleth, sauf only the
fyre of helle whiche contynuelly brenneth and shal
brenne without ende.

Wythin * therthe is plente of other places whiche ben   [* fo. 59]]
ful of fowle bestes & venymous, in suche wyse that the
water that renneth therby is alle enfected, and sourdeth
in somme places on therthe ; but who that drynketh
therof secheth his deth.

Of dyuerse fontaynes and welles that sourde on
therthe.[2] capitulo xxi°.[3]

Ther ben plente of fontaynes in other places, that
moche ofte chaunge their colour, and other of
whom come myracles ; but it is not wel knowen wherof
this procedeth.

In the londe of Samarye is a wel that chaungeth and
differenceth his colour four tymes in the yere ; hit is
first grene, and after it chaungeth in to Sangwynne ;
and after it becometh trowble, and after alle this it
becometh clere, nette and right syne,[4] in suche wyse
that men delyte them in beholdyng of it ; but no persone
dar drynke of it.

In this partye is yet another fontayne whiche spryngeth thre or four dayes the weke good and holsomme ;
and the other thre dayes it spryngeth not, but is alle
drye.

Ther is also a grete Ryuer that renneth sixe dayes
duryng in the weke. And on the sabotte[5] daye it
renneth not, ffor assone as the sabbotte day approcheth
he rebouteth[6] and goth in to therthe agayn.

---

[1] "This procedeth . . . fyre" : *Honorius Aug.* 1. 48.
[2] This chapter is translated from *Jacobus*, 85.
[3] O.F. text, Ch. XI[2].
[4] syne : O.F., p. 143, "fine," pure.
[5] sabbotte, 2nd ed. "sabotte." O.F. text, p. 143, "samedi,"
Saturday.
[6] rebouteth : O.F. "rebouter," to push. O.F. text (p. 143) has
se rembat, sinks.

By Acres the Cyte is founden a maner of sande, and there is founden also of the glayre of the see,[1] whiche ben medled to gydre. And of thyse two myxtyons is made good glasse and clere.[2]

[* fo. 59, vo.
h 3
In Egypte is the Rede See where the chyldren of Israhel passed ouer drye foote *for to come in to the londe of byheste. This see taketh his name of therthe ; ffor therthe is alle rede in the bottom & on the sydes in suche wyse that the water of this see semeth all reed.

In Perse is a ryuer longe & brood whiche in the nyght is so hard frozen that peple may goo ouer afoot and trauerse it. And on daye tyme it is cleer and rennyng.

Ther is in Espyre a welle of whiche the nature is moche meruayllous, the whiche quencheth brondes of fyre all brennyng, and after it setteth them a fyre agayn.

In Ethiope is another whiche by nyght hath so grete hete that no creature may thenne drynke therof. And all the daye it is so colde that it is frorn alle harde.

In Lorayne, nygh vnto Metz the cyte, is a water that renneth there, the whiche is soden[3] in grete payelles[4] of copper, and it becometh salt fayr and good. And this water furnyssheeth all the contre of salt. And this water sourdeth of a pitte whiche is called "the pytte of Dauyd."[5]

In this contre ben other fontaynes that ben so hoot that it brenneth all that it toucheth. In the same place sourde and sprynge other that ben as colde as yce. There been baynes wel attemprid and medlid with colde water and hoot. And they that bayne them in thise baynes, their scabbes and soores become all hool. Yet ther be of other fontaynes right black, whiche ben

[1] glayre of the see: O.F. text, p. 144: "une glaire de mer," gravel. "Glaire" is still used in that sense in some French dialects.

[2] "By Acres . . . clere": *Jacobus*, 85, "In Tyrensi autem et Acconensi territorio ex arenulis maris, ex sabulo videlicet et *glarea marina* subtili artificio vitrum efficitur purissimum."

[3] soden : boiled.

[4] payelles : O.F., p. 144, "paales," pans.

[5] the pytte of Dauyd: O.F., p. 144, "le puis Davi." This place, now Vic in Lorraine, was originally called "Bodasvic"; in Latin "Bodasius Vicus."

holden right holsom; and peple drynke of them in stede
of medecynes ; and they make oftymes grete purgacions,
and gretter than of a medycyne or a laxatyf.

Another fontayne ther is to ward the Oryent wherof
is made fyre grekyssh with other myxtyons that is put
therto. The whiche fyre, whan it is taken and light,
is so hoot that * it can not be quenchid with water, [* fo. 60]
but with aysel,[1] vryne, or with sonde only. The sarasyns selle this water right dere and derrer than they
doo good wyne.

Other fontaynes sourde in many other places, that
hele sore eyen and many soores and woundes. Other
fontaynes ther be that rendre to a man his mynde and
memorye. Other make men to forgete ; other that
refrayne peple fro lecherye ; other that meue them
therto. Other ther be that make wymmen to conceyue
and bere children ; and other that make them bareyne
and may bere none.

Ther ben somme ryuers that make sheep black, and
other that make them whyte as the lylye. On that other
syde ther ben many pondes or stagues in whiche may
nothyng swymme, man ne hounde ne other beeste, but
anon it synketh doun to the bottom. Ther ben other in
whiche nothing may synke, but contynuelly flote aboue.
Ther ben yet other fontaynes hoot that blynde the theues
whan they forswere them of the trespaas that they
haue commysed touchyng their thefte. And yf they be
charged & born wrongly on honde without reson and
thenne drynke of this water, certaynly they shal haue
better sight than to fore. Of all thise thynges can
noman rendre the reson, but that we ought to vnderstonde that alle this procedeth by myracle.

Yet ben ther other fontaynes whiche ben stylle and
clere, whiche that, whan men pleye ouer them with harpe
or other instrumentis that resowne in maner of consolacion by their sowne, the water of those wellis sprynge
vp with grete bobles & sprynge ouer in the waye.
Other fontaynes ben in other places, whiche ben right
peryllous.

[1] aysel : O.F. text, p. 144, "aisill," vinegar.

[* fo.60,vo.]
h 4

But for this present * we shal reste herwith all ffor
to telle of this that cometh by the waters whiche holde
their cours within therthe and also aboue; of whiche it
happeth other while so grete a quauyng that the erthe
meueth so strongly that it behoueth to fall all that
whiche is theron, thaugh it were a massyue tour.

Wherfor and how the erthe quaueth & trembleth.
capitulo xxii°.[1]

N ow vnderstande ye thenne what it is of the meuyng
of the erthe, and how the erthe quaueth and
shaketh, that somme peple calle "an erthe quaue" by
cause they fele therthe meue and quaue vnder their
feet.   And oftymes it quaueth so terrybly, and meueth,
that somtyme Cytees ben sonken in to therthe, that
neuer after be seen.

And this cometh of the grete waters that come within
therthe, so that by the puttyng out of the grete floodes
& waters growe somme tyme cauernes vnder therthe.
And the ayer that is shette fast withing, the which is
enclosed in grete distresse, yf therthe be there feble so
that it may not reteyne it all within, thenne is it constrayned to opene & cleue; ffor the ayer enforceth to
yssue out.   Wherof it happeth ofte that townes, cytees
and castellys ben sonken doun in to the abisme.

And yf therthe be of sucho force & strengthe that it
openeth not ne cleueth by the shouyng or heuyng of the
wyndes that ben within, thenne therthe meueth &
quaueth [2] so meruayllously that the grete walles and hye
towres that ben theron falle doun so sodenly in therthe
that it destroyeth & sleeth the peple that ben therin,
whiche * ben not aduysed ne pourueyed of suche daun-
gers; whiche is a grete sorow for the pour peple that
dwelle where suche meschief happeth, whan they be not
aduertysed at what tyme such tempeste shal come for
teschewe it.[3]

[* fo. 61]

[1] O. F. text, Ch. XII [2].
[2] "And this cometh ... quaueth": *Neckam*, II. 48 ; *Honorius
Aug.* I. 41, 42.
[3] "whiche is a grete . . . teschewe it": Caxton paraphrases
here an obscure passage of the O.F. text (p. 146), "dont li

But wyse men that doubte for to deye arme them and make them redy ayenst the deth, and gyue alle diligence for to seche to haue accordaunce vnto the souerayn iuge of their synnes & defaultes after their lawe and byleue that they haue, as they that haue none houre ne space to lyue where as they ben hool and weel at ease.

Thus the water and the wynde maken the right meuyng and quauyng by whiche the erthe cleueth and quaueth.

How the water of the see becometh salt.   capitulo xxiii°.[1]

N OW I wyll recounte and telle to yow how the water of the see becometh salt, whiche is so bittre that no persone may drynke, ne the beestis in lyke wyse.

Hit cometh by the sonne on hye; ffor it maketh so grete hete in somme place that the see is chauffed so strongly that therthe, whiche is vnder, draweth to hym a moysture bittre whiche taketh away all his sauour.   Ffor in the see ben right grete and hye montaynes and depe valeyes whiche ben ful of bitternesses greuous and infected.   And the erthe whiche is in the bottom of thise valeyes scumeth for the heete of the sonne vpward, whiche medleth with the water in the depe in suche wyse that it draweth the saltnes vp by the hete of the sonne, so longe til it be medlyd with that other.[2]   And thus is the water of the see salt with that * other.   [* fo. 61, vo.]

Thenne we shall here fynysshe to speke ony more of the watres fressh or salt, and shall recounte to you of the Ayer, whiche is one of the iiii Elementis, and of his propretees.

Here foloweth ôf the Ayer and of his nature.   ca. xxiiii°.[3]

T HE Ayer is sette aboue the water, and is moche more subtyl than the water or the erthe, and enuy-

---

pueples qui demeure la endroit, qui ne sevent pas a quele heure cele tempeste doit venir." Gossouin's usual sources do not contain this passage, and the O.F. MSS. all agree.

[1] O. F. text, Ch. XIII[2].

[2] "Hit cometh . . . other": *Neckam*, II. 1; *Honorius Aug.* I. 45; Adelard of Bath, *Quæstiones Naturales* (Louvain, 1480), Quaest. 51.

[3] O. F. text, Ch. XIV[2].

ronneth therthe on alle parties, and domyneth also hye
as the clowdes mounte. This Ayer whiche enuyronneth
vs on alle sydes is moche thycke. But we lyue therby
in like wyse as the fysshe lyueth by the water whiche
he draweth in, and after casteth it out agayn. In suche
maner the ayer prouffyteth to vs, ffor we drawe it in
and after we put it out ; and thus it holdeth the lyf
within the body. Ffor a man shold sonner deye without
Ayer than a fysshe shold doo without water, to whom
alleway the lyf is sone fynysshyd whan it is out of the
water.

Thayer maynteneth in vs the lyf by the moysture
that is in hym. And by the thycknes that is in hym
he susteyneth the byrdes fleeyng that so playe with
their wynges and meue them so moche al aboute therin
that they disporte them, ledyng their Joye therin and
their deduyt. Thus goon the birdes by thayer fleyng,
syngyng and preysyng their maker & creatour, lyke as
the fysshes that goon swymmyng in the water.

And ye may apperceyue in this maner : Take a rodde
and meue it in thayer ; and yf ye meue it fast and
roydly,[1] it shal bowe anon. And yf it fonde not thayer
[* fo. 62]   thycke, it * shold not bowe ne ploye, but shold holde hym
straight and right, how faste someuer ye meued it.

Of this Ayer the euyl esperites take their habyte
and their bodyes, whiche in somtyme put them in the
semblaunce of somme thinges, as whan they may
appere in som place for to deceyue som persone, man or
woman, or for to make them to yssue out of their
mynde, wherof they haue somtyme the myght ; or
whan by the arte of nygromancye he putteth hym in
somme semblaunce or in suche a fygure as he wille.[2]
But this is a scyence that, who that geuyth hym therto
to do euyl, hit gyueth hym the deth ; ffor yf he taketh
no hede therof, he shal be dampned body & sowle. But
we shal enquyre here after what cometh fro thayer in
to therthe.

[1] roydly : O. F. text (p. 148): "roidement," rapidly, violently.
[2] "Of this Ayer . . . wille": Saint Augustin (*De Gen. ad lit.*
III. ch. x. 14, *Patrol.* t. 34): "Daemones aeria sunt animalia,
quoniam corporum aeriorum natura vigent."

How the clowdes and rayn come comynly. ca. xxv°. [1]

NOW we shal speke of the clowdes for to knowe what
it is, and of the Rayne also.

The sonne is the foundement of all hete and of alle
tyme, all in suche wise as the herte of a man is the
foundement, by his valour that is in hym, of all natural
hete; ffor by hym he hath lyf, and all lyueth by hym,
that groweth on therthe as it pleseth to Our Lorde, as
here after shal be declared, yf ye wyl here and wel reteyne
the mater and substaunce of this present booke. Ffor
the sonne maketh the clowdes to mounte on hye, and
after it maketh the Rayne and to auale doun. And I
shal shewe to yow how it is doon, & shortly, by his
force. And vnderstande ye in what manere : Whan the
sonne spredeth his rayes vpon therthe & vpon * the   [* fo. 62, vo.]
mareys,[2] he dreyeth them strongly, and draweth vp the
moisture whiche he enhaunseth on hye. But this is a
moisture subtyl whiche appereth but lytyl, and is named
vapour ; and it mounteth vnto the myddle of thayer, and
there it assembleth and cometh to gydre and abydeth
there. And lytil & lytil it encreceth, that it cometh
thycke and derke in suche wise that it taketh fro vs the
sight of the sonne. And this thynge is the clowde.
But it hath not so moche obscurete that it taketh fro
vs the clernes of the day.

And whan it groweth ouer thycke, it becometh water
whiche falleth on the erthe, and the clowde abydeth
whyte. Thenne shyneth the sonne, whiche is on hye,
thurgh the clowde, yf it be not ouer black, lyke as
thurgh a glasse, and also lyke a candel within a
laterne, whiche gyueth vs lyght without forth, and yet
we see not the candel ; thus shyneth the sonne thurgh
the clowde which is vnder hym, and rendreth to vs the
clerenesse of the day as longe as he maketh his tourne
aboue therthe. And the clowde that alwaye so longe
abydeth and taketh more moisture so longe after that,
it becometh black & moyste. Thenne yssueth out the

---

[1] O. F. text, Ch. XV[2].

[2] mareys: O. F. text (p. 149): "marais," marshes.

water whiche cometh to therthe ; & thus groweth the
rayne.

And whan it is alle fallen to therthe, & the grete
moisture is. staunched,[1] the clowde hath lost his broun
colour that he byfore helde and the derknesse of whiche
she empesshid the day.[2]   Thenne apperith the cloude
clere and whyte whiche thenne is lyght and monuteth
on hye somoche that in thende she faylleth and is
deffeted by the hete of the sonne on hye whiche all
dreyeth vp.   Thenne thayer wexeth agayn pure & clere,
and the heuen * as blew as Azure.

[* fo. 63]

Of therthe groweth the rayn and the clowdes also, as
of a cloth that is weet and shold be dreyd by the fyre ;
thenne yssueth therof a moisture like a smoke or fumee,
and goth vpward.   Who thenne helde his hande ouer
this fumee, he sholde fele a vapour whiche sholde make
his honde moyst and weet ; yf it dured longe he sholde
appertly knowe that his hande were alle weet, and that
water shold droppe and falle therof.

And thus I saye to yow that in this maner growe
ofte the clowdes & raynes.   And Our Lord God multe-
plieth wel them, whan it pleseth hym, for to make the
seedes and fruytes growe that ben on therthe.

Of ffrostes and snowes.[3]   capitulo xxvi°.[4]

THE grete snowes & the grete frostes comen by the
grete coldes of thayer whiche is colde in the
myddle more than it is on ony other parte, like as ye
may see of the montaynes whiche ben in hye place, like
as the montaynes of Sauoye, of Pyemont, or in Wales
and in thise other montaynes[5] where ther is of custome
more snowe than is in places that ben in playn grounde.

[1] staunched : O. F. text, p. 149, "restanchier," to dry up.
[2] The passage from "the clowde hath" to "the day" is not in
O.F. text.
[3] Chapters similar to this one are found in Neckam, *De Laud.*
IV. 157, 188 ; *Honorius Aug.* I. 61.
[4] O. F. text, Ch. XV [2] (*b*).
[5] "like as the . . . other montaynes": O.F. text, p. 150 :
"si comme en ces mons de *mont Gieu,* et en ces autres hautes
montaingnes." Roy. 19 A IX. : "Si comme en ces montaignes
de *Savoye et de Pieumont,* et en ces autres hautes montaignes."
"Wales" is added by Caxton himself to the text of Roy. 19 A IX.

Alle this cometh of the coldnes of thayer whiche hath
lasse hete aboue than bynethe, by cause it is more
subtyl than that whiche is bynethe. And whan the
more subtyl is on hye, so moche reteyneth he lasse of
hete. But the more that thayer is thycke, somoche
more it chauffeth, and the sonner, where the sonne may
come. Of whiche cometh that yron and steel wexe more
hoot by the sonne than doth the * stone ; ffor of so
moche as the thynge is more hard and of more thyck
mater, so moche taketh it the fyre more asprely &
sonner than they that ben of lasse force.

[*fo. 63, vo.]

Thus saye I to yow of thayer that is aboue on hye,
whiche is more colde than this is bynethe, ffor as moche
as it is not so thycke as that is whiche is nyghe
therthe, and for the wynde that ofte groweth, whiche
maketh it ofte to be in meuyng ; ffor the water that
renneth faste eschauffeth lasse than that doth that
holdeth hym stylle : so doth thayer whiche is on hye.
And therby groweth the colde that freseth this moisture
anon as it is goon vp on hye, and falleth doun agayn y
frorn.[1]

Of haylle and of tempestes.   capitulo xxvii°.[2]

By this manere come*n* in the somer the grete haylles
and the grete tempestes ; ffor in thayer they
growe,[3] wherof oftyme cometh grete colde, so that the
moisture that is in thayer brought vp is drawen to be
frorn ; and it is in thayer assembled and amassed, ffor
the hete that chaceth after it. And the sonne causeth
it to lose and to falle on therthe. But it falleth not so
grete to the grounde as it is frorn aboue on hye, ffor it
cometh doun brekyng and amenuysyng in the fallyng.
And this is the tempeste whiche falleth ofte in the somer,
the whiche is greuous & ennoyous to many thynges.[4]

[1] Caxton distinctly prints "y frorn" in two words; the "y"
is evidently here the prefix of the past part. of "fresen."

[2] O.F. text, Ch. XV[2] (c).

[3] O.F. text, p. 150: "Car en air naissent aucun *vent* . . .,"
for there arise *winds* in the air . . . "*Wyndes* growe," instead
of "*they* growe," seems to be the proper reading required by the
context.

[4] "ffor in thayer . . . thynges": Neckam, *De Laud.* IV. 188 ;
Honorius Aug. I. 60.

Of lyghtnynges and of thonders.   capitulo xxviii°.[1]

*In thayer happen many thinges of whiche the peple speke not gladly ; ffor they retche not moche of suche thinges of whiche they can not wel come to the knowleche.

This that maketh therthe to quaue, and this that maketh the clowdes to thondre, that whiche maketh the erthe to opene, and this that [2] maketh the clowdes to sparkle and lyghtne whan the thondre is herde. Ffor thondres and lyghtnynges ben deboutemęns and brekyng out of wyndes that mete aboue the clowdes so asprely & sharply that, in their comyng, groweth ofte a grete fyre in thayr and this thondre [3] that falleth in many places, whiche the wyndes constrayne so terrybly that the clowdes cleue and breke ; and maketh to thondre and lyghtne. And falleth doun in so grete rage, by the wynde that destrayneth it so asprely, that it confoundeth alle that it atteyneth in suche wyse that nothyng endureth ayenst it. And it is of so heuy nature that somtyme it perseth therthe vnto the myddle. And somtyme it quencheth er it cometh to the grounde after that it is of poyse, and that is not of ouer stronge nature.[4]

Ffor whan the clowde is moche derke & thycke, and that ther is grete plente of water, the fyre passeth not so soone, but it is quenchid in the clowde by the grete quantyte of the water that is therin bifore it may perse thurgh, so that it may not approche therthe. But in the straynyng and brekyng that hit maketh thenne in

---

[1] O.F. text, Ch. XV [2] (*d*).

[2] O.F. text, p. 151 : "ce qui fait ouvrir la terre, *ce* fait les nues espartir" : what makes the earth open also makes the clouds produce lightning (*i. e.* earthquakes and lightning, etc., are all due to the same cause : the rushing of winds). Caxton's rather obscure sentence becomes clear if we follow the O.F. text and say : "that whiche maketh the erthe to opene, *this is that* maketh the clowdes to sparkle . . ."

[3] O.F. text, p. 151 : "Et ce *est* foudre qui chiet . . .", and this *is* the thunderbolt which falls . . .—The correct and more logical reading of the O.F. text would require a full stop after "thayr" and the insertion of "*is*" between "this" and "thondre"

[4] "after that . . . nature" : *i. e.* according to its weight (*i. e.* if it is of a light weight) and provided it is not too dense.

the clowde, groweth a sowne so grete and stronge that it is merueyllous to here. I declare to you for certayn that this is the thondre whiche is moche to be doubted and drad, in lyke wyse as of an hoot and brennyng yron that is put in a tubbe of water, * therof groweth a   [*fo. 64, vo.] noyse and a grete sowne, and also whan cooles ben quenchid.[1]

But the lyghtnyng of the thondre appereth and is seen er ye here the voys or sowne, ffor as moche as the sight of a man is more subtyl than the heerynge [2]; lyke as men see fro ferre ouer a water betyng of clothes or smytynge of marteaulx [3] or hamers, the strokes ben seen of them that smyte, or [4] the soun be herde of the stroke. Alle in lyke wyse may I saye to yow of the thondre, the whiche men see to fore and er they here it. And so moche the ferther it is aboue vs, so moche the ferther is the soun of the lyghtnyng after it is seen, er the soun be herd. And the sonner after the lyghtnyng is seen & the noys herd, somoche is the thondre more nyghe vnto vs.[5]

For to knowe how the wyndes growe and come. ca. xxix°.[6]

O f the wyndes may men enquyre reson of them that vse the sees. And the wyndes renne round aboute therthe oftymes, and entrecounte and mete in som place so asprely that they ryse vpon heyght in suche wyse that they lyft vp thayer on hye. And thayer that is so lyft and taken fro his place remeueth other ayer in suche facion that it retorneth as it were afterward, and gooth cryeng and brayeng [7] as water rennyng; ffor wynde is none other thyng but ayer that is meuyd so longe tyl his force be beten doun with the

---

[1] "This that maketh . . . quenchid": Neckam, *De Laud.* III. 97–118.

[2] "But the lyghtnyng . . . heerynge": *Philosophia Mundi*, III. 10.

[3] marteaulx: O.F. "martiaus," hammers.

[4] or = er, *i. e.* ere, before.

[5] "lyke as men . . . vnto vs": *Adelard of Bath*, Quaest. 68.

[6] O.F. text, Ch. XVI [2].

[7] cryeng and brayeng: O. F. text, p. 152, "ondoiant," undulating.

stroke.[1] Thus come ofte clowdes, raynes, thondres & lyghtnynges and the thinges tofore said.

Ther ben yet other resons how these werkes comen.

[˙ fo 65] But thise that beste serue to knowelege and lyghtly * to be vnderstonde, we haue drawen out shortly. And now shal cesse of this mater for to speke of the fyre whiche is aboue the ayer on hye.

Of the fyre and of the sterres that seme to falle.[2] ca. xxx°.[3]

Ye ought to knowe that aboue thayer is the fyre. This is an ayer whiche is of moche grete resplendour and shynyng, & of moche grete noblesse ; and by his right grete subtylte he hath no moisture in hym. And is moche more clere than the fyre that we vse, & of more subtyl nature, than thayer is ayenst the water or also the water ayenst the erthe.

This ayer in whiche is no maner moisture, it stratcheth vnto the mone. And ther is seen ofte vnder this ayer somme sparkles of fyre, & seme that they were sterres. Of whiche men saye they be sterres whiche goon rennyng, & that they remeue fro their places. But they be none ; but it is a maner of fyre that groweth in thayer of somme drye vapour which hath no moisture within it, whiche is of therthe ; & therof groweth by the sonne whiche draweth it vpon hye ; & whan it is ouer hye, it falleth & is sette a fyre like as a candel brennyng as vs semeth ; & after falleth in thayer moyste, and there is quenchid by the moistnes of thayer. And whan it is grete & the ayer drye, it cometh al brennyng vnto therthe.

Wherof it happeth ofte that they that saylle by the see or they that goon by londe haue many tymes founden & seen them al shynyng & brenning falle vnto therthe ; & whan they come where it is fallen,

---

[1] "Of the wyndes . . . stroke": *Philosophia Mundi*, III. 15 ; *Neckam* I. 18.

[2] Cf. for this chapter: Neckam, *De Laud.* I. 315, 329 ; *Philos. Mundi*, III. 12 ; *Honorius Aug.* I. 65-67.

[3] O.F. text, Ch. XVII [2] (*a*).

they finde none other thing but a litil asshes or
like thing, *or like som leef of a tree roten, that   [* fo.65,vo.]
i 1
were weet. Thenne apperceyue they wel, and byleue,
that it is no sterre; ffor the sterres may not falle,
but they muste alle in their cercle meue ordynatly &
contynuelly nyght & day egally.

[O.F. text, Ch. XVII² (*b*): "Du dragon qui samble cheoir et que
    ce est." This chapter is missing both in Roy. 19 A IX., and in
    Caxton. (See *Introduction* p. xix).]

Of the pure Ayer and how the seuen planetes ben sette.
capitulo xxxi°.¹

The pure ayer is aboue the fyre, whiche pourpriseth
    and taketh his place vnto the heuen.
   In this ayer is no obscurte ne dorknes, ffor it was

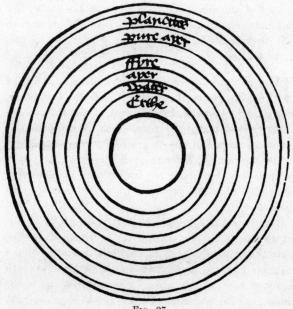

Fig. 27.

made of clene purete. It resplendissheth & shyneth so
clerly that it may to nothing be compared.
   In this ayer ben vii sterres whiche make their

¹ O.F. text, Ch. XVIII².

cours al aboute therthe, the whiche be moche clene
& clere, & be named þe vii planetes; of whome that
one is sette aboue that other, and in suche wyse
ordeyned that ther is more space fro that one to that
other than ther is fro the erthe to the mone[1] whiche is
ferther fyften [2] tymes than al the the [3] erthe is grete;
& euerich renneth by myracle on the firmament and
* maketh his cercle, that one grete and that other lytil,
after that it is and sitteth more lowe.   Ffor of
somoche that it maketh his cours more nyghe therthe, so
moche is it more short; and sonner hath perfourmed his
cours than that whiche is ferthest.   That is to saye that
who that made a poynt in a walle, & with a compaas
made dyuerse cercles aboute, alway that one more large
than another, that whiche shold be next the poynt shold
be leste of the other, and lasse shold be his cours; ffor
he shold sonner haue don his cours than the grettest, so
that they wente both egally; as ye may see by this
figure to fore.[4]

Thus may ye vnderstande of the vii planetes of whiche
I haue spoken that that one is vnder that other,
in suche wise that she that is lowest of alle the other is
leest of alle, & that is the mone.   But by cause that it
is next to therthe, it semeth grettest & most apparaunt
of alle the other [5]; & for thapprochement of therthe, &
by cause it goth so nygh, it hath no pure clerenes that
cometh of hym self proprely, by cause therthe is so
obscure.

But the clernes & lyght that it rendreth to vs she
taketh alway of the sonne, lyke as shold a myrrour
whan the rayes of the sonne smyteth therin, & of the
reflexion þe myrrour smyteth on the walle & shyneth
theron as longe as the rayes of the sonne endure in the
glasse; in lyke maner sheweth & lyghteth to vs the lyght

---

[1] "The pure . . . mone": *Honorius Aug.* I. 67–76.
[2] "fyften": O.F. text (p. 155): *xii* tauz (twelve times).   See
Introduction, p. xxii.
[3] "the" is repeated twice.
[4] Cf. *Fig. 27*, p. 123.
[5] "in suche wise . . . of alle the other": *Neckam* I. 13;
Honorius Aug. I. 67–76.

of the mone; & in the mone is a body polysshyd and
fair lyke a pommell right wel burnysshed, whiche re-
flaumbeth and rendrith lyght & clerenes whan the
rayes of the sonne smyteth therin.[1]

The lytil clowdes * or derkenes that is seen therin, [*fo.66,vo.]
so*m*me saye that it is therthe that appereth within ; and   *i* 2
that whiche is water appereth whyte, lyke as ayenst a
myrrour whiche receyueth dyuerse colours, whan she is
torned therto.   Other thinke otherwyse and saye that hit
happed and byfelle whan Adam was deceyued by thapple
that he ete, whiche greued alle humayne lignage, and
that thenne the mone was empesshed and his clerenesse
lassed and mynuysshid.[2]

Of thise vii sterres or planetes that ben there and
make their cours on the firmame*n*t, of whom we haue
here to fore spoken, ffirst were no moo knowen but
the tweyne, that is to wete the sonne and the mone ; the
other were not knowen but by Astronomye.   Neuertheles yet shal I name them for as we haue spoken of them
to yow.

Of thyse ther ben tweyne aboue the mone and byneth
the sonne, and that one aboue that other, of whom
eche hath on therth propre vertues.   And they be
named Mercurie and Venus.[3]

Thenne aboue the mone & thise tweyne is the sonne
whiche is so clere, fayr & pure that it rendreth lyght
& clerenesse vnto alle the world ; and the sonne is sette
so hye aboue that his cercle is gretter & more spacyouse
than the cercle of the mone, which maketh his cours
in xxx dayes, xii sithes somoche ; ffor the so*n*ne, whiche
gooth more ferther fro the erthe than þe mone, maketh
his cours hath ccclxv dayes : this is xii tymes somoche

---

[1] "But the clernes . . . smyteth therin": Baeda, *Elementorum philosophiae* II. (*Patrol*. t. 90, col. 1159–1160): Quamvis corpus lunae naturaliter sit obscurum tamen in quibusdam partibus suis est tunsum et politum ad modum speculi, in quibusdam scabrosum et rubiginosum. Ubi igitur politum est, ex radiis solis splendet ; sed ubi scabrosum, naturalem obscuritatem retinet.

[2] "The lytil . . . mynuysshid": *Neckam*, I. 14: "Merito enim praevaricationis primorum parentum, omnium planetarum et stellarum fulgor dispendium claritatis sustinuit. Luna vero, quae citima terris est, et aspectibus humanis familiarius occurens, maculam in se retinuit."

[3] "Of thyse . . . Venus": *Neckam*, I. 7.

& more ouer, as the calender enseigneth, & yet more the fourth part of a day, that be vi houres.[1] But for this that þe yere hath dyuersly his begynnyng, that one begynneth on þe daye & another on the nyght, whiche is grete ennoye to moche peple, this *fourth part of a day is sette, by cause alle way in four yere is a daye consumed whiche is aboue in that space; the which yere is named bysexte or lepe yere, whiche in iiii yere falleth ones ; and so is sette fro four yere to four yere alway more a daye.[2] And thenne is the sonne comen agayn in his first poynt : and that is in myd Marche, whan the newe tyme recomenceth and that alle thynges drawe to loue by the vertue of the retorne of the Sonne. Ffor in this season had the world first his begynnyng ; and therfore thenne alle thinge reneweth and cometh in verdure by right nature of the tyme and none other-wyse.

Aboue the sonne ther be thre sterres clere and shynyng, and one aboue another. That is to wete Mars, Jupiter and Saturnus. Saturne is hyest of the seuen, whiche hath in his cours xxx yere er he hath alle goon his cerkle.[3] & thyse iii sterres reteyne theyr vertues in thynges here bynethe ; & ye may see, yf ye beholde this figure, how they be in ordre eche aboue other ; whiche figure sheweth it well.[4]

How the vii planetes gyue the names to the vii dayes. capitulo xxxii°.[5]

*T*hise seuen planetes ben suche that they haue power on thynges that growe on therthe ; and habounde their vertues more than alle the other that ben on the firmament, and more appertly werke, lyke as thauncyent sage philosophres haue enserched by their wittes.

[1] "ccclxv . . . houres": O.F. text, p. 157 : "ccclxVI jourz. Ce est xii tanz plus et ·v· jours outre et enquores avoec le quart d'un jour : ce sont .vi. heures" : 366 days. That is to say 12 times more, and *five* days besides, and moreover the fourth part of a day, that is six hours.
[2] "Thenne aboue . . . daye": *Neckam*, I. 7 ; *Honorius Aug.* I. 67–76.
[3] "Mars . . . cerkle": *Neckam*, I. 7 ; *Honorius Aug.* I. 67–76.
[4] Cf. *Fig. 28*, p. 127.   [5] O.F. text, Ch. XIX [2] (a).

Of thise seuen planetes taken the dayes of the weke their names, as ye shall here.[1]   The mone hath the Monday, and Mars the Tewsday, Mercurye the Wednesday, Jupiter the Thursday, Venus the Vryday, Saturnus the

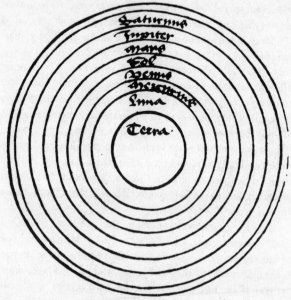

Fig. 28.

Saterday; and the holy Sonday hath his name of the Sonne whiche is the most fair.[2]   And therfor the Sonday is better than ony of the other dayes of the weke, ffor this day is sette and reseruyd from alle payne & labour. And on this day shold men doo thyng that shold playse Our Lord.

But syth in this chapytre we haue touched of the firmament, we shal speke after of somme caas that come on the heuen and therthe.

The Sonday is as moche to saye as the daye of pees and of praysynge, ffor the creatour of alle thynges cessed this day, the whiche made and created all.

---

[1] "Of thise . . . here": *Neckam*, I. 10; *Honorius Aug.* II. 28.
[2] "and the holy . . . fair": *Neckam*, I. 10: ". . . in die Dominica, quam Philosophi dicunt esse diem solis."

Of the meuyng and gooyng aboute of the ffyrmament
and of the sterres that ben therin.   capitulo xxxiii°.[1]

[* fo. 68]

A boue Saturne, whiche is the last planest & hyest
from vs of alle the vii planetes, is the heuen that
men see so full of sterres as it were sowen, whan it is
clere tyme and weder.   This heuen that is so sterred is
the firmament whiche meueth and goth round.[2]   Of whiche
meuyng is so grete Joye, so grete melodye and so swete,
that *ther is noman that, yf he myght here it, the neuer
after shold haue talente ne wylle to do thynge that were
contrarye vnto Our Lord in ony thynge that myght be,
so moche shold he desyre to come theder where he myght
alleway here so swete melodyes & be alway wyth them.[3]
Wherof somme were somtyme that sayde that lytil yonge
chyldren herde this melodye whan they lawghed in their
slepe; ffor it is sayde that thenne they here the Angels
of Our Lord in heuen synge, wherof they haue suche
Joye in their slepe.[4]

But herof knoweth noman the trouthe sauf God
that knoweth all, whiche setted the sterres on the
heuen and made them to haue suche power.   Ffor ther is
nothynge withyn the erthe ne withyn the see, how
dyuerse it be, but it is on the heuen fygured and compassed -by the sterres, of whiche none knoweth the
nombre sauf God only whyche at hys playsir nombreth
them & knoweth the name of eueriche of them, as he
that alle knoweth & alle created by good reason.[5]

At the regard of the sterres that may be seen, they
may be wel nombred & enquyred by Astronomye; *but
it is a moche maistryse; ffor ther ne is sterre so lytil
but that it hath in hym hole his vertue, in herbe, in flour

[* fo.68, vo.]
i 4

[1] O.F. text, Ch. XIX [2] (*b*).
[2] "Aboue Saturne . . . round": *Honorius Aug.* I. 83.
[3] "Of whiche meuyng . . . them": *Neckam,* I. 15 ; *Honorius Aug.* I. 80.
[4] "Wherof somme . . . slepe": This pretty legend is probably
founded on the following passage in Baeda, *Musica theorica*
(*Patrol.*, t. 90, col. 911): "Si autem aliquis in altero mundo
nasceretur (si possibile esset), ut Sanctus Augustinus affirmat, ut
in hunc mundum postea venisset, eam sine ullo impedimento
audiret, eique ultra vires placeret."
[5] "Ffor ther is . . . reason": *Neckam,* I. 7 ; *Honorius Aug.*
I. 90.

or in fruyt, be it in façion, in colour or otherwyse. Ther
is nothing in erthe that ought to be, ne therin hath

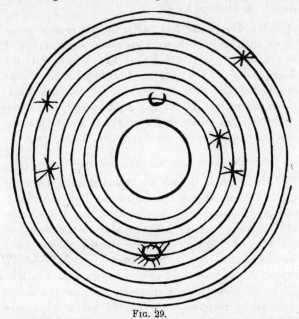

Fig. 29.

growyng, but somme sterre hath strengthe and puissaunce by nature, is it good or otherwyse, suche as God
hath gyuen to it.[1]

And for the firmament and for the planetes, take
this fygure to fore an that other syde,[2] and ye shal see
therin the sytuacion of them.

Bvt syth we haue descriued and spoken of the firmament in this second partye of this volume, we
shal speke of somme caases that come and happen on hye
and also lowe. And shal speke of the mesure of the firmament ffor to vnderstande the better the façion, and
how it is made and proporcioned, and of that whiche is
aboue. And also we shal speke of heuen.

Thus ffynyssheth the second partye
of this present volume.

[1] "ffor ther ne . . . gyuen to it": *Neckam*, I. 7 ; *Honorius
Aug.* I. 90. [2] Cf. *Fig. 29.*

Here begynneth the third parte of this present volume. And declareth first how the day and the nyght come.[1] capitulo p[io].[2]

IN this thirde and last partye of this present booke we shal fynysshe it wyth spekynge of the faites of astronomye. And I wyl declare to you first thw[3] the daye cometh and the nyght, and for to make you vnderstande * of the Eclipses, and also for to vnderstande other thinges, the whiche may moche prouffyte to them that wylle doo payne to knowe them, ffor to gouerne them the better after the disposicion of the tyme.

[* fo. 69]

Here declareth how the daye and nyght comen.

TROUTHE it is that the Sonne maketh this torne & cours aboute therthe in the daye and nyght, and gooth egally euery houre. And also longe as he abydeth aboue therthe, so longe haue we the deduyt of the day; & whan he is vnder therthe, thenne haue we the nyght; lyke as ye went tornyng a brennyng candell aboute your heed, or as ye shold bere it a lytil ferther of Round aboute an apple, and that the candel were alway brennyng; thenne the partye that were alway ayenst the candel shold alleway be lyght, and that other partye that is ferthest fro it shold be obscure and derke. Thus in lyke wise doth the sonne, by his propre nature, for to be day and nyght aboute therthe. He maketh the day to growe byfore hym, and on that other parte the erthe is vmbreuse & derke by hynde hym and where as he may not shyne. And this is the shadowe of the nyght whiche the deduyt of the day taketh away from vs.

But for as moche as the sonne is moche gretter than therthe, the shadowe goth lytil and lytil tyl at thende it cometh to nought, lyke the sown of a clocke endureth after the stroke.[4]

[1] This chapter is based on *Philosophia Mundi*, II, 27.
[2] O. F. text, Ch. I[3] (a).   [3] thw [sic] = how.
[4] "But for as moche . . . stroke": *Honorius Aug.* II. 30. Caxton's simile differs from O.F. text, p. 161 : ". . . a la maniere d'un *clochier* que l'en fait en ces mostiers": (the shadow becomes more and more slender) like a steeple such as is built on these monasteries.

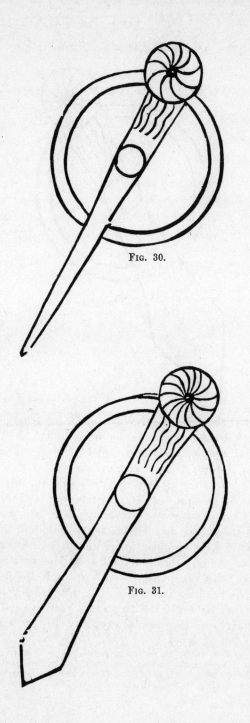

Fig. 30.

Fig. 31.

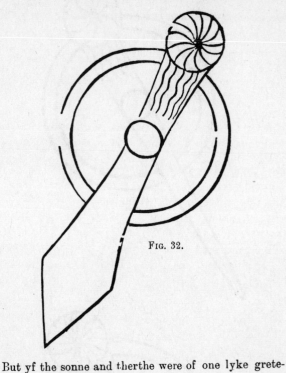

Fig. 32.

But yf the sonne and therthe were of one lyke gretenesse, this shadowe shold haue none ende, but shold be
[* fo. 69, vo.] all egal without declynyng. And yf *therthe were
gretter than the sonne, thenne the shadowe of þͤ sonne
shold goo enlargyng and be more; as ye may see
þͤ fourme by thise thre fygures folowyng[1]; & also ye
may preue it otherwise without fygures : Take somme
derke thing that may reteine lyght within it, as of
tree or of stone or other thynge what it be that may[2]
be seen thurgh; thenne sette that to fore your eyen,
[* fo. 70] ayenst *that thing that ye wold see, is it the heuen
or erthe or ony other thynge. Yf that thyng that ye
holde is more bredder and larger than your two eyen be
a sondre, it shal take away the syght ayenst that whiche

[1] Cf. *Figs. 30, 31, 32.*
[2] The sense seems to require a negation after "may," *i. e.*
"what it be that may *not* be seen thurgh." Caxton translates
literally the text of MS. Roy. 19 A IX., which has no negation.
Cf. O.F. text, p. 161: "qui soit tele que l'en *ne* puisse veoir
parmi."

is no bredder. And yf the thynge be alle egale in
lengthe as moche as ye may stratche your two eyen, as
moche shal it be taken fro you as the thinge shal haue
of gretnes, as ye may see by this figure bynethe an that
other syde. And yf the thinge haue lasse of gretnes
than the lengthe is bytwene your bothe eyen, it shal
take fro you lasse for to see, as wel nyghe as ferre, that
it is of largenes of that whiche ye wold see. And whan
ye put the thynge ferther fro your eyen, so moche the
more may ye see of that other part ouer and aboue you,
so that ye may se all. In lyke wyse is it of the sonne
withoute ony doubtaunce or variacion; ffor it passeth
therthe in gretnesse, so that it seeth the heuen al aboute,
the sterres, and all that is on the firmament.

Why the sterres ben not seen by day as wel as by
nyght. capitulo ii°.[1]

THE sterres of the firmament, on whiche the sonne
rendreth clernes, make contynuelly nyght and day
their tornyng & cours wyth the firmament round aboute
aboue as bynethe. But them that ben ouer vs we may
not see by daye; ffor the sonne by hys grete clernes
and lyght taketh from vs the sight of them,[2] in lyke
wyse as ye shold do of candellis that were ferre brennyng
from yow. And yf ther were a grete fyre brennyng
* bytwene you and the candellis, and had grete flawme   [* fo.70, vo.]
& lyght, it shold take away fro you your sight that ye
shold not see the candellis. And yf the fyre were take
away & put byhynde yow, ye shold incontynent see the
candellis to fore you brennyng. Thus in lyke wyse I
saye yow of the sterres that may not be seen by daye
as longe as the sonne maketh his torne and cours aboue
therthe. And whan the sonne is vnder therthe, the
sterres ben seen by vs.

But the sterres that ben ouer vs in the somer on the
day tyme, in wynter they be ouer vs in þe nyght; &
they that be vnder vs in the wynter be ouer vs in þe
somer; ffor tho sterres that we see in the somer by

---

[1] O. F. text, Ch. I [3] (b).
[2] "The sterres . . . sight of them": *Honorius Aug.* I. 89.

nyght, we may not see them on the day; ffor the sonne
that goth round aboute vs taketh fro tho sterres their
clernes that ben on þᵉ day tyme where the sonne is,
vnto the tyme that he draweth hym vnder.

But alle they be lyght, what someuer part they torne,
as wel by day as by nyght, as longe as the sonne
goth aboute hye and lowe shynyng, sauf the whiche ben
hyd by therthe fro vs: ffor, as longe at the shadowe
may comprise it, the sonne may gyue them no light.[1]
That ye may vnderstande by the figure.

Thus the shadowe discreaceth by the sonne whiche is
moche gretter than therthe, and fynysheth in lassyng.
And it endureth ferther fro therthe than the mone is
hye; but it faylleth aboue the mone.

Wherfor the sonne is not seen by nyght as it is by
day.   capitulo iii°.[2]

The erthe is suche that she deffendeth the day whiche
the sonne gyueth vs.   Yf therthe were so clere
[* fo. 71] that *men myght see thurgh, thenne myght the sonne
be seen contynuelly as wel vnder therthe as aboue.[3]
But it is so obscure and derke that it taketh away the
sight fro vs.   And it maketh the shadowe to goo alle
alway tornyng after the sonne, whiche maketh as many
tornynges aboute therthe as the sonne doth, whiche alle
way is ayenst it; ffor whan the sonne ariseth in the
mornyng in the est, the shadowe is in the weest; &
whan it is right ouer & aboue vs at mydday, thenne is
therthe shadowed vnder her.   And whan the sonne goth
doun in the west, the shadowe of it is in the eest; and
[* fo.71, vo.] thenne whan the *sonne is vnder, we haue thenne the
shadowe ouer vs, whiche goth drawyng to the west, so
longe til the sonne ariseth and shyneth & rendrith to
vs the day.   And this may ye see by thise two figures
to fore an that other syde.[4]

---

[1] "as longe at . . . light": as longe as they are within the
shadow, the sun cannot give them light.
[2] O. F. text, Ch. I³ (c).
[3] "The erthe . . . as aboue": *Honorius Aug.* II. 29.
[4] Cf. *Figs. 33, 34*, p. 135.

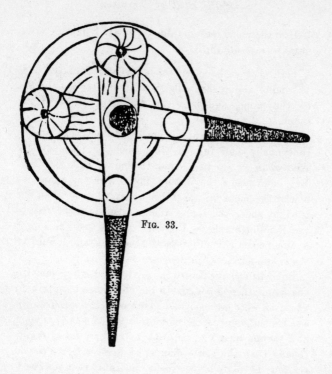

FIG. 33.

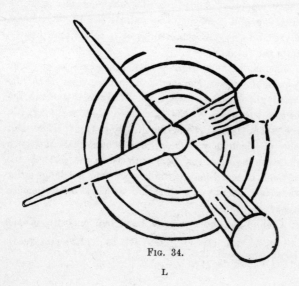

FIG. 34.

L

How the mone receyueth dyuersly her lyght and clerenesse.[1]   capitulo iiii°.[2]

Syth that ye haue vnderstond what it is of the daye
and of the nyght, wille ye thenne after see the fait
of the mone, and how she receyuyth lyght of the
sonne.

She receyueth lyght in suche maner that she is
contynuelly half full in what someuer place she be.
And whan we see her round, thenne we calle her full.
But how moche the ferther she is fro the sonne, so
moche the more we see of her apparayl; and whan she
is right vnder the sonne, thenne she apperithe not to
vs; ffor thenne she is bytwene therthe and the sonne,
& thenne she shyneth toward the sonne, and toward vs
she is alle derke. And therfore we see her not.

But whan she is passed the poynt, and is remeuid fro
the sonne, thenne begynneth her clerenesse to appere to
vs as she were horned; and so moche as she withdraweth
her fro the sonne, somoche more apperith she shynyng;
and thenne whan she apperith to be half ful of lyght,
thenne hath she gon a quarter of her cercle, whiche is
the fourthe parte of her torne and cours that she goeth
euery moneth. And thus alle way her clernesse en-
creacyng and growyng, she goth til she be alle rounde,
fayre and clere, in semblaunce of a rolle: and that we
calle the ful mone.

7]   Thenne is * she right vnder the sonne as she may
be, right ayenst the sight in suche wyse that alle
her lyght is torned toward vs. Thenne is therthe bytwene the sonne & the mone, so that we may not
see them bothe vpon therthe, but right litil. But
one of them may be seen, ffor whan that one goth
doun in the west, that other ariseth in the eest; & soo
at euen or morn may bothe be seen, but not longe; ffor
that one goth vnder therthe, & that other cometh
aboue.

Thenne the mone whiche hath ben opposite of the

---

[1] Cf. for this chapter: *Isidore*, III. 53; *Philosophia Mundi*,
II. 31; *Neckam*, I. 13.
[2] O. F. text, Ch. II [3].

sonne, & hath goon half her cours, the*n*ne she goth
on that other side approchyng the sonne; & begynneth
to lasse her light & mynusshe it til it be but half
agayn; & thenne hath she gon thre quarters of her
cercle, & is thenne as nygh the sonne on that syde as
she was at the first quarter on that other syde; & so
approcheth ner & ner til she appere horned as to fore;

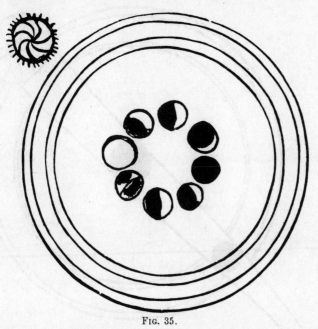

FIG. 35.

& thus she goth til she be al failled, that we may see
nomore the*n*ne of her; ffor the*n*ne is she vnder the so*n*ne,
as ye may see by thys present fygure.[1] & I saye nomore
herof but that she is the*n*ne bytwene þe sonne & therthe.

[* fo.72, vo.]

* How the eclipses of the mone happen.[2]   capitulo v°.[3]

It happeth ofte tymes that the mone muste nedes
lose her lyght. And that happeth whan she apperith most full; and she becometh as vanysshed away,
and derketh lytil and lytil til she be all faylled.

---

[1] Cf. *Fig. 35.*   [2] Cf. for this chapter: *Philosophia Mundi*, II.
32; *Neckam*, I. 13.   [3] O. F. text, Ch. III[3].

Ye haue herd here to fore how the mone taketh lyght of the sonne, that alle way she hath half her lyght hole. But whan it is so that she is in eclipse, thenne hath she no lyght in noo parte. And this happeth neuer but whan she is torned right so that the sonne gyueth her ful lyght; ffor the mone goth not al way so right at [1]

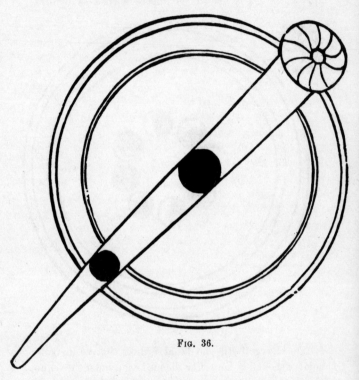

Fig. 36.

doth the Sonne, ffor somtyme she passeth in her cours by suche a way that therthe shadoweth her all; ffor therthe is gretter than the mone is, & therfore whan therthe is iuste bytwene the sonne and the mone, thenne she thus shadoweth her. Ffor bytwene the sonne and the mone is a lygne whiche declyneth somoche to the mone, by whiche the sonne smyteth his Rayes in her as longe as ther is no lettyng by

[1] at : as. Cf. also "as longe *at*," p. 134.

therthe. Ffor the more that therthe is bytwene them, the more is the mone shadowed; and the lasse that it is bytwene, somoche lasse is the shadowe. And the mone leseth the lasse of her lyght that she receyueth of the sonne, whan she is so shadowed.

Thus ye may vnderstonde : yf a lygne passed thurgh therthe by the poynt of the myddle of it, & stratched that one ende vnto the body of the sonne, in suche wyse by right sight that it endured on that other ende vnto the mone whiche euery moneth goth here and there, hyer and lower ; yf she were so euen ayenst the sonne, thenne shold she falle euery *moneth in that shadowe   [* fo. 73] whiche on alle partes shold empesshe her lyght whiche thenne myght not come to her for therthe in no wise ; ffor the ferther she is fro the right lygne, so moche hath & receyueth she the more of lyght. And whan she is so that therthe is ex opposito bytwene them, than loseth the mone her lyght.

Thus is seen somtyme the mone, in the myddle of his moneth, lose his lyght & derk whan she is most ful, and her lyght torned vnto derkenesse, whiche we calle the eclipse of the mone ; as ye may wel see and vnderstonde by this fygure [1] yf ye beholde it well.

How the Eclypse of the Sonne cometh.[2]   cap⁰ vi⁰.[3]

It happeth somtyme that the sonne leseth his clerenes & the lyght in the playn daye, ffor it goth as to declyne ; & is called in latyn eclipse. This eclipse procedeth bicause of defaulte of light ; and it happeth in this manere *that, whan the mone whiche is vnder the   [* fo.73, vo.] sonne cometh right bytwene vs and the sonne, thenne in   k 1 the right lygne, it behoueth that toward vs the mone taketh and reteygneth the lyght of the sonne on hye, so that it semeth to vs that is defaylled.[4] Ffor the mone is not so pure that the sonne may shyne ouer her and

---

[1] Cf. *Fig. 36*, p. 138.
[2] Cf. for this chapter : *Philosophia Mundi*, II. 30.
[3] O.F. text, Ch. IV [3].
[4] "whan the mone . . . defaylled" : when the moon is in a straight line between us and the sun, the moon keeps the light of the sun away from us, so that the sun seems to fail.

thurgh her as thurgh an other sterre : Alle lyke as of a
candell whiche is sette ferre fro your sight, and after ye
helde your honde right to fore the candell, thenne ye
shold not see nothyng therof. And the more right
ye holde your hand bytwene, the more lasse shold ye
see this candele. And somoche ye may sette your hand
right to fore your eyen, and so ferre, that ye shold see
nothyng therof.

In this maner I telle yow of the eclypse, that
bytwene the Sonne and the Mone is not one waye
comune ; but the mone goth an other waye whiche
destourneth her a lytil from the Sonne. Wherfore
vs byhoueth to vnderstande that the mone goth oftymes,
whan she is bytwene vs and the Sonne, somtyme aboue
and otherwhyle bynethe, here and there as she riseth
and declyneth. But whan she passyth in the right
lygne euen bytwene vs & the sonne, thenne taketh
the mone fro vs the lyght & clernes of the sonne in
suche wyse as we may not clerly see her in that paas ;
ffor thenne shadoweth she therthe, and kepeth the rayes
of the sonne that they may not shyne on therthe ; &
they that ben in this parte haue in their sight þe shadowe
behynde them.

But it apperith not comunely to alle men thurgh
al the world. Ffor the mone is not so grete nowher
nygh as all therthe ; therfor she shadoweth not all,
[* fo. 74] but only where * she is in the right lygne bytwene
therthe and the sonne. And thyder the philosophres
were wont to goo where as they knewe it ; ffor by their
wyt & studye they had lerned for to approue the daye
and tyme whan suche thynges sold happe ; by whiche
they preuyd plente of thynges, wherfore they preysed
moche Our Lord.

Thus see we here byneth the eclipse of the sonne
aboue vs, whan the mone is right vnder the sonne, for
as moche as she is bynethe the sonne and aboue vs.
And thenne the sonne passeth the right lygne and goth
departyng and wythdrawyng so moche that she apperith as she dyde afore ; and thenne the mone departed
is horned thre dayes after this Eclypse. And by this

fygure [1] ye may vnderstonde playnly this that ye haue herd here to fore.

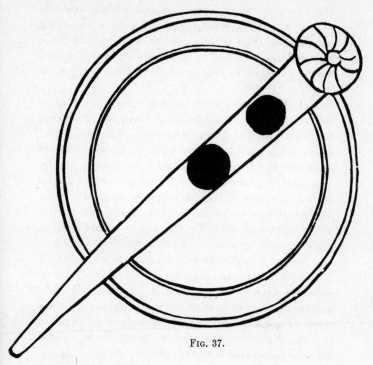

Fig. 37.

Of the eclipse that happed atte deth of Our Lord God. capitulo viiº. [2]

t   Hus [3] as the mone taketh away fro vs the light of   [fo.74, vo.] the sonne, so it happeth oftyme that therthe taketh   k 2 away the lyght of the mone as to fore is declared.   But the Eclipse of the mone may not be in no wise but whan she apperith most full, ne theclypse of the sonne may not be but whan the mone is all waned and faylled, and that we calle the coniuncion, but yf God, whiche may all thinge chaunge and deffete at is playsir, make it to come or happene otherwise; lyke as it happed at suche tyme as Our Sauyour Jhesu Cryste was on the

---

[1] Cf. *Fig. 37.*   [2] O.F. text, Ch. V [3]
[3] "Thus": the capital T is here replaced by a small t as initial.

crosse, at whiche tyme the lyght & bryghtnesse of the
day faylled fro mydday vnto þᵉ ix hour of the day ; &
thenne was the mone vnder therthe at the fulle as moche
as she myght be, whiche thenne in no wyse myght
empesshe the lyght of the sonne ; & the day at that tyme
was as derke and obscure as it had ben propre nyght,
whiche by nature at that tyme shold haue be bryght &
pure.

Ffor whiche cause seynt Dionyse, whiche at this tyme
is shryned in Fraunce, [1] & thenne beyng an estudyaunt
in Grece, a paynem, like a grete clerke as he was, ffor he
knewe moche of astronomye, whan he apperceyued this
grete obscurte & derknes, he had right grete meruaylle
& fonde by astronomye that this myght not be by
nature ne by reson that the eclipse of the sonne shold
happe & falle in suche season. Thenne saide he a derke
worde in this maner : "Or the god of nature suffreth
grete torment by wronge, or all þᵉ world discordeth &
shal desolue & faylle, as it that muste take an ende." [2]
& thought in hym self that he was a grete god that so
suffred, & that he had power & myght aboue all other
goddes, as he that byleuid on many goddes after his
lawe. Thenne this * holy Dionyse made an aulter in his
oratorye, alle aboue the other aulters, and also a parte
where as no persone repayred but he hym self only, by
cause he wold not be reputed in mysbyleue ; & whan
it was made & he had seen it, he called it " the aulter of
the god vnknowen," [3] & worshipped & adoured hym, and
helde hym for a right dere and grete god.

[* fo. 75]

It was not longe after this, that the holy doctour Seynt
Poul cam to this place where seynt Dionys was, as he
that knewe hym for a right grete clerke. And by
commynycacion and prechyng of seynt Poul he was
sone conuerted by the helpe of Our Lord, whiche
wrought so therin that thenne he had very knowleche

---

[1] Cf. *Introduction*, p. xvii.
[2] "Or the god . . . ende": *Suidas* (Life of Dionysius the
Areopagite, *Patrologia*, Series Græca, t. 117, col. 1251) mentions
this exclamation, addressed by Dionysius to his friend Apollo-
phanes : "ἤ τὸ θεῖον πάσχει, ἤ τῷ πασχόντι συμπάσχει." Dionysius
is also mentioned in the *Acts of the Apostles* (xvii. 23-34).
[3] *Acts of the Apostles*, xvii, 23.

how Our Lord had suffred his passion; ffor they were
bothe good clerkes, as is more playnly conteyned in
their legendes.

And thus was the noble clerke saynt Dionys bycomen
a good and very crysten man, whiche all his lyf to fore
had be a paynem; and he so employed his science & his
tyme, fro that day forthon, that it auaylled hym gretly
to the helthe of his sowle. This eclipse deceyuid hym
not ne this that he knewe astronomye; but he bycam
after a man of so good and holy lyf that he gate for his
reward the blysse of heuen.

Ye haue herd the fayt of eclipses. Yf ye wyl vnderstande them well, and ye shal not fare the werse ne
the lasse auaylle you [1]; ffor to knowe it may moche
prouffyte to euery persone; ffor suche demonstraunces
ben signefycacions of grete werkes & thynges that
ofte after happen & falle. This fynde wel astronomyers
by Astronomye, as somtym scarcete and deffaulte of
goodes, or of a grete derthe or warre, or deth of kynges
or prynces that falleth in the * world, as they may   [*fo. 75. vo.]
enquyre and serche by their science & reson.   *k* 3

This Eclipse that was so grete signefyed the deth of
Jhesu Cryst. And it ought wel to come otherwyse for
hym than for another; ffor he was and is by right lord
and kynge of alle the world, and may deffete and desolue
it, and ordeyne at his good playsyr.

The other eclipses comen by nature, whiche reteyne on
therthe their vertues of thinges that ben to come; ffor
it byhoueth alle to fynysshe and come to nought, alle
that is on therthe, & that shortly.

God made not the firmament ne the sterres for
nought whiche, as sayd is, goth tornyng ouer &
aboue vs; and gyueth to the sterres names and vertues
in heuen and in erthe, eche after his myght, on alle
thynges that hath growyng. Ffor ther is nothyng
but it hath somme power, for as moche as it hath

---

[1] "Yf ye wyl . . . auaylle you": "If you wish to understand
them, you will not be any the worse, nor will it be of less
advantage to you." We are guided in the punctuation of this
passage by the O.F. text (p. 172), which requires a stop after
"eclipses" and the omission of "and."

growyng, suche as it ought to haue by nature and by reson.

We shal now for this present leue for to speke ony more of the eclipses, and shal recompte and declare of the vertue of the firmament and of the sterres ; ffor who so wel knewe the vertue of them, he shold knowe the trouthe of alle suche thynge that is bynethe here on therthe by reson of nature, whether the thynge were obscure and derke or not.

Of the vertue of heuen and of the sterres.[1]   ca. viii°.[2]

Now wylle ye here of the science by the whiche men gete sapience for to knowe and enquyre the thinges that may happen in therthe by the werke of right nature whiche is figured by the world.

[* fo. 76]

The heuenes and the * sterres ben the very instruments of nature to the world, by whiche she werketh alle, as God wille, as wel nygh as ferre. & who that coude knowe her myght, he had knowlege of alle thyng that sayd is, as wel of the sterres that ben on heuen, whiche haue vertues on therthe, whiche God hath gyuen and graunted to euerich, and specyally to the sonne and to the mone whiche gyue lyght vnto the world, & wythout whom nóthyng lyuyng may be.[3] Ffor by them growe alle thynges that be in this world, and whiche haue ende and begynnyng. This consenteth and permyseth he that is almyghty.

Alle dyuersitees that be in persones, and whiche haue dyuersitees of makyng and of corsage, and alle that happeth by nature, be it in herbes, in plantes or in beestes, this happeth by the vertue celestyal whiche God gaf to the sterres, whan he first created the world, and that he sette them and endowed them wyth suche nature that he ordeyned them to goo round aboute the world ayenst the tornyng of the firmament. And by theyr

---

[1] Cf. for this chapter *Adelard of Bath*, Quaest. 74, " Utrum animatae sunt stellae."

[2] O.F. text, Ch. VI [3].

[3] " & who that coude ... may be.": *Neckam*, I. 7 ; *De Laud.* I

tornyng and by their vertue whiche lieth in heuen lyue alle thynges that ben vnder it.

And yf it pleasyd Our Lord that he wold holde the heuen al stylle in suche wyse that it torned not aboute, ther is nothyng in alle the worlde that myght meue hym. In hym shold be no vnderstondyng, nomore than in a dede body whiche feleth nothyng ne therin is no wytte, ne vnderstandyng, ne moeuyng, as he that hath no lyf ; in suche poynt shal euery thynge be whan the heuen shal leue his moeuyng. Alle thus shold they be & neuer moeue tyl that the heuen had agayn his moeuyng. And thenne sholde they be otherwyse.

But who that thenne *myght vse his wytte & see [* fo. 76, vo.] what he shal be, moche myght he see of semblaunces and *k* 4 of dyuerse contenaunces in other men that myght not remeue them ; ffor yf ther were no moeuyng on the heuen, ther is nothyng that myght lyue on erthe. Also God wyll that it so be, that all thyng hath establisshid by right.

Thus was the wylle of God, in whom alle vertues habounde, for to fourme the worlde ; ffor he made ne created neuer thynge, but that he gaf to it suche vertue as it ought to haue. Ellis he had made somthyng for nought and without reson. But he dyde not so ; ffor he neuer failled in no thinge.

He made and created all the sterres, and gaf to euerich his vertue. And who that wille not thus byleue, in hym is neyther memoire ne reson. Ffor we see openly that the mone taketh lyght whan we see her all full ; ffor the man hath thenne neyther membre ne vayne but that it is ful, whan it is in the cours, of humours and suche thinges.[1] And in lyke wise it happeth on alle bestes ; ffor they haue thenne their heedes and other membres more garnysshid of margh[2] and of humeurs. And the see also floweth and ebbeth

---

[1] "ffor the man . . . thinges." O.F. text, p. 174 : "car li nons n'a lors ne membre ne vainne qui plus ne soit plainne d'umeurs que quant *ele est en decours*" : for man has then neither limb nor vein which is not fuller of humours than when *she* (the moon) is *decreasing* (waning).—Caxton's "whan *it* is in *the cours*" is not a correct translation.

[2] margh : marrow.

in his cours euery moneth ; wherof it happeth that they
that ben nygh the see, whan they knowe that the mone
is ful, they wythdrawe them fro the see on hye, and
saue them & theyre meynage.　And in this poynt they
wythdrawe them and holde them in hye places vnto the
tyme that the see wythdraweth and lasseth agayn.　And
thus do they euery moneth.　But alle this happeth by
the mone whiche is one of the seuen planetes.

In lyke wyse is it seen of the sonne that, after
the wynter, whan he begynneth to mounte, he causeth
[* fo. 77] *the fruyt to be brought forth of therthe, and ap-
parailleth the trees wyth leues, and alle verdure to
come agayn ; and the byrdes begynne agayn their
songe for the swetenes of the new tyme.　And whan he
rebasshith and declyneth, he maketh the wynter to
bygynne, & causeth flowres and leuys to faylle and falle
so longe tyl he begynne to mounte agayn, as to fore is
said.

Syth that thise two sterres haue suche vertues, and
cause suche thynges to be don, the other whiche ben
pourtrayed on the heuen were not made to serue of
nought.　But to eueriche is ordeyned his vertue and his
right after his nature, wherfore they make dyuersytees
in thynges that ben on therthe, and the moeuynges of
tyme ; of whiche that one cometh soone and that other
late ; and the fruytes that come on therthe, somme
come sone and erly, and the other late, and ben otherwhile sonner rype in one yere than in an other, and
more assured of tempestes and other greuaunces ; and
thus chaunge in sondry maners.　Ffor one somer is softe
and moyste, and another is drye and wyndy.

Of the wynter it happeth oftymes that they chaunge,
so that one is colde, rayny, and more desplaysaunt that
thother ; and another shal be more Joyous & lasse damage-
able.　Thus is seen that the one is dere of somme vitaylle
or other thynges, and that other shal be plentyuous.　And
also it is ofte that ther is plente and good chepe in one
yere ; in an other yere it is had in grete chierte, & is of
grete scarsete ; this fallyth somtyme and ofte.

Alle thise dyuersytes cause the sterres whiche ben on

the heuen. But alle this is by the wylle of Our Lord that hath sette euerich in *his propre place where he maketh naturelly his cours, and euerich dyuersly. Ffor yf none other thynge has his vse in tymes sauf the sonne only wythout moo, as he that goth swyftly by the firmament euery yere, and mounteth as moche and as hye in one somer as in an other, and as moche descendeth in one wynter as in another euery day egally til that he come in to his right poynt, and Joyneth that other after hym where he was to fore, this knowe wel Astronomyers that he gooth euery yere aboute the heuen one torne, and where he is this day, in the same place he shal be this day a yere : ther by is it knowen that, yf none other had no power, thenne shold euery yere be lyk other ; & euery yere alway shold be lyke as the yere to fore was ; and euery moneth shold be lyke the same as eueriche shold come, that is to wyte one Janyuer lyke another Janyuer, and Ffeuerer lyke another Feuerer, and in lyke wyse alle the other x moneths ; ffor the sonne goth alle lyke in one moneth as he shal the next yere in the same moneth. And this day shold reassemble and be lyke vnto this day a yere in alle maner thynge, that is to wete of hete, of colde, of fair wether, of rayne and of other thynges euerich after their comyng all the yere dur-yng. Thenne sholde it falle by right nature that in all the somers and all the wynters that euer haue ben and shal be shold not come no dyuersytees. And all the tymes shold be lyke as they that by the Sonne shold be alway deme-ned, eschauffed and contynuelly gouerned ; ffor he goth egally alway, and endeth his cours euery yere, and holdeth his right way in one estate, as he that goth not out * of his waye.

Thus is he the right veyle and patrone of all the other sterres, ffor it is the most fyn of all the other by the grete clerenesse that is in hym, and in all thynges by hym[1] ; and he hath on therthe more power on thynges, of whiche may be enquyred of nature reson and right, than all the other sterres. Yet som-

---

[1] "and in all thynges by hym" : O.F. text, p. 176, "et toutes choses naissent par lui," and all things come to life through him.

tyme they restrayne his heetes and after they enlarge
them, after that they be fer or nygh, as he otherwhile
hath nede; lyke vnto a kynge whiche is the gretter lorde
and the more myghty in hym self for his hyghnesse than
ony other of his peple, neuertheles he hath somtyme nede
of them for to holpen and seruyd of them; ffor how
moche the nerrer he is to his peple, so moche more is he
stronge and puissaunt, and the ferther he wythdraweth
fro his folke, so moche the lasse he exployteth of his
werke.   In lyke wyse I saye to yow of the sonne whiche
is, as ye may vnderstonde, the grettest, the most myghty
and the most vertuous; of whiche he hath gretter power
in erthe than ony other sterre may haue.   But the other
haue their power euerich in his degree.

But syth we haue recounted to yow the shortest wyse we
may of the vertue of the firmament, we shal declare to you
herafter in short how the world was mesured as wel in
heyght as in depnesse, and on alle sides, of lengthe and
brede, by them that knewe the resons of the vii scyences.
Of whiche Geometrye is one, by whiche the sonne, the
mone, therthe and the firmament ben mesured as wel
wythin as wythoute, how moche it is of gretenes, and how
moche it is fro therthe to the firmament, and alle the
gretenes of the sterres; ffor this is preuyd by right
[*fo. 78, vo.]   * byholdyng.   And they that fonde this scyence perceyuid
that it myght not be knowen truly by astronomye, ne
the nature of the sterres withoute knowyng of their
mesures.   Therfore wolde they mesure them and preue
al their gretenesse.

Wherfore and how they mesured the world.   ca. ix°.[1]

Fyrst of alle the auncyent philosophres wolde mesure
the gretnes of the world all round aboute therthe
tofore ony other werke, by whiche they preuyd the
heyght of the sterres and the gretnes of the firmament
all aboute.   And they coude not fynde more greter
mesure to be mesured.

And whan they had mesured therthe how moche it
had of largenes all aboute, and how moche it had of

_____
[1] O.F. text, Ch. VII [3].

thycknes thorugh, they enquyred after of the mone, by
cause it was leste hye fro therthe & most nyhest therto.
And after they enquyred of the sonne how ferre it was
fro therthe, and how moche the body therof had of gretnes.
And they fonde it moche more than all therthe was.

And whan they had mesured thise thre thynges,
the Sonne, the Mone and therthe, they myght lightly
after enquyre of the other sterres, how moche euerich
is nygh or ferre, and the gretenes of euerich. Of whiche
they fonde none but his body were of more gretenes than
alle therthe is, excepte only thre of the planetes without
more, whiche ben Venus, Mercurye & the Mone whiche
is the thirde.[1]

And euery man may enquyre this, yf he knowe the
scyence of geometrye & the scyence of Astronomye
* with all; ffor that muste he knowe first to fore he [* fo. 79]
may fynde and knowe the trouthe. But for as moche
as alle be not good clerkis ne maistres of astronomye
that may proue this, we wil recounte here after how
moche the erthe is longe, and how thycke it is thurgh,
and also how moche the mone is aboue therthe, and the
sonne also whiche is aboue the mone, and how moche
eche of them hath of gretenes, lyke as the kynge
Tholomeus hath preued; and also we shal speke after
that of the sterres and of the firmament: Of alle this we
shal saye to you.

But first to fore all I shal recouute [2] to yow of the
faytes and dedes of the kynge Tholomeus whiche knewe
so many demonstraunces of apparicions, and somoche
loued astronomye that he wolde serche alle thyse thynges.
And we shal saye to you of somme thynges whiche
ben not contrarye to yow yf ye wyl wel vnderstande &
reteyne them, by whiche ye may lerne som good. And
thenne after we shal mesure to you the world the best
wyse we may.

Now entende ye of the kynge Tholomeus and of the
werkes of somme other philosophres for youre owne
prouffyt.

---

[1] "Of whiche they . . . thirde.": *Neckam*, I. 8.
[2] recouute = recounte.

Of the kynge Tholomeus and of somme other philosophres.   capitulo xᵒ.[1]

Tholomeuʒ was a kynge moche subtil in Astronomye.
This Tholomeus was kynge of Egipte [2], whiche helde
the contree longe tyme.   Ther were somtyme many
kynges that were named Tholomeus.   But emonge the
other this was he that knewe most of Astronomye and
[* fo. 79,vo.] *that most enserched of the sterres, and more vnderstode
of them than the other.   Of whiche he composed and
made plente of right fair volumes and bookes, and many
dyuerse instrumentes by whiche was founde appertly all
the gretenes of therthe, and the heyght of the firmament,
and how the sterres make their cours bothe by nyght &
by daye.

By hym were founden first the oryloges of the chirches,
whiche begynne the houres of the dayes & of the
nyghtes.   The dayes passe fast on [3]; wherfor the chirches
haue grete nede to haue good oryloges ffor to doo
therby alway the seruyse of Our Lord at hour com-
petent and due, as wel by day as by nyght; ffor God
loueth moche for to be adoured and seruyd entierly and
ordynately euery day.   Ffor the Orysons that ben sayd
and recyted euery day in the chirches playse more to Our
Lord than do they that ben said in many other places.
And therfor the oryloges ben necessarye in euery
chirche.

And men serue God the better in due tyme, and
fare the better, and lyue the lenger; ffor yf they
ruled soo them self to praye at a certayn hour, and at
an other hour in lyke wise to ete, and other thinges in
his right hour, it shold be a lyght thynge to doo and
plese God yf men wold applye them as wel to suche
thynges as they doo to doo that whiche confoundeth and
sleeth them; that is to wete that they be all enclyned to
conquere the richesses, of whiche they cesse not nyght
ne daye, and wenen to prolonge their lyf therby.   But

[1] O.F. text, Ch. VIII [3].
[2] See *Introduction*, p. xix.
[3] "The dayes passe fast on": O.F. text (p. 178), "les jours
acourcent," i. e. *the clocks shorten* the days.

they amasse and gete grete tresours, and pourchasse their
deth.[1] Ffor by the grete goodes that they assemble on
alle sides, they put them in suche thought and payne
that they lese * ofte their wytte & vnderstandyng and
also their mynde, so that they may not enclyne and
thynke on thoo werkes that towche their saluacion as
they ought to doo; and by suche werkes shold they be
in more ease and lyue lenger and plese better Our Lord,
and shold also haue more helthe of body and of sowle.
But they loue somoche the wynnyng of the goodes of
the world that they leue that whiche shold more
auayle and prouffyte them.

   I wote neuer wherfore they gete this hauoir and good,
ffor they lose therby the ease of the worlde; by cause
whan they wene to sette them in ease and to be in
pees, thenne cometh deth and maketh them to dye with
right grete sorowe. Ffor the grete couetyse of the
good, and the payne that they haue made alle way to
gete it without ordynaunce and mesure hath moche the
more hastelyer brought them to their deth. And so
ben many men deed that, yf they had ordeyned their
affaires and besynesse as they ought to do at euery hour
competently and by ordre, whiche yet had ben a lyue
and in good helthe.

   And lo, thus ye may see how they abregge their dayes
and auaunce their deth; ffor atte longe Nature may not
suffre dyuerse mayntenes [2] vnresonable ne the sodeyn
agrauacions ne griefs of whiche, by theyr folyes, they
trauaylle nature; and it displesyth moche vnto God.
And also no good may come therof. But gladlyer and
wyth better wylle they traueylle, and more dyligently, for
to wynne and gete the wordly goodes than the loue of God.
And neuer do they thynge by ordre. One day goon they
erly to the chirche, and another day late or at suche an
hour as they wene that it shall * not hurte them to
auaunce their gayne and wynnyng. Thus go they neuer
to chirche for to pray vnto God vnto the tyme that they

[* fo. 80]

[* fo. 80,vo.]

---

[1] This passage (that is to wete . . . pourchasse their deth) is
a word for word translation of MS. Roy. 19 A IX. This MS. gives
a paraphrase of the corresponding passage in MS. A.
[2] mayntenes: O.F. text, p. 179, "maintenirs," behaviour.

wene that they shal wynne nomore wordly goodes. But they wynne the lasse ; ffor they serue God in vayn. And God shal rendre to them their reward, and they shal bye right dere that they leue to serue hym, ffor he may rendre to them more meryte in one day than they may gete in a thousand yere.

Suche peple ben foles & euyl aduysed whan of nought they wene to serue hym that alle knoweth and alle seeth, ye the lest thought that they thynke. Yet ben ther somme, whan they goo to chirche, they goo not in entencion to praye God, but only for to gete the loos and goodes of the world ; and praye more for their richesses, that God sholde kepe and multepleye them, than they do for the saluacion of their sowles whiche ben in grete paryll to be perisshed.

And it is a grete meruaylle of suche maner of peple that thynke wel in their hertes and knowe wel that it is euyl that they do, yet for al that they amende them not. Of whiche it is grete pyte whan they so folowe the deuyll whiche is so feble a thyng fro whom alle euyllis sourden.[1] Truly the deuyl is ful of inyquyte, and withoute power and strengthe ouer ony persone of hym self ; ffor he may not vaynquysshe ne ouercome but hym that consenteth to his wyll. For who that wil conduyte and rule hym self well, the inyquytees of hym may not noye ne greue ne in no thynge traueylle hym of whiche he hath cause to sorowe, fore as longe as he will dispose hym to doo well. Thenne may wel be sayd "fy" ; ffor they ben more than faylled whan he ouercometh them
[* fo. 81]   * so febly, and taketh them in their euyll dedes and synnes, and ledeth them to perdicion, where neuer they shal be without payne ne neuer shal haue Joye, ne in nowise haue hope of mercy.

Of this purpos we shal saye nomore now, but recounte of kynge Tholomeus the whiche employed his tyme in the werkes of Our Lord God.

Out of his bookes were drawen the nombres of whiche the yeres ben ordeyned. And of the same is founde the cours of the mone, by whiche is seen whan she is

---

[1] sourden : spring, arise.

newe. Of whiche Julius Cezar, whiche of Rome was
Emperour, made a booke called the "sommes," the whiche
is ful necessarye in holy chirche; and it declareth the
golden nombre of the kalender; ffor by the kalender is
knowen the cours of the mone and of alle the yere; by
whiche is also knowen how we ought to lyne after reson
euery daye, that is to wete in etyng and drynkyng, and
in worshipyng Our Lord on hye dayes and symple, and
for to solempnyse suche dayes as holy chyrche hath
ordeyned and by blessyd sayntes establysshed. By the
kalender we knowe the holy tymes, as the ymbre dayes,
the lente, aduente, and the hye dayes and festes that we
ben most bounden to serue God ffor to gete his inestymable Joye and glorye whiche Our Lord hath promysed
vnto his good and trewe frendes whiche wyth good herte
serue hym.

Alle this lerneth vs the kalender the whiche was
drawen out of Astronomye whiche the good kynge
Tholomeus louyd so moche; and he knewe more than
ony other man sauf Adam whyche was the fyrst man;
ffor Adam knewe alle the seuen scyences lyberall
entyerly,* without fayllyng in a worde, as he that the [* fo. 81,vo.]
creatour made and fourmed with his propre handes.   *l* 1
And so wolde Our Lord haue hym souerayn in beaute,
in witte & in strengthe ouer al them that shold be
born after hym vnto the comyng of Jhesu Cryste sone
of God, the whiche had gyuen to hym suche vertues.
Ne neuer after Adam gaf he so moche to one man, ne
neuer shall. But anon as he had consented & commysed
the synne deffended, he lost somoche of his wytte and
power that anon he becam a man mortal. And he was
suche to fore er he had synned that he shold neuer haue
felte deth.

Ne alle we descended of hym shold not haue had
lasse meryte than he in Joye, in solaas, and in deduyt
of paradys terrestre, alle to gydre, and born and
nourysshed wythout synnes, and after in heuen gloryfyed. But syth they tasted of the fruyt whiche God
deffended them, his wytte and his entendement were so
destroyed and corumped by his synne that alle we

abyde entetched [1] and foylled ther by ; ne ther is nothing
vnder the fyrmament but it is werse sythen than to fore,
and of lasse valewe ; ye the sterres gyue lasse lyght
than they dyde to fore.

Thus alle thynges empayred of their goodnes &
vertues by the synne of Adam, which God had made
for man, as he that wolde make hym maistre of all
the goodes that he had made. But anon as he had
commysed the synne, he felte hym so bare of his witte
& entendement, strengthe & of his beaute, that hym
semed he was al naked, and that he had loste all
goodes, as a man put in exyle. But notwythstondyng
this, yet abode wyth hym more witte, strengthe and
beaute than euer ony man had * sythen.

[* fo. 82]

And to the regard of thise thre vertues that Adam
had, the kynge Dauid, that was so vertuous and wyse,
had ii sones [2] whiche myght be compared, that one to
the beaulte of Adam, and that other to his wysedom.
Absolon myght be compared to his beaulte, and Salomon
vnto his witte and wysedom, and Sampson the forte vnto
his strengthe. Thus were thise thre vertues in Adam so
parfyghtly that noman syth myght compare wyth hym,
ne the ii sones of Dauid, ne Sampson, ne none other. Ffor
as it is said tofore, he knewe the vii sciences liberall
better than alle the men that ben descended of hym, as
he to whom his God and maker had taught them to hym
and enseygned. And after that, they were sought by
many a man whiche rendred grete payne for to fynde
them and to saue them for cause of the flood, knowyng
that it sholde come to the world by fyre or by water.

How the scriptures and scyences were saued ayenst
the flood.[3] capitulo xi°.[4]

Syth Adam was deed ther were many men whiche
lerned the scyences of the vii artes liberall whiche
God had sente to them in therthe. Of whome somme

---

[1] entetched : O.F. text, p. 181, "entechiez," stained, tainted.
[2] O.F. text, p. 181 : "ot li rois David, qui tant fu sages, ·III·
filz." Gossouin evidently looks upon Samson as a son of David.
[3] This chapter is mostly taken from *Gervase of Tilbury*, I. 20.
See *Introduction*, p. xx.
[4] O.F. text, Ch. IX [3].

ther were that wolde enquyre what shold bycome of the
world, or euer it shold haue an ende.

And they founde verily that it shold be destroyed and
take ende twyes: At the first tyme by the flood of water.[1]

But Our Lord wold not they shold knowe whether it
shold be first destroyed by water or by fyre.   Thenne had
they grete pyte for the scyences * that they had goten,   [* fo. 82,vo.]
whiche they knewe and so shold perisshe but yf it were   *l* 2
kept and ordeyned fore by their wysedoms.   Thenne they
aduysed them of a grete wytte and bounte, as they that
wel wiste that after the first destruxion of the world ther
shold be other peple.   Wherfor they dyde do make grete
pylers of stone, in suche wyse that they myght pourtraye
and graue in euery stone atte leste one of the vii sciences
entierly, in suche wise that they myght be knowen to
other.

Of whiche somme saye that one of thise pylers was
of a stone as hard as marble, & of suche nature
that water myght not empayre it ne defface ne
mynuysshe it.   And they made other in a stronge maner
of tyles, all hole, wythoute ony Joyntures, that fyre
myght not hurte it in no wyse.   In thyse grete
colompnes or pylers, as sayd is, were entaylled & grauen
the vii scyences in suche wyse that they that shold
come after them shold fynde and lerne them.

Of them that fonde the science and the clergye after
the flood   capitulo xii°.[2]

As ye may vnderstonde, the seuen scyences lyberall
were founden by auncyent wyse men, out of whiche
all other sciences procede.   Thyse were they to whom Our
Lorde hath gyuen them and enseygned, doubtyng the
deluuye that God sente in to therthe, the whiche drowned
alle creatures, reseruyd Noe and them that he toke in to
the Arke wyth hym.   And after this the world was

---

[1] The passage after "twyes" is incomplete in MSS. A, Roy.
19 A IX., and in Caxton.   The correct reading, taken from other
MSS., is : "A l'une foiz *par feu ardant, a l'autre foiz* par le deluge
d'yaue": once by *burning fire, the other time* by the flood.—The
words in italics are missing, though quite essential to the sense in
the O.F. text (p. 182).

[2] O.F. text, Ch. X [3].

[* fo. 83] repeoplyd and made agayn by them that descended of
them.* Ffor after the tyme of Noe, the peple began to
make agayn howses and mansions, and to make redy
other werkis. But this was moche rudely, as they that
coude but right lytil vnto the tyme that thise sciences
were founden agayn. & thenne coude they better make
& doo that was nedeful & propice to them, & fynde
remedye for their euyllis.

The first that applyed hym and entermeted for to
enquyre and serche these sciences after the flood was
Sem, one of the sones of Noe, whiche had gyuen his
corage therto.   And in suche wyse he dyde therin
suche dyligence and so contynued that, by his wytte,
he fonde a parte of Astronomye. After hym was Abraham whiche also founde a grete partye[1]; and after
hym were other that vsed theyr lyf the best wise they
myght, so moche that they had the pryncyples and
resons of the seuen scyences.

And after cam Plato the sage and right souerayn
in philosophye, and his clerke named Aristotle
the wyse clerke. This Plato was the man aboue al
them of the world in clergye the most experte of
them that were to fore or after hym. He preuyd
first that ther was but one that was only souerayn,
whiche all made & of whom alle good thinge cometh ; yet
his bookes approue hyely that ther ne is but one souerayn
good, that is Our Lord God whiche made alle thynges.
And in this only veryte he preuyd the right trouthe ;
ffor he preued his power, his wisedom and his goodnes.
Thise thre bountees reclayme alle crysten men, that is
the fader, the sone, and the holy goste. Of the fader he
sayde the power and puissaunce ; of the sone, the
Sapyence ; and of the holy gost, the bienueullaunce.

[* fo. 83,vo.]
l 3 And Aristotle, whiche* cam after hym, holdeth plente
of thynges nyghe to hym, & knewe the thynges that he
had sayd, and ordeyned right wel the science of logyke,
ffor he knewe more therof than of other sciences.

Thise two notable clerkes fonde by their wysedom

---

[1] "The first that . . . partye": Josephus, *Antiq. Jud.* I. 2.
See *Introduction*, p. xx.

and connyng thre persones in one essence,[1] and preuyd·
it ; but they put it not in latyn, ffor bothe two were
paynems, as they that were more than thre hondred
yere to fore the comynge of Our Lord Jhesu Cryste.
And alle their bookes were in grekyssh lettres.

After cam Boece whiche was a grete philosophre
and right wise clerke, the whiche coude byhelpe
hym with dyuerses langages, and louid moche rightwisnes. This Boece translated of their bookes the most
partye, and sette them in latyn. But he deyde er he
had alle translated them ; wherof was grete dommage
for vs alle. Syth haue other clerkes translated ; but
this Boece translated more than ony other, the whiche
we haue yet in vsage. And compiled in his lyf
plente of fair volumes aourned of hye and noble philosophye, of whiche we haue yet grete nede for tadresse
vs toward Our Lord God.

And many other good clerkes haue ben in this world
of grete auctoryte whiche haue lerned and studyed alle
their tyme vpon the sciences of the vii Artes. Of
whiche haue ben somme that in their tyme haue do
meruaylles by Astronomye. But aboue alle them that
most antremeted and traueylled vpon the science of
Astronomye was Virgyle whiche comypled many
merueyllous werkes. And therfore we shal recounte a
lytil here folowyng of the meruaylles he dyde.*   [* fo. 84]

Here folowe in substauuce[2] of the meruaylles that
Virgyle wrought by Astronomye in his tyme by his
wytte.[3] capitulo xiii°.[4]

Virgyle, the wyse philosophre born in Itaile, was to
fore the comyng of Our Lord Jhesu Cryst. He sette
not lytil by the vii sciences, ffor he trauaylled and
studyed in them the most part of his tyme, somoche
that by astronomye he made many grete meruaylles.

Ffor he made in Naples a flye of copper whiche, whan he
had sette it vp in a place, that flye enchaced and hunted
away alle other flyes, so that ther mught abyde none in

---

[1] See *Introduction*, p. xx.   [2] Substauuce = substauuce.
[3] See *Introduction*, p. xx s.   [4] O. F. text, Ch. XI [3].

ony place ne durste none approche nyghe to that flye by the space of two bowe shote round aboute. And yf ony flye passed the bounde that Virgyle had compassed, incontynent it shold deye, and myght no lenger lyue.[1]

He made also an hors of brasse, the whiche guarisshed and heled alle horses of all their maladyes and seknesses of whiche they were entechid, also sone as the seke hors loked on the hors of brasse.[2]

Also he founded a meruayllous cyte vpon an egge by suche force and power that, whan the egge was meuyd, all the cyte quaued and shoke. And the more the egge was meuyd the more the cyte quaued and trembled.[3] The cyte in hye and lowe and in playn, the flye of copper and hors of brasse that Virgyle thus made, ben in Naples, and the cage where the egge is in, alle ben there seen. This hath be said to vs of them that be comen fro thens and that many tymes haue seen them.

Also he made that in one day alle the fyre thurgh out Rome faylled and was* quenchid, in suche wise that no persone myght haue none but yf he wente and sette it at the nature of a woman with a Candel or otherwyse. And she was doughter of themperour, and a grete lady whiche to fore had don to hym a grete sklaundre and dysplaysir. And all they that had fette fyre at her myght not adresse it to other; but euerych that wolde haue fyre muste nedes go fetche it there as the other had fette it. And thus auenged he hym on her for the displaysir that she had don to hym.[4]

And he made a brygge vpon a water, the grettest that euer was made in the worlde; and is not knowen of what mater it is made, whether it be of stone or of wode. But ther was neuer werkman so subtyl, ne carpenter, ne mason, ne other that coude somoche knowe ne enserche wythin therthe ne wythin the water, that

[*. fo. 84,vo.] l 4

---

1 "Ffor he made . . . lyue": *Gervase of Tilbury,* III. 10.
2 "He made . . . brasse": *Chronica di Parthenope,* XX.
3 "Also he founded . . . trembled": *Chronica di Parthenope,* XXXI.
4 "Also he made . . . to hym": Solinus, *Memorabilia* (ed. Francfort 1603, p. 143).

they myght knowe and fynde how that brygge was there
sette, ne how it was susteyned in no maner, ne atte
endes ne in the myddys; and men passed ouer frely aud [1]
all wythout lettyng.[2]

He made also a gardyn all aboute round closyd wyth
thayer, wythout ony other closure, whiche was as thycke
as a clowde. And this gardyn was right hye fro
therthe.[3]

He made also two tapres and a lampe a lyght and
brennyng in suche wise that it contynuelly brennyd
wythout quenchyng, and mynusshed ne lassed no thyng.
Thise thre thinges he enclosed within therthe in suche
wyse that noman can fynde it ffor all the craft they
can doo.[4]

Yet made he an heed to speke, which answerd of alle
that whiche he was demanded of, and of that whiche
shold happen and come in therthe. So on a day he
demanded of the heed how he shold * doo in a certayn [*fo. 85]
werke where as he shold goo vnto. But the heed
answerd to hym in suche wyse that he vnderstode it
not wel; ffor hit sayde that yf he kept wel the heed,
he shold come agayn all hole. And with this answere
he wente his way wel assured. But the Sonne, whiche
that day gaf grete hete, smote hym on the heed and
chauffed his brayn, of whiche he toke none hede, that
he gate therby a sekenes and maladye wherof he deyde.
Ffor whan he had the answere of the heed, he vnderstode
not that he spack of his heed, but vnderstode of the
heed that spack to hym; but it had be better that he
had kept wel his owne heed.[5]

And whan he felte hym self agreuyd wyth sekenesse,
he made hym to be born out of Rome ffor to be beryed

---

[1] aud = and.
[2] "And he made . . . lettyng": *Neckam*, II. 174.
[3] "He made also . . . therthe": *Neckam*, II. 174; *Gervase of Tilbury*, III. 13.
[4] "He made also two tapres . . . can doo": William of Malmesbury, *De Gestis Regum Anglorum*, (ed. Stubbs, London, 1887), vol. I. p. 259. See *Introduction*, p. xxi.
[5] "Yet made he . . . heed": Puymaigre (*Notice sur l'Image du Monde.* Metz, 1854) states, without, however, giving chapter and page, that this story is to be found in the works of *Bacon* and *Albert the Great*.

in a castel beyng toward Sezyle, and a myle nyghe to the See. Yet ben there his bones whiche ben better kept than others ben. And whan the bones of hym ben remeuyd, the See begynneth to encreace and swelle so gretly that it cometh to the castel. And the hyer they be reysed vp, the hyer groweth the See, in suche wyse that the castel shold be drowned yf they were not anon remysed and sette in their place. But the*n*ne whan they be sette agayn in their place, anon the see aualeth and gooth a way there as it was to fore.[1] And this hath be oftymes proued ; and yet endure the vertues of hym, as they saye that haue ben there.

Virgyle was a moche sage and subtyl clerke and ful of grete engyne, ffor vnto his power he wold preue all the vsages of clerkes, as moche as was possible for hym to knowe. . He was a man of lytil stature ; a lytil courbed was he on the back by right nature, and wente his heede [*fo. 85,vo.] hangyng * doun and beholdyng the ground.

Virgyle dyde and made many grete meruaylles whiche the herers shold holde for lesynges yf they herde them recounted ; ffor they wolde not byleue that another coude doo suche thynge as they coude not medle wyth. And whan they here speke of suche maters or of other that they see at their eyen and that they can not vnderstonde né knowe not therof, anon they saye that it is by thelpe of the fende that werketh in suche maner, as they that gladly myssaye of peple of recommendacion. And also saye it is good not to conne suche thynges. But yf they knewe the science and manere, they wold holde it for a moche noble and right werke of nature, and without ony other espece of euyll. And whan they knowe not ne vnderstonde the thinge, they saye moche more euyl than well.

Certaynly who that knewe well Astronomye, ther is nothyng in the world of whiche he coude enquyre by reson but he shold haue knowleche therof. And many thynges shold he doo that sholde seme myracles to the

---

[1] "And whan he . . . to fore." This story is to be found in the works of *Chancellor Conrad of Querfurt* (ed. Borch, Dresden, 1880, p. 10).

peple whiche that knewe nothynge of the science. I
saye not but ther myght be wel don euyll by hym that
coude it; ffor ther is none so good science but that
myght be entended therin somme malyce, and that he
myght vse it in euyll that wolde so applye hym therto.
God made neuer so good a gospel but somme myghte
torne it contrarye to trouthe; & ther is no thynge so
true but somme myght so glose that it shold be to his
dampnacion, who that wolde payne hym to do euyll,
how wel it is no maystrye to do yll.

Euery man hath the power to drawe hym self to do
well or to doo euyll, whiche that he wylle, as he that
hath fre * liberte of that one and of that other.   Yf [* fo. 86]
he gyue hym self to vertues, this goodnes cometh to
hym fro Our Lord; and yf he be inclyned to doo euyll,
that bryngeth hym at thende to sorow and to payne
perpetuell.   Neuer shal the euyl disposed man saye well
of that he can not wel vnderstonde & knowe.   Ther is
no craft, arte, ne scyence but it is good to be knowen,
whan a man wyll gyue and applye hym self therto.
But late hym do nothyng ayenst God by whiche he lese
his grace.

Alle thynge is knowen by Astronomye, sauf suche
thynge as God wylle that it be not knowen.   And so
it is better to lerne that, than to lerne to amasse and
gadre to gydre grete tresours.   Ffor who that coude
Astronomye proprely, he shold haue all that he wold
haue on erthe; ffor hym shold faylle nothyng, what
someuer he wold and yet more.   But they had leuer
haue the monoye; and they knowe not that it is of
Astronomye, ne wherfore monoye was founden, how wel
that they applye all their entendement for to haue it.
But they retche not for to lerne, sauf that whiche they
knowe shal redounde to their singuler prouffyt.   And
yet for alle that we shal not leue but that we shal
recyte somme caas for them that haue talente for to
lerne.   And late hym herkne and take hede that wyll
vnderstonde it.

Here it declareth for what cause monoye was first establisshid.[1]   capitulo xiiii°.[2]

The monoyes were establisshed first, for as moche as they had not of alle thinges necessarye to gydre.
[*fo. 86,vo.] *That one had whete, another had wyn, and another cloth or other wares ; he that had whete had not wyn withoute he chaunged one for another ; and so muste they dayly chaunge one for another ffor to haue that they had not, as they that knewe none other mene.

Whan the philosophres sawe this, they dyde so moche that they establisshed, wyth the lordes somtyme regnyng, a lytil lyght thynge whiche euery man myght bere with hym to bye that was nedeful to hym and behoefful[3] for his lyf.   And so ordeyned by aduyse to gydre a thynge whiche was not ouer dere, ne holden for ouer vyle, and that it were of somme valure for to bye and vse wyth all true marchandyse one wyth another by vertue of suche enseygne,[4] and that it were comune ouerall and in all maner.

And establed thenne a lytil moneye whiche shold goo and haue cours thurgh the world.   And by cause it lad men by the waye, and mynystred to them that was necessarye, it was called monoye ; that is as moche to saye ȧs to gyue to a man al that hym behoueth for his lyuyng.   "Monos" in grekyssh langage is as moche te[5] saye as "one thyng only"; ffor thenne was but one maner of monoye in all the world.   But now euery man maketh monoye at his playsir, by which they desuoy and goo out of the waye more than yf ther were but one coyne only ; ffor by this cause is seen ofte plente of dyuerse monoyes.

Thus establisshed not the philosophres ; ffor they establisshed for to saue thestate of the world.   And I saye it for as moche yf the monoye were out of grotes

---

[1] Cf. for this chapter *Neckam*, II. 52.
[2] O.F. text, Ch. XII [3].   [3] behoefful : profitable.
[4] "and that it were . . . enseygne": which should be of some value for buying and exchanging goods by means of a token. (enseygne = O.F. *ensaingne*, a coin, token.)
[5] te = to.

and pens of siluer so thenne it shold be of lasse weyght
and lasse of valewe ; and that shold * be better for to   [* fo. 87]
bere by the way for poure folke, and better shold be
easid for the helpe of their nedes to their lyuyng.   And
for none other cause it was ordeyned first ; ffor the
monoyes be not preysed but for the gold and syluer that
is therin.   And they that establisshed it first, made it
right lytil and lyght, ffor the more ease to be born al
aboute where men wold goo.   Ffor now in late dayes as
in the begynnyng of the Regne of kynge Edward, and
longe after, was no monoye curraunt in Englond but
pens and halfpens and ferthynges.   And he ordeyned
first the grote and half grote of . syluer, and noble, half
noble and ferthyng in golde.[1]

Here foloweth of phylosophres that wente thurgh the
world.[2]   capitulo xv°.[3]

Thus the philosophres, by the moyen of their
     monoye, wente where they wolde thurgh the
world, and the marchantes in their marchandyses, or in
pylgremages, or in pourchacyng and enquyryng somme
places that they wolde knowe.   Of whom ther were many
whiche were philosophres and that wolde haue experi-
ence of alle thinges ; and they wente by see and by
londe for tenserche the very trouthe of the secrete
thinges of heuen and of erthe.   They rested them not
by the grete fyres ne brassed [4] not, as som doo now in
thyse dayes in the worlde, the whyche gyue them to
doo no good ne applye to no vertues but yf it be to haue
the loos and preysyng of the world.   But they wente
serchyng by the see and the londe on alle parties * for   [* fo.87,vo.]
to knowe the better the good and the yuell, and for to
conne discerne that one fro that other ; by whiche they
endured many grete trauaylles for to gete the sauyng of

---

[1] The passage from "Ffor now . . . ." to ". . . in golde." is
not in the O.F. text.
[2] Cf. Philostrates' *Life of Apollonius of Tyanae* (ed. Kaiser,
Leipzig, 1870), III. 16 seq. ; *Neckam*, II. 21.
[3] O.F. text, Ch. XIII [3].
[4] brassed : O.F. text (p. 188) : *rostissoient*, roasted.   This is
 vidently the sense in which Caxton uses "brassed," which
ₑsually means "to harden by the fire."

u

their sowles.   And at this day alle men seche to gete
Richesses and tresour, and the name to be callyd
maistre for to gete louyng and honour of the world
whiche so hastely faylleth.

Certaynly an euyl man may not thinke on hye
thynges; ffor who that is of erthe, to therthe entendeth,
and who pretendeth to God, God attendeth to hym.
Ffor God hym self saith : "Who that is of therthe,
speketh of therthe ; and who that cometh fro heuen,
vnto heuen pertended."   He wythout other is lord and
sire of and aboue other.

The philosophres, that wel coude vnderstonde this
worde, had moche leuer to suffre trauaylles and mesayses
for to lerne than tendende[1] to worldly honours ; ffor they
helde for more dere and worthy the sciences and the
clergyes than alle the seygnouryes of the world.

Plato, whiche was a puissaunt and a recommended
maistre of Athenes, lefte his noble estate and his place,
by cause he wolde of suche renommee lyue, that he
serched many londes and contrees.[2]   And had leuer
haue payne, mesayse and trauayll for tenserche trouthe
and for to lerne science, than for to haue seygnourie
and domynacion in the world, ne renommee for to be
maister ; ffor he wold saye nothyng but yf he were
certayn therof, ffor ony vayne glorye of the world.

Apolynes, whiche was so grete a prynce, lefte his
empire and his Royamme, and departed al poure and
naked for to lerne the scyences.   And he was taken and
[* fo. 88] solde oftymes to straunge men.   Ne neuer was ther *
none of them so valyant, of alle them that bought and
solde, that he sette ought therby, so that he myght
alleway lerne.   And more trauaylled on alle partyes for
to lerne and knowe God and the world, whiche he
loued better than ony other worldly thyng ; and he
wente so ferre that he fonde syttyng in a Trone of

[1] tendende = *entende*, to give attention to.
[2] "by cause he wolde . . . contrees."   This passage seems to
mean "for he wished to have the renown of having been through
many countries."   The O.F. text (p. 188), says : *Car il n'ot cure
de tele renommée ; ainz cercha maintes contrées,*" i. e. For he did
not care about such glory ; he would rather travel about many
countries.

golde an hye philosophre and of grete renommee, the
whiche enseygned and taught his discyples wythin his
trone where he satte, and lerned them of the faytes of
nature, of good maners, the cours of the dayes and of
the sterres, and the resonne and signefiaunce of thynges
touchyng sapyence and wysedom.   This philosophre was
named Hyarchas.

After, Appolynes serched by many contrees so ferre
that he fonde the table of fyn golde, whiche was of
so grete renommee that it was named the table of the
Sonne, wherin alle the world was pourtrayed.   Therin
saw he aud[1] lerned many faytes and many meruaylles
whiche he louyd more than ony Royamme.   He erred so
ferre by strange londes that he passed the flood of
Ganges and alle Ynde; and in thende so ferre, that he
myght fynde nomore waye.   And where someuer he
cam, he fonde & lerned alleway suche as myght auaylle
and prouffyte to hym self and other for tauaunce hym
tofore God.

Thus the kynge Alysaundre also suffred trauaylles
without nombre for to lerne.   But he wente fro place
to place in estate ryall, and with puissaunce of peple ;
wherfor he myght not so wel lerne ne enquyre the
trouthe of thynges.

Virgyle also wente thurgh many contrees for to enquyre
and serche the trouthe of alle thynges.

Tholomeus, whiche of Egypte was kynge,* was not all   [* fo.88, vo.]
quyte of his parte,[2] but wente by many contrees and
Royammes[3] for to lerne, experymente and see all the
good clerkes that he myght fynde.

---

[1] aud = and.

[2] "was not all quyte of his parte": O.F. text (p. 189): *n'en
clama pas quite sa partie,* i. e. did not consider himself free from
this duty.

[3] After "Royammes" Caxton has left out several lines of the
O.F. text (p. 189): "Ainz ala par maintes contrées, *tant qu'il ot
trouvées maintes merveilles.   Sainz Pols, qui fu moult preudomme,
ala par maintes contrées* pour plus aprendre et pour vëoir touz
les bons clers que il porroit trouver . . .": but wente by many
contrees and Royammes, *so much that he discovered many wonders.
Saint Paul, who was a very wise man, went through many countries*
for to lerne, experymente, and see all the good clerkes that he
myght fynde.—Caxton's oversight was probably due to the
repetition of "ala par maintes contrées."

Saynt Brandon neuer lefte for to laboure [1] by see
and by lande, ffor only to see and lerne; and he sawe
plente of grete meruaylles, ffor he cam in to an yle of
the see, where he sawe certayn byrdes whiche spack as
spyrites, whiche sayde to hym som thyng whiche he
demanded of them the vnderstondyng. And so ferre
he erred that he fonde one so perylous a place and so
ful of spyrites in so terryble tormentis, that they coude
not be nombred ne estemed. Emonge whom he sawe
one that answerd to hym and sayde that he was Judas
that betrayed Jhesu Cryst, whiche euery day was tormented an hondred tymes, and deye he myght not.
And plente of other grete meruaylles he sawe, as alonge
is recounted in the legende of his lyf.

Ther were many other philosophres that serched the
world, as moche as was possible for them to doo, for to
knowe the better the good and the euyll; and spared
for nothyng, ffor they beleuyd not lyghtly a thinge tyl
they knewe it wel by experyence, ne alle that they fonde
in their bookes to fore they had preuid it, for to knowe
God the better and to loue hym. But they serched by
see and by lande, tyl they had enserched all; and thenne
after retorned agayn to their studyes alle way for to
lerne the vertues & good maners. And thus loued
somoche philosophye ffor to knowe them self the better
in good and iust lyf.

But by cause that many tymes we haue spoken of
philosophye, and that somoche good cometh therof that
a man may haue therby vnderstondyng to knowe
* and loue God, therfore we shal telle to yow what it
signefyeth.

[* fo. 89]

What thynge is philosophye, and of thanswer that
Plato made therof. capitulo xvi°. [2]

Veray Philosophye is to haue knowleche of God
and fyn loue of sapyence, and to knowe the
secretes and ordinaunces of dyuyne thynges and of

---

[1] "laboure": O.F. text (p. 189): *errer*, to roam, to wander
about, to travel.
[2] O.F. text, Ch. XIV [3].

humayne ffor to knowe God and his power, and what a
man ought to be so that he myght conduyte hym that it
myght be to God agreable. Who that wel knewe
God and his mysteryes, he shold wel conne entierly
philosophye.

Alle they ben good philosophres that of them self
haue knowleche. Of whom Plato answerd to somme
that demanded hym in commun, and sayd to hym that
he had lerned ynowh and neded nomore, ffor he had
estudyed alle his tyme for to lerne; and it was sayd to
hym : " Maystre, it is wel in yow for to saye to vs
somme good worde procedyng of hye entendement, as ye
haue don other tymes." Thenne Plato, how wel that he
was the most experymented of all other, answerd sayeng,
as in his herte troubled, that he had nomore lerned sauf
as moche as he that felte hym self lyke vnto a vessel
that day and nyght is all voyde & empty. Thus moche
answerd Plato and nomore, how wel he was at that tyme
the most grete clerke that was knowen in alle the world,
and of moche perfounde science.

They that on thise dayes wil medle take non hede
to answere thus, but make semblaunt to be moche grete
clerkis & * experte, for to gete the loos and preysyng
of the world whiche ledeth them to dampnacion and
bryngeth theyr folye in to their hedes, so that they
entende nomore to vertues than doo beestis. Ffor they
be not alle clerkes that haue short typettis ; ffor ther
be many that haue the Aray of a clerke, that can not
wel vnderstande that he redeth ; ne yet somme that be
prestis can not wel and truly rede neyther.[1] And whan
suche knowe ony thynge that them seme be of valewr,
thenne wene they to knowe all. But moche remayneth
of their folyssh consayte. They be of the nature of
proud foles that ben surquydrous, that seche nothyng
but loos and preysyng of the peple, and traueylle them
self for to deceyue the world : this shal they abye dere
ones.

It were better for them to lerne suche scyence that

[* fo. 89, vo.] m 1

---

[1] " Ffor they be . . . " to ". . . rede neyther " is not in O.F.
text.

shold make them to vnderstande trouthe and right,
lyke as thyse auncyent wyse men dyde, the whiche
so lytil preysed the world that alle their tyme they
ocupyed in lernyng of phylosophye. Thus estudyed
auncyently the phylosophres to fore their deth for
tadresse them and other to their maker and creatour.
And in dede traueyllyd moche for tadresse alle peple
to vertue.

They ordeyned the monoyes that they bare for to
haue their lyuelode in byeng and payeng, ffor men
gyue not allewaye.

And for couetyse of the peple that haue fere of
their despences, it corumpeth right and nature ; ffor
by reson and right euerych ought to take his lyuyng.
And therfore was monoye establysshid for to susteyne
to euerich his lyuyng whan they wente by the waye.

[* fo. 90]
But they loue their kareynes [1] and bodyes moche more *
than nede is, and reteyne and kepe more goodes and
richesses that they nede for their ordynarye, whyche
they lete rote and faylle by them, and see that many
poure persones haue grete nede therof. The monoyes
were not founde for this cause, but for to haue their
liuyng vnto the tyme that deth cometh and taketh alle
that he ought to take at the playsyr of God.   And
thus shold they be more easyd than they now be, and
euerych shold haue that hym lacked,• and they shold
leue to doo so many synnes.

But they be not so wyse as were they that by their
witte fonde agayn Astronomye, of whom Tholomeus was
one ; and trauaylled so moche that he knewe and proued
the cours of the sterres that ben on the heuen, and
mesured them all on hye ; wherof we' haue spoken here
to fore.

And now we shal recounte from hensforth the gretenes
of therthe and of heuene, of the Mone, of the Sonne,
of the Sterres and of the planetes, whiche thynges
be not comune vnto alle men ; lyke as' the kynge
Tholomeus hym self mesured them vnto the abysme,
and preuyd by reson in a book that he compyled named

---

[1] kareynes : carrion.

Almageste, whiche is as moche to saye as an hye werke.
Thenne wyl ye here what he saith herto, whiche many
another hath also proued after hym by his booke in
whyche he gaf the crafte & scyence to proue and see it
by reson.

How moche therthe is of heyght rounde aboute and
of thyckenes by the myddle.[1] capitulo xvii. [2]

* The Auncyent philosophres mesured the world on [*fo. 90, vo.]
    alle parties by their science, Arte and wytte,   m 2
vnto the sterres all on hye, of whiche they wolde knowe
the mesure ffor to knowe the better their nature.   But
first they wolde mesure therthe and preue his gretenes.
And thenne, whan they had mesured therthe al aboute
by a crafte that they knewe, and proued by right reson,
they mesured it rounde aboute lyke as they sholde haue
compassed it al aboute wyth a gyrdle, and thenne they
stratched out the gyrdle al alonge.   And thenne that
whiche wente out of lengthe of the gyrdle, they fonde it
in lengthe xx·M·cccc· and ·xxvii· myles [3] ; of whyche
euery myle conteyneth a thousand paas, and euery paas
fyue foot, and euery fote xiiii ynches.[4]   Somoche hath
the erthe in lengthe round a boute.

By this fonde they after how thycke therthe is in the
myddle.   And they fonde the thycknes therof, lyke as
it shold ben clefte in the myddle fro the hyest to the
lowest or fro that one syde to that other, vi·M· and v·C·
myles.   By this laste mesure, whyche is after nature
right, they mesured iustely the heyght of the firmament ;
ffor they coude nowher fynde a gretter mesure ffor
textende the gretenesse of alle thynges whiche ben
enclosed wythin the heuene.

---

[1] Cf. for this chapter : Ptolemy, *Almageste* (ed. Halma. Paris,
1813) V. 15, 16 ; *Neckam*, I. 8.

[2] O.F. text, Ch. XV [3].

[3] O.F. text, p. 192 : " ·xxVIII· milles."

[4] Both MSS., A and Roy. 19 A IX., give "xiiii pouces." The
correct reading, found in other MSS., is " XII pouces."

How the Mone and the Sonne haue eche of them
their propre heyght.[1] capitulo xviii°.[2]

Therthe, as the auncyent philosophres saye, after they
had mesured it they mesured þe sterres, the plan-
[* fo. 91.]   etes* and the firmament.

And first they mesured the mone & preuyd his
gretnesse. And they fonde the body of therthe, without
and withinne, that, after their comune mesure, it was
more grete than the body of the mone was by xxix[3]
tymes and a lytil more. And they fonde that it was
in heyght aboue the erthe xxiiii[4] tymes and an half as
moche as therthe hath of thycknes.

Also in lyke wyse preuyd they touchyng the sonne
by very demonstraunce and by reson, that the Sonne
is gretter than alle therthe is by an hondred syxty and
sixe sythes. But they that knowe nothynge herof,
vnnethe and wyth grete payne wyl byleue it. And
yet it is suffysauntly preuyd as wel by maystryse of
scyence as by verray connyng of Geometrye. Of whyche
haue ben many, syth the phylosophres that fonde this
first, that haue studyed and trauaylled for to knowe the
trouthe, yf it were soo as is sayd or not ; somoche that
by quyck reson they haue preuyd that thauncyent phylosophres had sayd trouthe as wel of the quantyte of the
Sonne as of the heyght. And as to the regard of hym
that compyled this werke, he sette all his entente &
tyme, by cause he hadde so grete meruaylle therof, tyl
he had perceyuyd playnly that of whiche he was in
doubte ; ffor he sawe appertly that the Sonne was gretter
than al therthe wythout ony defaulte by an C·lxvi· tymes,
and thre partyes of the xx parte of therthe, with al this
that[5] thauncyent philosophres sayde. And thenne byleuid

---

[1] Cf. *Ptolemy*, V. 15, 16 ; *Neckam*, I. 8.
[2] O. F. text, Ch. XVI [3].
[3] O.F. text, p. 193 : "XXXix tanz."
[4] O.F. text, p. 193 : "XXXiiii tanz." Most MSS. give "xxiiii
tanz." The correct reading is found in the Turin MS. of the Image
du Monde. The whole number, in the O.F. text, reads "·xxxiiii·
tanz et demi que la terre n'a d'espès parmi, *et les ·v· douzainnes
avoec*" : *i. e.* 34$\frac{11}{12}$ times the "thickness" of the earth. Caxton
has left out the "five twelfths" mentioned in O.F. text.
[5] O.F. text, p. 193 : "les iii parties vintiesmes de la terre avoec
tout *ce, si comme* li ancien le distrent" : and thre partyes of the
·xx· parte of therthe with al this, *as* thauncyent .

he that whiche was gyue hym to vnderstonde. And he
had neuer put this in wrytyng, yf he had not certaynly
knowen the trouthe & that he playnly had proued * it.
And it may wel be knowen that it is of grete quantyte,
whan it is so moche ferre fro vs & semeth to vs so lytil.
Ne he shall neuer be so ferre aboue vs but in lyke wyse he
shal be as ferre whan he is vnder or on that other side
of vs. And for trouthe it is fro therthe vnto the Sonne,
lyke as the kynge Tholomeus hath prouyd it, ffyue
hondred lxxx and v tymes as moche as therthe may
haue of gretenes and thyckens thurgh.

[*fo. 91, vo.]
m 3

Here foloweth of the heyght of the sterres and of theyr
gretenesse.   capitulo xix°. [1]

Now wyll I recounte to you briefly of the sterres of
the firmament, of whiche ther is a right grete
nombre; and they ben alle of one lyke heyghte, but
they ben not all of one gretenes. And it behoueth ouer
longe narracion that of alle them wolde descryue the
gretenes. And therfore we passe lyghtly ouer and
shortly; how wel I aduertyse you and certefye, that
ther is none so lytil of them that ye may see on the
firmament but that it is gretter than all therthe is. But
ther is none of them so grete ne so shynyng as is the
Sonne; ffor he enlumyneth alle the other by his
beaulte whiche is so moche noble.

Ffro therthe vnto the heuen, wherin the sterres ben
sette, is a moche grete espace; ffor it is ten thousand and
·lv· sythes as moche, and more, as is alle therthe of
thycknes. And who that coude acompte after the nombre
and fourme, he myght knowe how many ynches it is of
the honde of a man, and how many feet, how many myles,
and how * many Journeyes it is from hens to the firmament or heuen.   Ffor it is as moche way vnto the heuen
as yf a may [2] myght goo the right way without lettyng,
and that he myght goo euery day xxv myles of Fraunce,
whiche is ·l· englissh myle,[3] and that he taried not on
the waye, yet shold he goo the tyme of seuen ·M·i·C· and

[* fo. 92]

---

[1] O.F. text, Ch. XVII [3].
[2] may: O.F. text, p. 194, "uns hons," a man.
[3] "of Fraunce" to "myle" is not in O.F. text.

·lvii· yere and an half er he had goon somoche waye
as fro hens vnto the heuen where the sterres be inne.

Yf the firste man that God fourmed euer, whiche was
Adam, had goon, fro the first day that he was made and
created, xxv myles euery day, yet shold he not haue
comen theder ; but shold haue yet the space of ·vii·C·xiii·
yere to goo, at the tyme whan this volume was perfourmed by the very auctour : And this was atte
Epyphanye in the yere of grace ·i·M·ii·C· and ·xlvi·.[1]
That tyme shold he haue had so moche to goo, er he
shold comen theder.

Or yf ther were there a grete stone whiche shold falle
fro thens vnto therthe, it shold be an hondred yere er it
cam to the grounde. And in the fallyng it shold descende in euery hour, of whiche ther be xxiiii in a day
complete, xliii myle and a half.[2] Yet shold it be so longe
er it cam to therthe. This thing hath be proued by
hym that compiled this present volume, er he cam thus
ferre in this werke. This is wel ·xl· tymes more than
an hors may goo, whiche alle way shold goo without
restynge.[3]

Here foloweth of the nombre of Sterres.   capitulo xx°.[4]

(*fo. 92, vo.]
m 4

To the regard of the Sterres we shal saye to yow the
nombre lyke as the noble kynge Tholomeus *nombred them in his Almageste ; to whome he gaf the propre
names, and sayd that ther were a thousand and xxii,
all clere and that myght be all seen, without the vii
planetes ; and may be wel acompted without ony paryll.
In alle ther be ·i·M· and ·xxix· whiche may wel be seen,
withoute many other whiche may not wel be seen ne

[1] O.F. text, p. 195 : "·xlv·"
[2] O.F. text, p. 195 : "·lx· milles et ·xiiii· et une demie,"
i. e. 74½ miles.
[3] The following passage from O.F. text, p. 195, has been
omitted by Caxton at the end of this chapter : "Ore qui veult
si puet entendre, s'une pierre porroit descendre en une heure autant
comme il pose. Car meilleur glose n'i sai faire." *i.e.*: Now whoever wishes it can understand this by means of a stone which falls
in an hour as fast as is natural to it. I cannot explain it any
better.
[4] O.F. text, Ch. XVIII [3].

espyed.[1] Ther may not wel moo be espyed but so many
as sayd is, ne appertly be knowen. Now late hym
beholde that wil see it ; ffor noman, trauaylle he neuer
somoche ne studye, maye fynde nomore. Neuertheles ther
is no man lyuyng that may or can compte so moche, or can
so hye mounte in ony place, though he be garnysshid of a
moche gentil instrument & right subtyl, that shold
fynde moo than the kynge Tholomeus fonde, by whiche
he knewe & myght nombre them,[2] and where eueryche
sitteth, & how ferre it is from one to an other, be it of
one or other or nygh or ferre, and the knowlege of the
ymages of them, the whiche by their semblaunce fourmed
them. Ffor the sterres whyche be named ben all fygures
on the heuene, and compassed by ymages and that all
haue dyuerse beynges. And euerych hath his fourme
and his name. Of whiche ben knowen pryncypally xlvii
within the firmament. And of them ben taken xii of
the most worthy whiche ben called the xii Sygnes. And
they make a cercle rounde aboute the vii planettes, where
as they make their torne.

We ben moche ferre from heuen merueyllously.
Aud [3] late euery man knowe that he that deyeth in
dedly synne shal neuer come theder. And the blessyd
sowle whyche is departed fro the body in good estate,
not withstondyng the longe way, is sone *come thether,   [* fo. 93]
ye truly in lasse than half an hour, & vnto the most
hye place to fore the souerayn iuge which sitteth on the
right syde of God the fader in his blessyd heuen ; the
whiche is so ful of delytes of alle glorye and of all
consolacion that ther is noman in this world lyuyng that
may ne can esteme ne thinke the Joye & the glorye
where this blessyd sowle entreth.

And ther is no man that can esteme ne thinke the
capacite &   retnes of heuene, ne may compare it ne

---

[1] "To the regard . . . espyed" : *Ptolemy*, VIII. 1.
[2] "Neuertheles . . . nombre them" : O.F. text, p. 195 : "Mais
nus hons nes porroit conter, *tant* seüst monter en haut lien, *fors
que* par ·i· gentill estrument moult soustill que Tholomeus trouva ;
par quoi l'en les connoist et conte . . ." : But no man could
count them, *however* high he might ascend, *except* with the help
of an excellent and very ingenious instrument which Ptolemy
invented ; whereby one can know and count them.
[3] "Aud" = and.

valewe it to the capacyte and gretnes of all therthe, or
so moche as may compryse fro therthe to the firmament,
as to the regard of the inestymable gretenes aboue the
firmament; ffor that greteness is inestymable without
ende and without mesure. Certes the firmamente ou
hye is so spacyous, so noble and so large, that of alle his
wytte may not a man vnnethe thinke or esteme the
nombre of lyke masses as all therthe is that shold fylle
it, yf they were alle in one masse. Who is he that
coude or myght comprehende or compryse the gretenes
of them, whan they alle be assembled, and euerich as
grete as all therthe? Neuertheles we shal saye to you
therof as moche as we may wel ymagyne.

Of the gretenesse of the firmament, and of the heuen
whiche is aboue it. capitulo xxi°.[1]

Yf the erthe were so grete and so spacyouse, and so
moche more for to resseyue an hondred thousand
tymes as moche peple as euer were in this world, & euery
man of them were so myghty for to engendre another
*man euery day duryng an hondred thousand yere, and
that euery man were as grete as a Geaunt, and euery man
had his hows as grete as euer had ony kynge, & woodes,
Ryuers, champaynes, gardyns, medows, pastures and
vyneyerdes, euerych aboute his castell or place for to
lyue wyth, and that eche had so grete foyson that
eueriche myght holde an hondred maynyes for to serue
hym, and euerich of this maynee helde xx other, and had
therto grete romme and pourpris in their manoyr: alle
thyse myght moche plentyuously be rescyuyd within the
firmament; and yet sholde ther be moche place voyde,
more than all they myght pourprise and take for to playe
and dysporte them therin yf they wolde.

Thenne ought we wel to knowe that Our Lord God is
moche myghty & of a right hye affayre whan he can make
of nought so noble a thynge as the heuene and the Sonne
and all the other thynges that ben on the heuene, in
thayer, on the erthe and in the See. Suche a lord and
suche a maistre ought wel to be God, that can make so

---

[1] O.F. text, Ch. XIX[3].

noble thynges of whiche we haue very knowleche. And
we ought parfyghtly to loue hym.

And well may euery man thinke that the thinge that
is aboue is moche gentyl and moche noble, whan it that
is vnder is. so subtyl; ffor that whiche is aboue is
more grete an hondred thousand tymes than it whiche
is bynethe, and ouer moche more than can be knowen or
may be compted by ony nombre, or may be thought;
ffor this is a thynge that in no manere shal haue
ende ne terme. Therfore I may wel vnderstonde that
ther is nothing that may pourprise ne esteme in gretenes ne otherwyse this whiche is *aboue the firmament,   [* fo. 94]
where the heuene taketh his place, ne may be re-
plenesshid ne fylled with nothing that may be, but yf it
be wyth the goodes of Our Lord God fyllyd. But
the right debonayre Lorde is so moche full of all goodes
that be [1] fylleth alle other thynges whiche ought to haue
parte and meryte in goodes. And the euyll departeth fro
the good in suche wyse that it is voyde and disgarnysshed from all goodes what someuer it be, and that it
shal be lyke as it were nought; wherof is redde herof
that synne is nought ffor as moche as it is voyde
and disgarnysshed of all goodnes, and rendred the body
and sowle so moche febled and disgarnysshid of alle
goodes, of alle vertues and of alle graces, that that one
is totally destroyed and perisshed wyth that other; ffor
alle way the euyll cometh to nought, and contrarye the
good goth alway growyng and in amendyng. And therfore ther is none euyl but synne, whiche is nought; ffor
ye may vnderstande that it cometh to nought as donge.

Ther is nothing that ought to be made right, but only
this that ought to be permanent. And therfor it is good
a man to holde hym nyghe the good, ffor the good
amendeth allwayes. And who that customly doth gladly
the good werkes, they ben the cause to lede hym to
heuene, as he that hath none other wythdraughte ne other
dwellyng place. And therfor he muste enhabite there.
Hym behoueth to come in to heuene for to reteyne there
his place, and also for to fylle it.

---

[1] O.F. text, p. 197: "qu'*il* aemplist," that *he* fylleth.

Ther is noman in the worlde that can doo so moche
good but that he shal alway fynde his place and his
repayre propice after his merytes, ffor as moche as this
[*fo. 94, vo.] so moche noble a *place is withoute ende and without
terme, in suche wyse that no goodes, what someuer they
be, shal neu*er* haue terme ne ende, ne neuer shal haue
defaulte. But it is contynuelly ful of alle consolacion,
of alle delyces, of alle goodes, of alle Joye and of
alle gladnesse, wythout hauyng ony thynge voyde ; of
whiche they that deserue it of Our Lord shal haue ful
possession of alle the inestymable goodes.

Of helle I may frely saye to you that ther is
nothyng sauf sorowe and martirdom truly the most
anguysshous, the most horryble, and somoche sorowful,
that ther is no lyke. And yf so were that the chyldren
that haue ben syth Adam were all dampned, yet it
myght not be fylled by them, though they were twyes
so many more. And they that be therin perisshed shal
be dampned and perpetuelly tormented ; ffor after that
they be dampned, they shal abyde euer as longe as
God shal be, whiche is wythout begynnyng and wythout
endyng. And therre they shal brenne in fyre eternel
withoute hope of alegeau*n*ce, of ony mercy, of ony hope to
haue ony better, but alleway werse fro tyme to tyme.
As it is so that the saued sowles desire the day of dome
and of iugement for to be gloryfyed in body and sowle,
the dampned sowles redoubte & drede it, thynkynge that
after that day they shal be perpetuelly tormented in
body and in sowle. And to that dredeful day they be
not tormented in the body, but in the sowle.[1]

And I haue recyted this thynge shortly to this
ende that it may be knowen certaynly that ther is no
good deede but it shal be rewarded, ne none euyl dede
but that it shal be punysshed. This is the wille of
[* fo. 95] the creatour & maker of all thinges, *wythoute whom
ther is none that in ony maner hath ony power ; and
he is somoche a debonayer lorde, ful of souerayn
puissaunce and of grete and of infynyt goodes, that ther

[1] The passage from "And therre . . ." to "but in the sowle"
is not in O.F. text, but only in Roy. 19 A IX.

is no comparison to hym, as he that all thynge created, made and establisshid of nought at his playsir and will.

But syth we haue spoken to yow of the inestymable gretenesse of the firmament, wherin the sterres be sette, whiche alle way is in moeuyng, so shal ye vnderstonde that ther is an heuen aboue where they that ben there moeue nothyng, but ben contynuelly in one estate; lyke as somme man remeuyd hym from som place to another, the fyrst place meuyd hym not. But he that shold goo so al aboute, lyke round aboute a cercle, shold ofte go fro place to place er he come to his place, and so longe he myght goo that he shold come right to the place fro whens he departed first. But that place shold not meue, but holde hym alle way in one poynt.

Now wylle ye thus vnderstonde of this heuen, that ther is no maner place that is remeuyd fro the sterres ne fro the firmament; but they holde them also fermly all as they most maye. This heuen muste be vnderstonde by them whiche ben Astronomyers. This is that gyueth to vs his colour blew, the whiche estendeth aboue thayer, the whiche we see whan thayer is pure and clere alle aboute. And it is of so grete attemperaunce that it may haue no violence. This is the heuen that encloseth the firmament. Now I shal saye yow all appertly that this that ye may vnderstonde here tofore by heeryng may not be taken, ne knowen, ne be proued yf it be trouthe or non, ne may not be by ony arte of demonstraunce, lyke* as may be seen by eyen; ffor the [* fo. 95, vo.] wytte of a man hath not the power. But neuertheles we shal saye to you this that we truly may fynde by wrytyng in certayn places, lyke as somme Auncyent philosophres haue ymagyned and thought, of whiche they fonde certayn resons.

Here after foloweth of the heuen crystalyn and of the heuene imperyall.   capitulo xxii°.[1]

Aboue this heuen that we may see blew, as sayd is, after that thauncyent clerkes saye, ther is another heuene alle rounde aboute that aboue and bynethe, lyke

[1] O.F. text, Ch. XX[3].

as it were of the colour of whyte crystall, clere, pure
and moche noble ; and is called the heuen crystalyn.

And aboue this heuen crystalyn, alle rounde aboute
that, is an other heuen of the colour of purple, lyke as
the deuynes saye. And that is called the heuen Imperyal. This heuene is garnysshid and ful of alle
beaultees, more than ony of the other that we haue
named ; and there is thayer seuen tymes more fayr and
more clere than is the sonne. Ffro this heuen Imperyal
fylle the euyl angeles by their pryde, the whiche were
disgarnysshid of alle glorye and of alle goodes. And
ther ben the blessyd Angeles of Our Lord.

Here foloweth of the Celestyal heuene. capitulo xxiii°.[1]

Yff ye wil vnderstande for to knowe of this heuene
Celestyall whyche is aboue alle the other, ye shal
*vnderstonde that this place is right worthy and blessyd
in alle thynges ; wherfor ther may nothyng growe but
all goodnesses and swetnesse by reson and right. This
is the propre place of the holy trynyte, where as God
the fader sytteth in his right worthy mageste. But in
that place faylleth thentendement of ony erthely man ;
ffor ther is nowher so good a clerke that may thynke
the tenth parte of the glorye that is there.

And yf Our Lord pourpryseth ony place, hym behoueth
to haue that by right ; but he is so comune ouerall that
he seeth euery man that hath deseruyd it ayenst hym ;
and seeth all thynges here and there. He seeth all
aboute as he that hath all thynges in his kepyng. Of
whiche ye may take ensample by somme, whan ye here
them speke, that alle they of whom they here the tale,
they here his worde : many men vnderstonde al attones,[2]
and in one tyme heere ; euery man hereth al the worde.
In lyke wyse may ye vnderstande that God is ouerall
and regnyng ouerall in euery place, and is in alle places
anon & attones. And the lyght and clerenes that
groweth of hym enlumyneth alle thynges bothe here
and there, and also soone that one as that other.

[* fo. 96]

[1] O.F. text, Ch. XXI[3].
[2] al attones : all at once.

Example, yf ye sette aboute many thynges a lyght; also soone shal the resplendour goo on the syde by yonde it as on the syde on this syde it.

Whan suche thinges haue lyke vertue, ouer moche more ought he to haue, that all thynge made and created, and that alle goodes hath wythin hym; his heuen stratched oueral, as he whiche of all is lord and maistre. In heuen ben alle thangeles, alle tharchangeles and alle the sayntes whiche synge all to gydre tofor God * glorye and lawde wyth right grete Joye and con- [* fo. 96, vo.] solacion. Ther is none that may compryse, ne herte of man mortal may vnderstande what thynge is heuene, and how moche grete Joye they haue, to whom he hath gyuen and graunted it.

The best clerk of the world, the most subtyl and the best spekyng wyth all that euer was lyuynge in erthe, or euer shal be in ony tyme of the world, and thaugh he had a thousand tongues spekynge, and euerych of the tongues spack by hym self, and also had a thousand hertes within his body, the most subtyle and the most memoratyf that myght be taken and founden in alle the world, and best chosen to vnderstaude & to experymente; and yf this myght be and happe that alle this myght be to gydre in the body of a man; and after myght thynke alway the best wyse that they coude descryue & deuyse thestate of heuen; and that euery tongue myght saye and declare the intencion of euery herte: yet myght they neuer in no maner of the world saye ne recounte the thousand parte of the grete Joye that the pourest and leest of them that shal be there shal haue.

And foul he be that shal not be there; ffor they that shal be in heuene wold not be alle the dayes of the world lordes and kynges of alle the Monarchye of the worlde erthly, thaugh all their commandementz myght be obserued and don, not for to ben one only hour out of heuen; ffor there is the lyf perdurable, and there is the parfyght and inestymable Joye that euer was and euer shal be. There is euery thynge establisshed and certayn for euer more, without ende and without

begynnyng, ne neuer shal faylle ; ne there shal neuer be
ony doubtaunce *of deth, ne of maladye, of sorow, of
anguyssh, ne of drede, of angre, of trauayll, of payne,
ne of pouerte, of caytyfnes, ne of ony trybulacion that

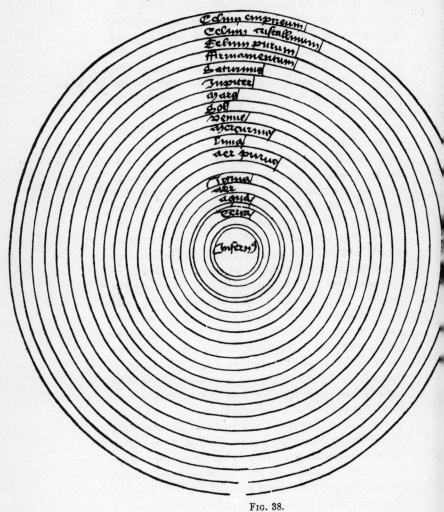

Fig. 38.

euer may happe in ony manere of the world to hym
that shal haue his mansyon in heuene. But he shal be
contynuelly in Joye, in solace, in alle delices, and in

alle goodes perdurable and wythout ende. And he
shal haue more consolacion than ony man can thynke
ne esteme, thaugh he employe alle his engien for to
vnderstonde it.

Now for to knowe what it is of heuene and of helle,
after our declaracion to fore sayd, and wyth this the
firmamente, the sterres and the seuen planetes, I presente
them to you here on that other syde of this leef by a
fygure, by whyche ye may moche prouffyte yf ye wille
wel applye and employe therto your entendemente.[1] *   [* fo.97, vo.|
                                                              n l

* Her foloweth the recapitulacion of the thynge tofore   [* fo. 98]
said.   capitulo xxiiii°.[2]

W yth this we shal make an ende of our book,
the whiche at his begynnynge speketh of Our
Lord God, wherfore he fourmed the world, and why he
loued man so wel that he fourmed hym to his semblaunce, and gaf hym power to doo wel and euyl. After,
why he made hym not suche that he myght not synne
dedely, and how first were founden the vii sciences and
the artes. Sith it speketh of thre maner of peple that
thauncyent philosophres put in the world[3]; how nature
werketh, and what she is, & how she dyuersefyeth in
euerych of her werkes. Also ye haue herde of the
facion of the world and of the dyuysion of the four
elementes whiche ben round aboute and holde them on
the firmament, and how the erthe holdeth hym within
the firmament. Also ye haue herde of the lytilnes of
therthe vnto the regard of heuen, and also how the
sonne maketh his cours al aboute therthe, and the other
planettes in lyke wyse; alle this haue ye herd in the
first partye.

In the seconde partye is declared to yow whiche

[1] Cf. *Fig. 38*, p. 180.   [2] O.F. text, Ch. XXII[3].
[3] Both in Roy. 19 A IX., and in Caxton there is a passage
missing between "in the world" and "how nature . . .":
O F. text, p. 202, "Comment clergie est remuée, et comment ele
vint en France." This corresponds to Ch. VI, part 1: Of thre
maner of peple and *how clergye cam first in to the Royamme of
Fraunce.* "Comment ele vint en France. De nature" is also
missing in MS. A.

parte of therthe is inhabyted, & of the dyuysion
of mappa mundi. And first it speketh of paradys
terrestre and of the contrees & regyons of Ynde, &
of the dyuersytees that ben ther; of men, of bestes, of
trees, of stones, of byrdes, & of somme fysshes that ben
there; and where helle the dolourous place is & stondeth,
and of the grete paynes that they endure that ben
dampned & ben there. After ye haue herd of the
*fo. 98, vo.]
n 2second element, that is of the water; of the *flodes &
of the fontayues[1] hoot and colde, holsom & euyll, whiche
ben in dyuerse contrees, & how the see bicometh salt;
how the erthe quaueth & synketh; and after of the
Ayer, how hit bloweth & rayneth; of tempestes & of
thondres, of ffyre, of layte, & of the sterres whiche
seme as they fylle; of pure ayer & of the vii planettes;
how the bysexte cometh; of the firmament & of his
tornyng, and of the sterres that ben round aboute
therin.

In the thirde partye ye haue herde how the day
& nyght come; and of the mone & of the sonne,
how they rendre their lyght, and how eche of them
leseth their clerenes by nyght & by day somtyme, &
of the Eclipses that thenne happe, wherby the day
bycometh derke; and of the grete eclypse that fylle
atte the deth of Our Lord Jhesu Cryste, by whiche saynt
Dionys was after ward conuerted; & of the vertue of
the firmament & of the sterres, & how the world was
mesured, & the heuen & therthe; of the kynge Tholomeus & of his prudence; of Adam & of somme other;
and how clergye & the vii sciences were kepte ayenst
the flood, and how all this was founden agayn after the
flood; and of the merueylles that Virgyle made by his
wytte & clergye; and for what cause moneye was so
named & establisshed; and of the philosophres that
wente thurgh the world for to lerne; what thinge is
philosophye & what Plato answerde therto; how moche
þe erthe, the mone & the sonne haue of gretenes,
euerych of hym self; & thestages of the sterres, of
their nombre, & of their ymages; the heyght & gretenes

---

[1] fontayues = fontaynes, fountains.

of the firmament, & of the blew heuen whiche is aboue
that; & of the heuene crystalyn, & of the heuen
Imperial.[1]

And as ye haue herde in thende of the *heuene   [* fo. 99]
celestyal & of his estate, and of God whiche maye be
oueral by his glorye & his bonute, of all thise thinges
ye haue herde vs recounte & telle, & rendrid to you
many fayr resons briefly; ffor the prynces & other
peple.ben nothyng curyous to here longe gloses without
grete entendement, but loue better shorte thinges, as
they that ben not of longe tyme but passe briefly; ffor
in a shorte tyme they be fynysshed & ende. And alle
we shal come more shortly than we wolde to nought,
ffor this world passeth fro tyme to tyme lyke as the
wynde, & faylleth fro day to day, & makith to euerych
a lytil seiournyng; ffor it is so ful of vanyte that ther
nys but lytil trouthe therin. And it happeth oftymes
that he that weneth lengest to seiourne here is he that
leest while abydeth & that sonnest taketh his ende.

And therfor I counseylle euery man that eche payne &
trauaylle hym self to lyue wel & truly for the litil tyme
that he hath for to abyde in this world full of tribula-
cions & myseryes; ffor ther is none that knoweth what
hour or tyme þe deth shal come renne on hym. & it
ofte happeth that he or she that weneth yet to lyue &
playe in this world vi or viii or x yere, that he deyeth
in lasse than fyue dayes & fyndeth hym self dampned &
cast doun in to the brennyng fornays of helle. & thenne
is he in a good hour born & wel aduysed, whan at his
ende he is taken in the seruyse of Our Lord, & nothyng
in the worldly voluptuositees & dampnable; & that his
maker hath lente to hym to vnderstonde hym, & that he
haue tyme & space. Ffor God shal rendre to hym so
riche a yefte & so fayr that he shal haue all goodes at
his abandon[2] wyth the Joye perdurable of heuene; the

---

[1] The "Recapitulation," in MS. Roy. 19 A IX., stops at "comment clergie est remuée," and only starts again at "Si avez oÿ en
la fin del celestiel paradis" (O.F. text, p. 203): Caxton, fo. 98
"how nature werketh" to fo. 98 vo., "And as ye haue herde in
thende of the heuene celestyal . . ."
[2] "at his abandon": O.F. text (p. 203): *a bandon*, freely.

[* fo.99, vo.] whiche * to vs be graunted by the creatour & redemptour
of the worlde, in whom alle pyte & mercye haboundeth,
& in whom be alle goodes & vertues what someuer haue
ben, ben, and shal ben perdurably wythout ende.

Thus fynysshith the boke called thymage or myrrour
of the world, the whiche, in spekynge of God & of his
werkes inestymable, hath bygonne to entre in mater
spekynge of hym & of his hye puissances & domyna-
cions, and taketh here an ende; ffor in alle begynnynges
& in all operacions the name of God ought to be called,
as on hym without whom alle thinges ben nought.
Thenne he so ottroye and graunte to vs so to bygynne,
perseuere and fynysshe, that we may be brought &
receyuyd in to his blessyd glorye in heuene, vnto the
blessyd Trynyte, ffader, Sone, and holy gost, whiche
lyueth and regneth without ende in secula seculorum.
Amen.

And where it is so that I haue presumed and emprised
this forsayd translacion in to our englissh and maternal tongue in whiche I am not wel parfyght, and yet
lasse in frensshe, yet I haue endeuourd me therin, atte
request and desyre, coste and dispence of the honourable
and worshipful man, Hughe Bryce, Cytezeyn and
Alderman of London, whiche hath sayd to me that he
entendeth to presente it vnto the puissaunt, noble and
vertuous lorde, My lorde Hastynges, Chamberlayn vnto
our souerayn lord the kynge, and his lieutenaunt of the
toun of Calays & Marches there. In whiche translacion
[* fo. 100.] * I knowleche my self symple, rude and ygnoraunt,
wherfor I humbly byseche my sayd lord Chamberlayn
to perdonne me of this rude and symple translacion

How be it, I leye for myn excuse that I haue to my
power folowed my copye and, as nygh as to me is
possible, I haue made it so playn that euery man resonable may vnderstonde it yf he aduysedly and ententyfly
rede or here it. And yf ther be faulte in mesuryng of
the firmament, Sonne, Mone, or of therthe, or in ony
other meruaylles herin conteyned, I beseche you not
tarette the defaulte in me but in hym that made my

copye; whiche book I began first to translate the second day of Janyuer, the yere of Our Lord .M.CCCC.lxxx., and fynysshyd the viii day of Marche the same yere, and the xxi yere of the Regne of the most Crysten kynge, kynge Edward the fourthe, vnder the Shadowe of whos noble proteccion I haue emprysed & fynysshed this sayd lytil werke and boke. Besechynge Almyghty God to be his protectour and defendour agayn alle his Enemyes, and gyue hym grace to subdue them, and inespeciall them that haue late enterprysed agayn right and reson to make warre wythin his Royamme; and also to preserue and mayntene hym in longe lyf and prosperous helthe; and after this short & transitorye lyf he brynge hym and vs in to his celestyal blysse in heuene. Amen.[1]

[1] 2nd. ed. adds on next line "Caxton me fieri fecit." The end of this work, from "ffor in alle begynnynges . . ." to ". . . in heuene. Amen." differs completely from the O.F. text, and from MS. Roy. 19 A IX. It is Caxton's own.

INDEX OF PROPER NAMES AND OF SUBJECTS DEALT WITH IN THE MIRROUR

ffrostes, pp. 118, 119 : frost.
Ffrygye, p. 85 : Phrygia.
ffyrmament, pp. 128, 129, 174 *seq.* : the firmament.
fish (I) which sailors mistake for an island, pp. 88, 89 : the whale.
—— (II) with long hairs, p. 88.
flood, pp. 154 *seq.* : the Deluge.
flye, pp. 52, 60, 157, 158 : the fly.
fontaynes, pp. 111 *seq.* : fountains.
foxe, p. 100 : the fox.
fyre, pp. 104, 122 : fire.

Galyce, p. 93 : Galicia.
Ganges, pp. 72, 165; *Ungages,* p. 68 : the Ganges.
gardyn, p. 159 : garden.
Gascoynge, p. 110; *Gascoyne,* p. 93 : Gascony.
George (Seynt), p. 87 : Saint George.
Georgie, p. 87 : Georgia, a country in Asia Minor.
Georgiens, p. 87 : inhabitants of Georgia.
Germanye, p. 92 : Germany, or Germania.
Ghelres, p. 93 : Geldern.
glasse, p. 112 : glass.
Gomor, p. 83 : Gomorrah.
Goths, p. 70; *Gog,* p. 70 : Gog.
goshawke, p. 103 : the goshawk.
grapes one cluster of which is a load for two men, p. 90.
Grece, pp. 86, 93, 142 : Greece.
Grekes, pp. 86, 88 : Greek.
grekyssh, pp. 113, 157, 162 : Greek.
Groyne, p. 71 : people in India.
gryffon, p. 70 : the griffin.
gynger, p. 91 : ginger.
Gyon, p. 69 : the Nile.

Hastynges (Wylliam, Lord), pp. 6, 184 : William, Lord Hastings.
haylle, p. 119 : hail.
heed, p. 159 : head.
heer, p. 57 : hair.
Helayne, p. 85 : Helen, carried off by Paris.
Herme, p. 86 : the river Hermus.
Hermenye, p. 69 : Armenia.
herte, p. 100 : the hart, stag.
heuen, pp. 171 *seq.*: the sky, heavens.
heyron, p. 102 : the heron.
Holande, p. 93 : Holland.
Hongrye, p. 92 : Hungary.

hors, pp, 73, 97, 158 : the horse.
Hosterich, p. 92 : Austria.
hostryche, p. 102 : the ostrich.
hounde, p. 101 : the hound, dog.
huppe, p. 103 : the lapwing.
Hyarchas, p. 165 : chief of philosophers in India.
hyrchon, p. 101 : the hedgehog.

iacobyns, p. 32 : jacobins (Dominican friars).
Irlonde, pp. 93, 98 : Ireland.
island (I) where no woman can live, p. 98.
—— (II) where men cannot die, p. 98.
—— (III) which burns night and day, p. 98.
—— (IV) where a night lasts six months, p. 98.
Islonde, p. 98 : Iceland.
Israhel, p. 112 : Israel.
Itaile, p. 157 : Italy.

Jacob, p. 86 : Saint James.
Jacobyns, pp. 86, 87 : a nation in Asia Minor.
Jason, p. 94 : Jason.
Johan Baptiste, p. 86; *Johan Baptest,* p. 87; *John Baptyst,* p. 87 : John the Baptist.
Jewe, pp. 42, 86 : Jew.
Jherusalem, pp. 87, 93 : Jerusalem.
Jhesu Cryste, pp. 25, 82, 157, etc.; *Jhesus,* pp. 87, 90; *Jhesu Cryst,* pp. 93, 166 : Jesus Christ.
Judas, p. 166 : Judas.
Jupiter, pp. 126, 127 : the planet Jupiter.
Jus (Mount), pp. 93, 100 : the Great St. Bernard.

kalender, p. 153 : the calendar.

lambe, p. 102 : the lamb.
lampe, p. 159 : lamp.
lapwynche, p. 103 : the lapwing.
larke, p. 103 : the lark.
Lombardye, p. 93 : Lombardy.
londe of byheste, p. 112 : Holy Land.
London, pp. 6, 7, 184 : London.
Lorayne, pp. 31, 110, 112 : Lorraine.
lybans, p. 91 : the ebony-tree.
Lybe, p. 93 : Libya.

EARLY ENGLISH TEXT SOCIETY

THE Subscription to the Society, which constitutes full membership for private members and libraries, is £3. 3s. (U.S. members $9.00) a year for the annual publications, due in advance on the 1st of JANUARY, and should be paid by Cheque, Postal Order, or Money Order made out to 'The Early English Text Society' and crossed 'National Provincial Bank Limited', to the Hon. Secretary, R. W. Burchfield, 40 Walton Crescent, Oxford. Individual members of the Society are allowed, after consultation with the Secretary, to select other volumes of the Society's publications instead of those for the current year. The Society's Texts can also be purchased separately from the Publisher, Oxford University Press, through a bookseller, at the prices put after them in the List, or through the Secretary, by members only, for their own use, at a discount of 2d. in the shilling.

The Early English Text Society was founded in 1864 by Frederick James Furnivall, with the help of Richard Morris, Walter Skeat, and others, to bring the mass of unprinted Early English literature within the reach of students and provide sound texts from which the New English Dictionary could quote. In 1867 an Extra Series was started of texts already printed but not in satisfactory or readily obtainable editions.

In 1921 the Extra Series was discontinued and all the publications of 1921 and subsequent years have since been listed and numbered as part of the Original Series. Since 1921 nearly a hundred new volumes have been issued; and since 1957 alone more than seventy volumes have been reprinted at a cost of £30,000.

In this prospectus the Original Series and Extra Series for the years 1867–1920 are amalgamated, so as to show all the publications of the Society in a single list. In 1963 the prices of all volumes down to O.S. 222, and still available, were increased by one half, and the prices of some texts after O.S. 222 were also increased, in order to obtain additional revenue for reprinting.

LIST OF PUBLICATIONS

Original Series, 1864–1966. Extra Series, 1867–1920

O.S. 1. Early English Alliterative Poems, ed. R. Morris. (*Reprinted 1965.*) 42s.   1864
   2. Arthur, ed. F. J. Furnivall. (*Reprinted 1965.*) 7s. 6d.   ,,
   3. Lauder on the Dewtie of Kyngis, &c., 1556, ed. F. Hall. (*Reprinted 1965.*) 12s. 6d.   ,,
   4. Sir Gawayne and the Green Knight, ed. R. Morris. (*Out of print, see O.S. 210.*)   ,,
   5. Hume's Orthographie and Congruitie of the Britan Tongue, ed. H. B. Wheatley. (*Reprinted 1965.*)
      12s. 6d.   1865
   6. Lancelot of the Laik, ed. W. W. Skeat. (*Reprinted 1965.*) 42s.   ,,
   7. Genesis & Exodus, ed. R. Morris. (*Out of print.*)   ,,
   8. Morte Arthure, ed. E. Brock. (*Reprinted 1961.*) 25s.   ,,
   9. Thynne on Speght's ed. of Chaucer, A.D. 1599, ed. G. Kingsley and F. J. Furnivall. (*Reprinted
      1965.*) 55s.   ,,
   10. Merlin, Part I, ed. H. B. Wheatley. (*Out of print.*)   ,,
   11. Lyndesay's Monarche, &c., ed. J. Small. Part I. (*Out of print.*)   ,,
   12. The Wright's Chaste Wife, ed. F. J. Furnivall. (*Reprinted 1965.*) 7s. 6d.   ,,
   13. Seinte Marherete, ed. O. Cockayne. (*Out of print, see O.S. 193.*)   1866
   14. King Horn, Floriz and Blauncheflur, &c., ed. J. R. Lumby, re-ed. G. H. McKnight. (*Reprinted
      1962.*) 30s.   ,,
   15. Political, Religious, and Love Poems, ed. F. J. Furnivall. (*Reprinted 1965.*) 55s.   ,,
   16. The Book of Quinte Essence, ed. F. J. Furnivall. (*Reprinted 1965.*) 10s.   ,,
   17. Parallel Extracts from 45 MSS. of Piers the Plowman, ed. W. W. Skeat. (*Out of print.*)   ,,
   18. Hali Meidenhad, ed. O. Cockayne, re-ed. F. J. Furnivall. (*Out of print.*)   ,,
   19. Lyndesay's Monarche, &c., ed. J. Small. Part II. (*Out of print.*)   ,,
   20. Richard Rolle de Hampole, English Prose Treatises of, ed. G. G. Perry. (*Reprinted 1920.*) 10s.   ,,
   21. Merlin, ed. H. B. Wheatley. Part II. (*Out of print.*)   ,,
   22. Partenay or Lusignen, ed. W. W. Skeat. (*Out of print.*)   ,,
   23. Dan Michel's Ayenbite of Inwyt, ed. R. Morris and P. Gradon. Vol. I, Text. (*Reissued 1965.*)
      50s.   ,,
   24. Hymns to the Virgin and Christ; The Parliament of Devils, &c., ed. F. J. Furnivall. (*Out of print.*) 1867
   25. The Stacions of Rome, the Pilgrims' Sea-voyage, with Clene Maydenhod, ed. F. J. Furnivall. (*Out
      of print.*)   ,,
   26. Religious Pieces in Prose and Verse, from R. Thornton's MS., ed. G. G. Perry. (*See under 1913.*)
      (*Out of print.*)   ,,
   27. Levins' Manipulus Vocabulorum, a rhyming Dictionary, ed. H. B. Wheatley. (*Out of print.*)   ,,
   28. William's Vision of Piers the Plowman, ed. W. W. Skeat. A–Text. (*Reprinted 1956.*) 30s.   ,,
   29. Old English Homilies (1220–30), ed. R. Morris. Series I, Part I. (*Out of print.*)   ,,
   30. Pierce the Ploughmans Crede, ed. W. W. Skeat. (*Out of print.*)   ,,
E.S. 1. William of Palerne or William and the Werwolf, re-ed. W. W. Skeat. (*Out of print.*)   ,,
   2. Early English Pronunciation, by A. J. Ellis. Part I. (*Out of print.*)   ,,
O.S. 31. Myrc's Duties of a Parish Priest, in Verse, ed. E. Peacock. (*Out of print.*)   1868
   32. Early English Meals and Manners : the Boke of Norture of John Russell, the Bokes of Keruynge,
      Curtasye, and Demeanor, the Babees Book, Urbanitatis, &c., ed. F. J. Furnivall. (*Out of print.*) ,,
   33. The Book of the Knight of La Tour-Landry, ed. T. Wright. (*Out of print.*)   ,,
   34. Old English Homilies (before 1300), ed. R. Morris. Series I, Part II. (*Out of print.*)   ,,
   35. Lyndesay's Works, Part III: The Historie and Testament of Squyer Meldrum, ed. F. Hall.
      (*Reprinted 1965.*) 12s. 6d.   ,,
E.S. 3. Caxton's Book of Curtesye, in Three Versions, ed. F. J. Furnivall. (*Out of print.*)   ,,
   4. Havelok the Dane, re-ed. W. W. Skeat. (*Out of print.*)   ,,
   5. Chaucer's Boethius, ed. R. Morris. (*Out of print.*)   ,,
   6. Chevelere Assigne, re-ed. Lord Aldenham. (*Out of print.*)   ,,
O.S. 36. Merlin, ed. H. B. Wheatley. Part III. On Arthurian Localities, by J. S. Stuart Glennie. (*Out of
      print.*)   1869
   37. Sir David Lyndesay's Works, Part IV, Ane Satyre of the thrie Estaits, ed. F. Hall. (*Out of print.*) ,,
   38. William's Vision of Piers the Plowman, ed. W. W. Skeat. Part II. Text B. (*Reprinted 1964.*) 40s. ,,
   39. The Gest Hystoriale of the Destruction of Troy, ed. D. Donaldson and G. A. Panton. Part I.
      (*Out of print.*)   ,,
E.S. 7. Early English Pronunciation, by A. J. Ellis. Part II. (*Out of print.*)   ,,
   8. Queene Elizabethes Achademy, &c., ed. F. J. Furnivall. Essays on early Italian and German
      Books of Courtesy, by W. M. Rossetti and E. Oswald. (*Out of print.*)   ,,
   9. Awdeley's Fraternitye of Vacabondes, Harman's Caveat, &c., ed. E. Viles and F. J. Furnivall.
      (*Out of print.*)   ,,
O.S. 40. English Gilds, their Statutes and Customs, A.D. 1389, ed. Toulmin Smith and Lucy T. Smith, with
      an Essay on Gilds and Trades-Unions, by L. Brentano. (*Reprinted 1963.*) 55s.   1870
   41. William Lauder's Minor Poems, ed. F. J. Furnivall. (*Out of print.*)   ,,
   42. Bernardus De Cura Rei Famuliaris, Early Scottish Prophecies, &c., ed. J. R. Lumby. (*Reprinted
      1965.*) 12s. 6d.   ,,
   43. Ratis Raving, and other Moral and Religious Pieces, ed. J. R. Lumby. (*Out of print.*)   ,,
E.S. 10. Andrew Boorde's Introduction of Knowledge, 1547, Dyetary of Helth, 1542, Barnes in Defence of
      the Berde, 1542–3, ed. F. J. Furnivall. (*Out of print.*)   ,,
   11. Barbour's Bruce, ed. W. W. Skeat. Part I. 21s.   ,,

2

3

O.S. 75. **Catholicon Anglicum,** an English-Latin Wordbook, from Lord Monson's MS., A.D. 1483, ed., with Introduction and Notes, by S. J. Herrtage and Preface by H. B. Wheatley. (*Out of print.*) 1881

76, 82. **Ælfric's Metrical Lives of Saints,** in MS. Cott. Jul. E VII, ed. W. W. Skeat. Parts I and II. (*Reprinted as one volume 1966.*) 60s. ,,

E.S. 37. **Charlemagne Romances : 4. Lyf of Charles the Grete,** ed. S. J. Herrtage. Part II. (*Out of print.*) ,,

38. **Charlemagne Romances : 5. The Sowdone of Babylone,** ed. E. Hausknecht. (*Out of print.*) ,,

O.S. 77. **Beowulf,** the unique MS. autotyped and transliterated, ed. J. Zupitza. (*Re-issued as No. 245. See under 1958.*) 1882

78. **The Fifty Earliest English Wills,** in the Court of Probate, 1387–1439, ed. F. J. Furnivall. (*Reprinted 1964.*) 42s. ,,

E.S. 39. **Charlemagne Romances : 6. Rauf Coilyear, Roland, Otuel, &c.,** ed. S. J. Herrtage. (*Out of print.*) ,,

40. **Charlemagne Romances : 7. Huon of Burdeux,** by Lord Berners, ed. S. L. Lee. Part I. (*Out of print.*) ,,

O.S. 79. **King Alfred's Orosius,** from Lord Tollemache's 9th-century MS., ed. H. Sweet. Part I. (*Reprinted 1959.*) 45s. 1883

79 b. **Extra Volume.** Facsimile of the Epinal Glossary, ed. H. Sweet. (*Out of print.*) ,,

E.S. 41. **Charlemagne Romances : 8. Huon of Burdeux,** by Lord Berners, ed. S. L. Lee. Part II. (*Out of print.*) ,,

42, 49, 59. **Guy of Warwick :** 2 texts (Auchinleck MS. and Caius MS.), ed. J. Zupitza. Parts I, II, and III. (*Reprinted as one volume 1966.*) 84s. ,,

O.S. 80. **The Life of St. Katherine,** B.M. Royal MS. 17 A. xxvii, &c., and its Latin Original, ed. E. Einenkel. (*Out of print.*) 1884

81. **Piers Plowman :** Glossary, &c., ed. W. W. Skeat. Part IV, completing the work. (*Out of print.*) ,,

E.S. 43. **Charlemagne Romances : 9. Huon of Burdeux,** by Lord Berners, ed. S. L. Lee. Part III. (*Out of print.*) ,,

44. **Charlemagne Romances : 10. The Foure Sonnes of Aymon,** ed. Octavia Richardson. Part I. (*Out of print.*) ,,

O.S. 82. **Ælfric's Metrical Lives of Saints,** MS. Cott. Jul. E VII, ed. W. W. Skeat. Part II. (*See* O.S. 76.) 1885

83. **The Oldest English Texts, Charters, &c.,** ed. H. Sweet. (*Reprinted 1966.*) 63s. ,,

E.S. 45. **Charlemagne Romances : 11. The Foure Sonnes of Aymon,** ed. O. Richardson. Part II. (*Out of print.*) ,,

46. **Sir Beves of Hamtoun,** ed. E. Kölbing. Part I. (*Out of print.*) ,,

O.S. 84. **Additional Analogs to 'The Wright's Chaste Wife',** O.S. 12, by W. A. Clouston. (*Out of print.*) 1886

85. **The Three Kings of Cologne,** ed. C. Horstmann. (*Out of print.*) ,,

86. **Prose Lives of Women Saints,** ed. C. Horstmann. (*Out of print.*) ,,

E.S. 47. **The Wars of Alexander,** ed. W. W. Skeat. (*Out of print.*) ,,

48. **Sir Beves of Hamtoun,** ed. E. Kölbing. Part II. (*Out of print.*) ,,

O.S. 87. **The Early South-English Legendary,** Laud MS. 108, ed. C. Horstmann. (*Out of print.*) 1887

88. **Hy. Bradshaw's Life of St. Werburghe** (Pynson, 1521), ed. C. Horstmann. 18s. ,,

E.S. 49. **Guy of Warwick,** 2 texts (Auchinleck and Caius MSS.), ed. J. Zupitza. Part II. (*See* E.S. 42.) ,,

50. **Charlemagne Romances : 12. Huon of Burdeux,** by Lord Berners, ed. S. L. Lee. Part IV. (*Out of print.*) ,,

51. **Torrent of Portyngale,** ed. E. Adam. (*Out of print.*) ,,

O.S. 89. **Vices and Virtues,** ed. F. Holthausen. Part I. (*Out of print.*) 1888

90. **Anglo-Saxon and Latin Rule of St. Benet,** interlinear Glosses, ed. H. Logeman. (*Out of print.*) ,,

91. **Two Fifteenth-Century Cookery-Books,** ed. T. Austin. (*Reprinted 1964.*) 42s. ,,

E.S. 52. **Bullein's Dialogue against the Feuer Pestilence, 1578,** ed. M. and A. H. Bullen. (*Out of print.*) ,,

53. **Vicary's Anatomie of the Body of Man, 1548,** ed. F. J. and Percy Furnivall. Part I. (*Out of print.*) ,,

54. **The Curial made by maystere Alain Charretier,** translated by William Caxton, 1484, ed. F. J. Furnivall and P. Meyer. (*Reprinted 1965.*) 10s. ,,

O.S. 92. **Eadwine's Canterbury Psalter,** from the Trin. Cambr. MS., ed. F. Harsley, Part II. (*Out of print.*) 1889

93. **Defensor's Liber Scintillarum,** ed. E. Rhodes. (*Out of print.*) ,,

E.S. 55. **Barbour's Bruce,** ed. W. W. Skeat. Part IV. (*Out of print.*) ,,

56. **Early English Pronunciation,** by A. J. Ellis. Part V, the present English Dialects. (*Out of print.*) ,,

O.S. 94, 114. **Ælfric's Metrical Lives of Saints,** MS. Cott. Jul. E VII, ed. W. W. Skeat. Parts III and IV. (*Reprinted as one volume 1966.*) 60s. 1890

95. **The Old-English Version of Bede's Ecclesiastical History,** re-ed. T. Miller. Part I, 1. (*Reprinted 1959.*) 45s. ,,

E.S. 57. **Caxton's Eneydos,** ed. W. T. Culley and F. J. Furnivall. (*Reprinted 1962.*) 30s. ,,

58. **Caxton's Blanchardyn and Eglantine,** c. 1489, ed. L. Kellner. (*Reprinted 1962.*) 42s. ,,

O.S. 96. **The Old-English Version of Bede's Ecclesiastical History,** re-ed. T. Miller. Part I, 2. (*Reprinted 1959.*) 45s. 1891

97. **The Earliest English Prose Psalter,** ed. K. D. Buelbring. Part I. (*Out of print.*) ,,

E.S. 59. **Guy of Warwick,** 2 texts (Auchinleck and Caius MSS.), ed. J. Zupitza. Part III. (*See* E.S. 42.) ,,

60. **Lydgate's Temple of Glas,** re-ed. J. Schick. (*Out of print.*) ,,

O.S. 98. **Minor Poems of the Vernon MS.,** ed. C. Horstmann. Part I. (*Out of print.*) 1892

99. **Cursor Mundi.** Preface, Notes, and Glossary, Part VI, ed. R. Morris. (*Reprinted 1962.*) 25s. ,,

E.S. 61. **Hoccleve's Minor Poems,** I, from the Phillipps and Durham MSS., ed. F. J. Furnivall. (*Out of print.*) ,,

62. **The Chester Plays,** re-ed. H. Deimling. Part I. (*Reprinted 1959.*) 37s. 6d. ,,

O.S. 100. **Capgrave's Life of St. Katharine,** ed. C. Horstmann, with Forewords by F. J. Furnivall. (*Out of print.*) 1893

4

O.S. 101. **Cursor Mundi.** Essay on the MSS., their Dialects, &c., by H. Hupe. Part VII. (*Reprinted*
1962.) 25s. 1893
E.S. 63. **Thomas à Kempis's De Imitatione Christi**, ed. J. K. Ingram. (*Out of print.*) ,,
64. **Caxton's Godeffroy of Boloyne, or The Siege and Conqueste of Jerusalem**, 1481, ed. Mary N.
Colvin. (*Out of print.*)
O.S. 102. **Lanfranc's Science of Cirurgie**, ed. R. von Fleischhacker. Part I. (*Out of print.*) 1894
103. **The Legend of the Cross**, &c., ed. A. S. Napier. (*Out of print.*) ,,
E.S. 65. **Sir Beves of Hamtoun**, ed. E. Kölbing. Part III. (*Out of print.*) ,,
66. **Lydgate's and Burgh's Secrees of Philisoffres** ('Governance of Kings and Princes'), ed. R. Steele.
(*Out of print.*)
O.S. 104. **The Exeter Book** (Anglo-Saxon Poems), re-ed. I. Gollancz. Part I. (*Reprinted* 1958.) 45s. 1895
105. **The Prymer or Lay Folks' Prayer Book**, Camb. Univ. MS., ed. H. Littlehales. Part I. (*Out
of print.*) ,,
E.S. 67. **The Three Kings' Sons**, a Romance, ed. F. J. Furnivall. Part I, the Text. (*Out of print.*) ,,
68. **Melusine**, the prose Romance, ed. A. K. Donald. Part I, the Text. (*Out of print.*) ,,
O.S. 106. **R. Misyn's Fire of Love and Mending of Life** (Hampole), ed. R. Harvey. (*Out of print.*) 1896
107. **The English Conquest of Ireland**, A.D. 1166–1185, 2 Texts, ed. F. J. Furnivall. Part I. (*Out of print.*) ,,
E.S. 69. **Lydgate's Assembly of the Gods**, ed. O. L. Triggs. (*Reprinted* 1957.) 37s. 6d. ,,
70. **The Digby Plays**, ed. F. J. Furnivall. (*Out of print.*) ,,
O.S. 108. **Child-Marriages and -Divorces, Trothplights**, &c. Chester Depositions, 1561–6, ed. F. J. Furnivall.
(*Out of print.*) 1897
109. **The Prymer or Lay Folks' Prayer Book**, ed. H. Littlehales. Part II. (*Out of print.*) ,,
E.S. 71. **The Towneley Plays**, ed. G. England and A. W. Pollard. (*Reprinted* 1966.) 45s. ,,
72. **Hoccleve's Regement of Princes, and 14 Poems**, ed. F. J. Furnivall. (*Out of print.*) ,,
73. **Hoccleve's Minor Poems, II**, from the Ashburnham MS., ed. I. Gollancz. (*Out of print.*) ,,
O.S. 110. **The Old-English Version of Bede's Ecclesiastical History**, ed. T. Miller. Part II, 1. (*Reprinted*
1963.) 30s. 1898
111. **The Old-English Version of Bede's Ecclesiastical History**, ed. T. Miller. Part II, 2. (*Reprinted*
1963.) 30s. ,,
E.S. 74. **Secreta Secretorum**, 3 prose Englishings, one by Jas. Yonge, 1428, ed. R. Steele. Part I. 36s. ,,
75. **Speculum Guidonis de Warwyk**, ed. G. L. Morrill. (*Out of print.*) ,,
O.S. 112. **Merlin.** Part IV. Outlines of the Legend of Merlin, by W. E. Mead. (*Out of print.*) 1899
113. **Queen Elizabeth's Englishings of Boethius, Plutarch**, &c., ed. C. Pemberton. (*Out of print.*) ,,
E.S. 76. **George Ashby's Poems**, &c., ed. Mary Bateson. (*Reprinted* 1965.) 30s. ,,
77. **Lydgate's DeGuilleville's Pilgrimage of the Life of Man**, ed. F. J. Furnivall. Part I. (*Out of
print.*) ,,
78. **The Life and Death of Mary Magdalene**, by T. Robinson, c. 1620, ed. H. O. Sommer. 9s. ,,
O.S. 114. **Ælfric's Metrical Lives of Saints**, ed. W. W. Skeat. Part IV and last. (*See* O.S. 94.) 1900
115. **Jacob's Well**, ed. A. Brandeis. Part I. 18s. ,,
116. **An Old-English Martyrology**, re-ed. G. Herzfeld. (*Out of print.*) ,,
E.S. 79. **Caxton's Dialogues**, English and French, ed. H. Bradley. 18s. ,,
80. **Lydgate's Two Nightingale Poems**, ed. O. Glauning. (*Out of print.*) ,,
80A. **Selections from Barbour's Bruce** (Books I–X), ed. W. W. Skeat. 20s. ,,
81. **The English Works of John Gower**, ed. G. C. Macaulay. Part I. (*Reprinted* 1957.) 60s. ,,
O.S. 117. **Minor Poems of the Vernon MS.**, ed. F. J. Furnivall. Part II. 27s. 1901
118. **The Lay Folks' Catechism**, ed. T. F. Simmons and H. E. Nolloth. (*Out of print.*) ,,
119. **Robert of Brunne's Handlyng Synne, and its French original**, re-ed. F. J. Furnivall. Part I.
(*Out of print.*) ,,
E.S. 82. **The English Works of John Gower**, ed. G. C. Macaulay. Part II. (*Reprinted* 1957.) 60s. ,,
83. **Lydgate's DeGuilleville's Pilgrimage of the Life of Man**, ed. F. J. Furnivall. Part II. (*Out of
print.*) ,,
84. **Lydgate's Reson and Sensuallyte**, ed. E. Sieper. Vol. I. (*Reprinted* 1965.) 42s. ,,
O.S. 120. **The Rule of St. Benet in Northern Prose and Verse, and Caxton's Summary**, ed. E. A. Kock.
(*Out of print.*) 1902
121. **The Laud MS. Troy-Book**, ed. J. E. Wülfing. Part I. 27s. ,,
E.S. 85. **Alexander Scott's Poems**, 1568, ed. A. K. Donald. (*Out of print.*) ,,
86. **William of Shoreham's Poems**, re-ed. M. Konrath. Part I. (*Out of print.*) ,,
87. **Two Coventry Corpus Christi Plays**, re-ed. H. Craig. (*See under* 1952.) ,,
O.S. 122. **The Laud MS. Troy-Book**, ed. J. E. Wülfing. Part II. 36s. 1903
123. **Robert of Brunne's Handlyng Synne, and its French original**, re-ed. F. J. Furnivall. Part II.
(*Out of print.*) ,,
E.S. 88. **Le Morte Arthur**, re-ed. J. D. Bruce. (*Reprinted* 1959.) 45s. ,,
89. **Lydgate's Reson and Sensuallyte**, ed. E. Sieper. Vol. II. (*Reprinted* 1965.) 35s. ,,
90. **English Fragments from Latin Medieval Service-Books**, ed. H. Littlehales. (*Out of print.*) ,,
O.S. 124. **Twenty-six Political and other Poems from Digby MS. 102**, &c., ed. J. Kail. Part I. 18s. 1904
125. **Medieval Records of a London City Church**, ed. H. Littlehales. Part I. (*Out of print.*) ,,
126. **An Alphabet of Tales**, in Northern English, from the Latin, ed. M. M. Banks. Part I. 18s. ,,
E.S. 91. **The Macro Plays**, ed. F. J. Furnivall and A. W. Pollard. (*Out of print*; *see* 262.) ,,
92. **Lydgate's DeGuilleville's Pilgrimage of the Life of Man**, ed. Katherine B. Locock. Part III.
(*Out of print.*) ,,
93. **Lovelich's Romance of Merlin**, from the unique MS., ed. E. A. Kock. Part I. (*Out of print.*) ,,
O.S. 127. **An Alphabet of Tales**, in Northern English, from the Latin, ed. M. M. Banks. Part II. 18s. 1905
128. **Medieval Records of a London City Church**, ed. H. Littlehales. Part II. 18s. ,,
129. **The English Register of Godstow Nunnery**, ed. A. Clark. Part I. 18s. ,,

5

E.S. 94. Respublica, a Play on a Social England, ed. L. A. Magnus. (*Out of print. See under* 1946.) 1905
95. Lovelich's History of the Holy Grail. Part V. The Legend of the Holy Grail, ed. Dorothy Kempe. (*Out of print.*) „
96. Mirk's Festial, ed. T. Erbe. Part I. 21*s*. „
O.S. 130. The English Register of Godstow Nunnery, ed. A. Clark. Part II. 27*s*. 1906
131. The Brut, or The Chronicle of England, ed. F. Brie. Part I. (*Reprinted* 1960.) 25*s*.
132. John Metham's Works, ed. H. Craig. 27*s*.
E.S. 97. Lydgate's Troy Book, ed. H. Bergen. Part I, Books I and II. (*Out of print.*) „
98. Skelton's Magnyfycence, ed. R. L. Ramsay. (*Reprinted* 1958.) 45*s*. „
99. The Romance of Emaré, re-ed. Edith Rickert. (*Reprinted* 1958.) 22*s*. 6*d*. „
O.S. 133. The English Register of Oseney Abbey, by Oxford, ed. A. Clark. Part I. 27*s*. 1907
134. The Coventry Leet Book, ed. M. Dormer Harris. Part I. (*Out of print.*)
E.S. 100. The Harrowing of Hell, and The Gospel of Nicodemus, re-ed. W. H. Hulme. (*Reprinted* 1961.) „
30*s*.
101. Songs, Carols, &c., from Richard Hill's Balliol MS., ed. R. Dyboski. (*Out of print.*) „
O.S. 135. The Coventry Leet Book, ed. M. Dormer Harris. Part II. 27*s*. 1908
135 *b*. Extra Issue. Prof. Manly's Piers Plowman and its Sequence, urging the fivefold authorship
of the *Vision*. (*Out of print.*) „
136. The Brut, or The Chronicle of England, ed. F. Brie. Part II. (*Out of print.*) „
E.S. 102. Promptorium Parvulorum, the 1st English-Latin Dictionary, ed. A. L. Mayhew. 37*s*. 6*d*. „
103. Lydgate's Troy Book, ed. H. Bergen. Part II, Book III. (*Out of print.*) „
O.S. 137. Twelfth-Century Homilies in MS. Bodley 343, ed. A. O. Belfour. Part I, the Text. (*Reprinted*
1962.) 25*s*. 1909
138. The Coventry Leet Book, ed. M. Dormer Harris. Part III. 27*s*.
E.S. 104. The Non-Cycle Mystery Plays, re-ed. O. Waterhouse. (*Out of print.*) „
105. The Tale of Beryn, with the Pardoner and Tapster, ed. F. J. Furnivall and W. G. Stone. (*Out
of print.*) „
O.S. 139. John Arderne's Treatises on Fistula in Ano, &c., ed. D'Arcy Power. 27*s*. 1910
139 *b, c, d, e, f, Extra Issue.* The Piers Plowman Controversy: *b*. Dr. Jusserand's 1st Reply to Prof.
Manly; *c*. Prof. Manly's Answer to Dr. Jusserand; *d*. Dr. Jusserand's 2nd Reply to Prof.
Manly; *e*. Mr. R, W. Chambers's Article; *f*. Dr. Henry Bradley's Rejoinder to Mr. R. W.
Chambers. (*Out of print.*) „
140. Capgrave's Lives of St. Augustine and St. Gilbert of Sempringham, ed. J. Munro. (*Out of print.*) „
E.S. 106. Lydgate's Troy Book, ed. H. Bergen. Part III. (*Out of print.*) „
107. Lydgate's Minor Poems, ed. H. N. MacCracken. Part I. Religious Poems. (*Reprinted* 1961.) „
40*s*.
O.S. 141. Erthe upon Erthe, all the known texts, ed. Hilda Murray. (*Reprinted* 1964.) 30*s*. 1911
142. The English Register of Godstow Nunnery, ed. A. Clark. Part III. 18*s*. „
143. The Prose Life of Alexander, Thornton MS., ed. J. S. Westlake. 18*s*. „
E.S. 108. Lydgate's Siege of Thebes, re-ed. A. Erdmann. Part I, the Text. (*Reprinted* 1960.) 24*s*. „
109. Partonope, re-ed. A. T. Bödtker. The Texts. (*Out of print.*) „
O.S. 144. The English Register of Oseney Abbey, by Oxford, ed. A. Clark. Part II. 18*s*. 1912
145. The Northern Passion, ed. F. A. Foster. Part I, the four parallel texts. 27*s*. „
E.S. 110. Caxton's Mirrour of the World, with all the woodcuts, ed. O. H. Prior. (*Reprinted* 1966.) 42*s*. „
111. Caxton's History of Jason, the Text, Part I, ed. J. Munro. 27*s*. „
O.S. 146. The Coventry Leet Book, ed. M. Dormer Harris. Introduction, Indexes, &c. Part IV. 18*s*. 1913
147. The Northern Passion, ed. F. A. Foster, Introduction, French Text, Variants and Fragments,
Glossary. Part II. 27*s*. „
[An enlarged reprint of O.S. 26, Religious Pieces in Prose and Verse, from the Thornton MS.,
ed. G. G. Perry. (*Out of print.*)] „
E.S. 112. Lovelich's Romance of Merlin, ed. E. A. Kock. Part II. (*Reprinted* 1961.) 30*s*. „
113. Poems by Sir John Salusbury, Robert Chester, and others, from Christ Church MS. 184, &c., ed.
Carleton Brown. 27*s*. „
O.S. 148. A Fifteenth-Century Courtesy Book and Two Franciscan Rules, ed. R. W. Chambers and W. W.
Seton. (*Reprinted* 1963.) 25*s*. 1914
149. Lincoln Diocese Documents, 1450–1544, ed. Andrew Clark. 27*s*. „
150. The Old-English Rule of Bp. Chrodegang, and the Capitula of Bp. Theodulf, ed. A. S. Napier.
22*s*. 6*d*. „
E.S. 114. The Gild of St. Mary, Lichfield, ed. F. J. Furnivall. 27*s*. „
115. The Chester Plays, re-ed. J. Matthews. Part II. (*Reprinted* 1959.) 37*s*. 6*d*. „
O.S. 151. The Lanterne of Light, ed. Lilian M. Swinburn. (*Out of print.*) 1915
152. Early English Homilies, from Cott. Vesp. D. XIV, ed. Rubie Warner. Part I, Text. (*Out of
print.*) „
E.S. 116. The Pauline Epistles, ed. M. J. Powell. (*Out of print.*) „
117. Bp. Fisher's English Works, ed. R. Bayne. Part II. (*Out of print.*) „
O.S. 153. Mandeville's Travels, ed. P. Hamelius. Part I, Text. (*Reprinted* 1960.) 25*s*. 1916
154. Mandeville's Travels, ed. P. Hamelius. Part II, Notes and Introduction. (*Reprinted* 1961.) 25*s*. „
E.S. 118. The Earliest Arithmetics in English, ed. R. Steele. 27*s*. „
119. The Owl and the Nightingale, 2 Texts parallel, ed. G. F. H. Sykes and J. H. G. Grattan. (*Out
of print.*) „
O.S. 155. The Wheatley MS., ed. Mabel Day. 54*s*. 1917
E.S. 120. Ludus Coventriae, ed. K. S. Block. (*Reprinted* 1961.) 30*s*. „
O.S. 156. Reginald Pecock's Donet, from Bodl. MS. 916, ed. Elsie V. Hitchcock. 63*s*. 1918
E.S. 121. Lydgate's Fall of Princes, ed. H. Bergen. Part I. (*Out of print.*) „

Forthcoming volumes

Other texts are in preparation including three further English versions of the Ancrene *Riwle.*

June 1966.

Publisher: LONDON · THE OXFORD UNIVERSITY PRESS, ELY HOUSE, W. 1